THE TOSCANINI
MUSICIANS KNEW

B. H. HAGGIN

The Toscanini Musicians Knew

HORIZON PRESS · New York · 1967

Contents

Relevant Dates in the Toscanini Career

1885–Graduated from the conservatory in Parma as a cellist.

1886–Conducted his first performance of opera—*Aida*—in Rio de Janeiro.

1895–Became conductor at the Teatro Regio in Turin, where he conducted the first Italian performance of *Die Götterdämmerung*.

1896–Conducted his first orchestral concert, which opened with Schubert's Symphony No. 9, in Turin.

1898–Became principal conductor at La Scala in Milan, where he conducted Strauss's *Salome* and Debussy's *Pelléas et Mélisande*, among other new works.

1908–Began to conduct at the Metropolitan Opera in New York.

1913–Conducted the Metropolitan Opera Orchestra, Chorus and soloists in Beethoven's Ninth Symphony at his first orchestral concert in New York.

1915–Left the Metropolitan and returned to Italy.

1920–Conducted the La Scala Orchestra in an American tour.

1921–Became musical director of La Scala when it reopened after the war.

1926/7–Conducted the New York Philharmonic as guest conductor.

1928–Became a principal conductor of the New York Philharmonic. Selected players of the Philharmonic and the New York Symphony for the New York Philharmonic-Symphony.

1929–Resigned from La Scala.

1930–Conducted the New York Philharmonic-Symphony in a tour of Europe.

1930/1–Conducted at the Bayreuth Festival.

1930–Conducted the Philadelphia Orchestra as guest conductor.

1933/4/5/6/7–Conducted the Vienna Philharmonic in concerts and operas in Vienna and Salzburg.

1935/7/8/9–Conducted the BBC Symphony in England.

1936–Resigned from the New York Philharmonic-Symphony.

1936/7–Conducted the Palestine Symphony.

1937–Began to conduct the NBC Smphony in NBC broadcasts.

1940–Conducted the NBC Symphony in a tour of South America.

1941-42–Absented himself from NBC for the season, except for a few war-bond concerts.

1941/2–Conducted the Philadelphia Orchestra as guest conductor.

1942–Conducted the New York Philharmonic-Symphony in a Beethoven series in the spring and additional concerts in the fall.

1944–Conducted the Philadelphia Orchestra the last time, in a pension fund concert.

1945–Conducted the New York Philharmonic-Symphony the last time, in a pension fund concert.

1946–Conducted the inaugural concert in rebuilt La Scala.

4

1950–Conducted the NBC Symphony in a transcontinental tour.

1952–Conducted the Philharmonia Orchestra in London.

1954–Conducted the NBC Symphony's last broadcast, his last public appearance.

THE TOSCANINI
MUSICIANS KNEW

Introduction by B. H. Haggin

In the spring of 1962 my friend Mel Evans told me the idea he had had once for a book about Freud that would have been made up of what those who had known Freud and worked with him remembered of their experiences. Evans thought such a book about Toscanini—containing what the musicians who had played and sung with him remembered about him as a conductor and a person—would be valuable and fascinating; and to convince me he began to improvise stories he imagined these musicians telling. I said I couldn't see how one would make a book out of hundreds of anecdotes; but Evans urged me not to reject his idea until we had been able to ask one of the musicians what he thought of it.

At that point I recalled an incident at the Manhattan School of Music two weeks before. As I was inching my way toward the exit of the auditorium through the crowd that had come to hear Nadia Boulanger speak, I saw a man smiling at me in recognition; and when I reached him I said: "Please forgive me. I know your face, but I can't remember your name." "After seeing me day after day, week after week, all those years!" he answered reproachfully. "And after I bought ten copies of your book on Toscanini! Without even getting a discount!" And *more in the same vein, until at last he revealed that he was David Walter of the NBC Symphony's bass section, whom I had seen at Toscanini's rehearsals.*

I now telephoned to Walter, who was quite willing to meet Evans and me at lunch, where we asked him what he thought of Evans's idea.

"All the books about Toscanini until now," he said, "have been written by outsiders, only one of whom"—with a nod in my direction—"gave any sign of understanding. And I think it is very important to have a book by the insiders—the musicians who actually rehearsed and played with Toscanini—so that there will be an authoritative statement by those who experienced his greatness to give people in the future a correct idea of what that greatness was." (This was a year before the appearance of This Was Toscanini, *with the illuminating text of Samuel Antek of the NBC Symphony and a large number of the marvelous photographs of Robert Hupka.)*

And he began right then and there to tell us what he re-membered, continuing with one fascinating or moving recollec-tion after another, until it occurred to him to ask what time it was. "Four o'clock!" he exclaimed. "I have a pupil waiting for me!" And he rushed off, after arranging to talk to me again the following week.

"You see?" said Evans.

"I do and I don't," I answered. "The stories are marvelous; but I still can't visualize how to make a book out of hundreds of stories."

I hurried home to write down all I remembered of what Walter had told us; and the following week I took notes as Walter talked for two hours more. And then the problem of how to handle this material was solved when I read in The New Yorker *the monologues of a number of actors that Lillian Ross had made out of her interviews with them. What each musician told me in answer to my questions, I would make into such a monologue; and the book would be the series of these mono-logues.*

I proceeded in this way with the material Walter had given me, and gave him what I produced. He substituted a better word or phrase here and there; cut out a few statements he thought it better not to make in public; and authorized me to publish the corrected text, which now follows.

Statement by David Walter

In 1940 Toscanini had become dissatisfied with the bass section that Rodzinski had picked for the NBC Symphony in 1937; and auditions were to be held. At that time I was principal bass in the Pittsburgh Symphony under Reiner; and I was among the principals of a number of orchestras who were invited to audition. But as it happened I played in the NBC Symphony even before I auditioned.

On April 1, 1940, I received a call from NBC: the principal bass was ill from the shots he had been given for the coming South American tour, and a man was needed to complete the section. I couldn't make it that day; so they got a bass-player named Smith. A man was moved up from second stand to first, and Smith was put in at second stand. It was a rehearsal of Tchaikovsky's *Pathétique*, which as you know begins with a fifth—E and B—played by the basses; and when they played it Toscanini stopped them and said "Out of tune!", and called on them to play one stand at a time. The first stand played and satisfied him; and he went on to the second. But Smith was so terrified to find himself in this exposed position that he couldn't draw his bow across the strings; so there was only the B from the other man. *"Ma che è questa! What is this!"* said Toscanini.

"Play!"; and he started again. This time Smith's hand shook so badly that he produced an unsteady sound. There was a violent exclamation from Toscanini, and another start; and this time Smith's bow flew out of his hand and landed where he couldn't reach it; so again the B came out without the E. And at that point Toscanini blew up and walked out.

The next day I was able to accept the NBC call; and when I got there well ahead of rehearsal time I found the entire bass section in the room off Studio 8H carefully tuning their instruments—after which they practiced the opening passage of the *Pathétique* with the bassoon who had the melody. When the rehearsal began the basses played their fifth perfectly, and Toscanini exclaimed: *"Ecco!"*—which I didn't understand until I was told what had happened the day before. And this was my introduction to Toscanini.

I stayed with the orchestra to the end of the season; and it so happened that in that month there wasn't a single outburst of the famous Toscanini temper, so that I began to wonder about all those stories about this gentle old man. And early in May I formally auditioned for him. I began by playing something I thought would have special impact on him—the *Agnus Dei* of Verdi's *Requiem*, in which all the violins, violas and cellos play with only one bass. When I played this bass part Toscanini came and stood near me; and at the end he asked: "Are you American?" I said yes; and he said with a smile: "You play like European"—which I later figured out to mean that he heard evidence of the kind of musical training, particularly in *solfège* and *cantabile* style, that European bass-players got from the start but ours often didn't. Then I played the recitatives in the last movement of Beethoven's Ninth; and Toscanini moved over to the piano and began to play the orchestral part with me. He kept going past the recitatives, so I had to keep going with him; and luckily he stopped just as my memory was about to give out (the orchestra's personnel manager had taken away my music).

13

I was accepted, and joined the orchestra officially in time for the South American tour, which began in June.

On the ship Toscanini walked the decks day and night, and was always approachable and affable and talked freely with the men. He was amusingly observant: once when a poker game broke up at 3 in the morning we found him on deck, and he asked: "It went well?" And he was touchingly human: one cool day we were all on deck in thin short-sleeved sport shirts; and Toscanini, who also was in such a shirt, said solicitously to Bachman, who was of course considerably younger: "Go, Bachman, put on your coat." "What about you, Maestro?" said Bachman. "Oh, I am younger than you," said Toscanini. And I remember a later incident: one of the men was killed by a bus the last day of the tour; and the news was kept from Toscanini until a couple of days before the ship got to New York. When he was told he became terribly upset, feeling that he was responsible for the man's death—that if he hadn't made the tour the man would be alive. As a result we didn't see him again for the rest of the trip; and he canceled the party that had been planned for the last day.

I mention these incidents to show that at this time he was close to us, whereas in later years he became more distant. One reason for this was the deterioration of his sight. I recall an incident involving our solo bassoon, Kohon, whose wife died, and who had to put in a substitute for the rehearsal on the day of her funeral. The substitute sat only a few feet away; but Toscanini didn't see that it wasn't Kohon sitting there; and he said: "No, my dear, no, no, NO! You are not the old Kohon; you do not play like the old Kohon today. No, no, NO!" But in addition, in those later years the entourage that made itself Toscanini's protector against the intrusion of the outside world included his orchestra among the intruders. So at the few parties for the orchestra that he gave in the fifties it was a pleasure to see him his old affable, congenial self again. But I

14

must add that the last party, after his retirement, was very different. There were to be three such parties; and about a third of the men were at the first one. He didn't come down to join us; and eventually Ghignatti and Cooley went upstairs to see him. They reported that he was in tears, exclaiming "My poor orchestra! My poor orchestra!"—feeling that he was responsible for the disbanding of the orchestra, and that he couldn't face us. And the other two parties were canceled.

But to get back to the ship on the way to South America: Toscanini, as I said earlier, talked freely to us, and not only about music. We discovered he was a man who had read a great deal—principally an enormous number of the *fin de siècle* novels that were called romances. I might add that he was also a man who could appreciate the attractiveness of the lady harpist who was with the orchestra on this tour. And so it was exciting to discover that he was a rounded human being.

But of course much of his talk was about music; and the men egged him on with questions to get him to tell the endless and fascinating stories about operas and composers and performances—operas we had never heard of, or this performance in November, 1902, or that one in May, 1905, in which, no matter how much had been good, he remembered the contralto or the second oboe or the seventh cellist who had been terrible. "Did you conduct in England, Maestro?" "O-o-oh, ye-e-es! Oboes were very bad!" What about the premiere of one of the Puccini operas—the soprano, the tenor, the baritone? Toscanini described the soprano, shook his head over his recollection of the typical example of the species *tenori* that he considered the lowest of all, but broke out into a furious denunciation of the baritone. Someone managed to ask what had become of him. "Ah, poor man," Toscanini said sadly, "I think he died in 1915." Someone asked: "Why do you get so excited about him after so many years?" "Because," Toscanini answered vehemently, "I am angry when I remember what he did to Puccini!"

Statement by David Walter

I had a demonstration of that extraordinary memory when we got to Buenos Aires. Ricordi had put on an exhibition of Toscaniniana, among which was a photograph of Toscanini taken many years before that fascinated me: it showed him in his prime, in a proud stance, his mustache fiercely pointed, and wearing a terrifically high collar. I was able to buy a copy, and found the courage to ask him to sign it. He took it from me, examined it with great interest, and said: "Yes, I remember this photograph. It was taken by good photographer, in April, 1913—no, *May*, 1913."

In Rio we rehearsed Beethoven's Seventh. I got to know the Seventh from a popular recording when my family bought its first phonograph in 1929; and later I played it as a student and professional with various conductors; but now when I heard for the first time all the different things in Toscanini's performance I was so excited that I could hardly contain myself. I remember in particular the shock of the second movement. It is often referred to as the *slow* movement; and you know the usual slow tempo [Walter sang the opening of the movement in this tempo]. So you can imagine the effect on me when Toscanini began the movement in *his* tempo [Walter demonstrated Toscanini's faster tempo]. He set a tempo that conformed to the meaning of Beethoven's direction, *Allegretto*, not to the traditional preconception of 'slow movement'.

This was the first of countless demonstrations of his respect for the composer's text. The printed score didn't tell you everything; but Toscanini believed it was what you had to start with; and he made you think of the exact meanings of the words you found there—for example the word '*andante*', which most people think means 'slow', whereas its literal translation is 'going', and its meaning in music is 'with flowing movement'. I remember his stopping us once at the beginning of the second movement of Beethoven's *Eroica*: "Is written *Marcia funebre*. You play *funebre*; I want *marcia!*" And this exactness extended to every-

16

thing else in the score—dynamics, time values, phrasing.

For example, he was bothered by the usual execution of *fp* which made the *p* almost inaudible. The *p*, he insisted, meant *p*: if the composer had meant *pp* he would have written it. *"Piano, ma voce,"* he would say, meaning a *piano* that was full-bodied. He also insisted on the difference between *f* and *ff* in Beethoven—for example the *f* of this passage [bars 109-112] of the first movement of the *Eroica*, and the *ff* of its more heavily scored repetition. The same with time values. He insisted on a precise execution of the basic rhythm of the first movement of Beethoven's Seventh:

with a short sixteenth-note and a little pressure on the eighth, instead of the usual unprecise

He insisted on exactness in the rhythm of the Funeral Music in Wagner's *Götterdämmerung*:

on which he based the plastic melodic phrase. And the exact delineation of rhythm all the way through the opening statement of Strauss's *Don Juan*:

gave that statement an effect I have never heard in other performances, which are careless about the triplet and the dotted eighth and sixteenth in the second measure. I must add, however, that the exact execution Toscanini insisted on from each woodwind at the beginning of Ravel's *Daphnis and Chloë* Suite achieved something different from the usual impressionistic effect of the passage played without this exactness. I would say what was most outstanding in Toscanini's work was his organization of time and rhythm and dynamics into form; and this made him, in my opinion, most effective in music with clearly delineated rhythmic and formal structure, as against music which made its effect with color. In other words, he was a classicist rather than an impressionist. And so he did well with Ravel's *Bolero*; and if he had played modern music I think he would have done well with Bartók's *Concerto for Orchestra* and Stravinsky's neo-classical works.

But to get back to his exactness about everything in the score: although every marking had to be observed, this had to be done with flexibility and imagination. The opening phrase of Mozart's G-minor was marked with only *p*; but this didn't mean one played it in an anemically unmodified *p*: one made the modifications in the *p* that were necessary to give the phrase a singing quality. The Scherzo of the *Eroica* is marked *pp*; but when we played it with Toscanini it wasn't a light and delicate scherzo: it had an energy and bite that made it a *heroic* scherzo. And the horn passage of the Trio wasn't suave and graceful: it was powerful and noble.

A marking meant one thing in one work, and a different thing in another. I remember the first time I played in Beethoven's Ninth with Toscanini—how surprised I was by the violins' statement of the theme of the slow movement, which is marked *mezza voce*, but which this time had a full-bodied sound it hadn't had in other conductors' performances. The movement is marked *Adagio molto e cantabile*; and the violins played the

18

theme in a *mezza voce* that was *cantabile*. And Toscanini's *Adagio molto* actually was a little faster than that—a *con moto* tempo that gave the theme cohesiveness and a structure it hadn't ever had before in my experience: for the first time I heard a long integrated melody instead of the usual series of melodic fragments; and this meant that when the variations on the theme came later in the movement I could hear them as variations. There are those who talk about musical architectomics; but Toscanini produced it without knowing the word.

What he did was to make you sharply aware of the differences in the size of a *forte*, the strength of an accent, the rapidity of a *crescendo* or *decrescendo*, in different works. Even the most expert orchestral musician became more alert and sensitive playing with him. And so without being at all didactic, Toscanini was, in effect, a great teacher.

This was in addition to having extraordinary powers as a conductor. Even for a good conductor whom he respects and likes, the average player does about fifty percent of what he is capable of; but with Toscanini you felt you had to do your best every moment. I have known only two other conductors who made you feel that way: one was Cantelli, the other is Casals. Actually you did more than your best for Toscanini: he got you to extend yourself, so that however well you played, with him you found yourself playing better. In Rossini's Overture to *Cenerentola* there is a fast passage for the basses that is extremely difficult to finger; and in most performances one or two men may make an enormous effort and play it accurately; but with Toscanini the section played it perfectly, and in his faster tempo.

One of the reasons for this effect on the player was Toscanini's superb knowledge of what he was doing. And another was his tremendous involvement in it—emotional and physical. Conductors—particularly older conductors, but even younger ones—will spare themselves; but Toscanini didn't: he fully con-

19

ducted a *forte*; he fully conducted a *fortissimo*; and he didn't relax even for a *piano*. He simply didn't know any way of easing up: at the time he was having trouble with his right arm he continued its large sweeping movements even when they caused him to grimace and curse for pain. And this affected and inspired the player. There are climaxes in Tchaikovsky in which the basses are asked to saw away *ff* for forty or fifty measures. If the men don't care they make a great show of effort but actually play *f* at most; if they care they arrange to spell each other: one man at a stand plays *ff* for ten measures, then eases up while the other man plays *ff* for ten measures. But with Toscanini fully conducting *ff* throughout the passage, every man in the section played *ff* in every one of those forty or fifty measures. With Toscanini doing his utmost, you couldn't do less.

Those large sweeping movements of the right arm that I mentioned were one of the means of getting you involved as intensely as he was: they swept you on. I should add that Toscanini's conducting movements didn't beat time in accordance with the traditional skeletal configurations of time-beating in conducting manuals; they delineated the musical flow, and in doing this broke the prison of those configurations. And so while they were the most expressive movements and gestures of any conductor, they didn't always answer the orchestral player's well-known question, "Where's the beat?" Nor did they give you all entrance cues, but only the ones that were musically important; which meant that at times you *had* to count measures attentively to know when to come in.

I said before that you were affected by Toscanini's knowledge of what he was doing; and I should add that you were affected also by his knowledge of what *you* were doing. He made you feel that he knew you and knew your part so much better than you did that you couldn't dare to do less than your best. I remember an occasion when he flashed an angry look in the direction of the basses at one point, and afterwards there were five men, each of whom was sure *he* had been the culprit Toscanini had caught in the error and glared at.

You played beyond the limit of your ability—out of fear of his knowledge and fear of his anger, but also out of fear of not fulfilling yourself. So men took their parts with them to practice them at home, and came to rehearsals early to practice them some more. I remember arriving for a rehearsal and finding the woodwinds practicing those enormously difficult passages in the Scherzo of Tchaikovsky's *Manfred,* which usually have to be taken a little more slowly then they are marked; with the result that at the rehearsal the passages were played brilliantly in the right tempo.

Working with him was therefore always very exciting; but what I recall as most exciting were the first years, and on the other hand the last ones, when he seemed to get his second wind. I think of the last Beethoven performances, which not only were less dramatic and more introspective, but had new details that represented new thought and analysis. When we did the Seventh the last time he told us he had been up all night with the score, and mentioned specific details of our earlier performances that he now realized had been mistakes: "*I* was stupid; *you* were stupid; only Beethoven was not stupid!" That this man, at this age, should feel there was still something to look for and learn in a piece of music he had played so many times—this not only was moving, but inspired you to do more work yourself.

It meant that although he was old in years his mind and spirit were young; and that was the way he felt. This could be amusing. I remember his helping Ansermet up the steps of the podium and saying to someone afterwards: "Poor man, he has aged." And there was the incident at Sun Valley, which we visited on our transcontinental tour in 1950. We had a barbecue in the afternoon, with superb food and lots of liquor; and we were sitting with Toscanini afterwards, very relaxed, when one

of the men said: "Maestro, you are looking wonderful today"—
as in fact he was: some of the men had been afraid to take the
ride on the ski-lift even once; but he had insisted on taking it
twice; and he was still in a glow of excitement. "No," he answered mournfully, "I am old man." And he went on to remind
us of the Italian saying that a man lived only to the age of his
mother—which meant that he, at eighty-two, had only a couple
of years left. "But Maestro," the man persisted, "think of Verdi,
who lived to be eighty-seven. Surely you can expect to live as
long as he did!" "Verdi!" Toscanini exclaimed. "He was sick
old man! I am strong; I will live longer than Verdi!"

One more thing I must speak of is Toscanini's concentration. When he was going over a point of phrasing with Mischakoff or one of the solo winds, he was completely oblivious to the
talking around him; and as a result we got to be known as the
noisiest of orchestras. Once, however, he did notice the noise,
and exclaimed: "Eh! . . . Why you talk?!! Ah, you are *uomini
senza gentilezza . . . senza educazione . . . senza cultura . . .*"

This mixture of languages was habitual: being multilingual,
he would begin a sentence in one language and finish it in
another. *"Bitte, cominciamo"*; or *"Non tedeschi!* You play like
Germans!" Or "You are *primi violini,* but you play like *prime
donne"*—followed by a crescendo of excoriation which halted
momentarily as he searched for a climactic epithet, and then
shouted: *"Farmacisti!"*—a reference to the insignificant Italian
village apothecaries who applied leeches and so on.

His language when he became angry could get violent and
coarse. But I would like to say that the outbursts of rage have
been made too much of. They provided colorful stories; but
they have given people a false idea of what went on at rehearsals.
The fact is that most of the time Toscanini worked with the
orchestra with quiet and superb efficiency. And on one occasion
we learned how his outbursts were to be taken. As his words got
angrier and angrier he tried to break his baton between his

hands; and it bent but wouldn't break. "DOLAN!!!" he roared to the orchestra's librarian, who brought another baton. This one broke easily; and the storm was over. One of the men ventured to express concern over his getting so upset; but Toscanini reassured him: "Don't worry; is good for my blood." After that, whenever he got into a rage we would say: "It's all right; it's good for his blood." Though I recall a different comment once when I commiserated with the tympanist, a very gentle older man, about the way Toscanini had shouted at him. "Yeah," he answered, "if he hadn't been right I'd have told him off."

There were men in the orchestra who would have preferred a peaceful existence without Toscanini to the strenuous one with him. We had a guest conductor once—an unassuming man who made no demands and let us off from rehearsal early; and one of our principal wind-players said: "That's a conductor you could live with." But speaking for myself—and I know others would agree—I can say that when I was worn out at the end of a Toscanini rehearsal I didn't mind, because it had been an endlessly fascinating and exciting and instructive experience.

Alan Shulman

HAGGIN:

Listening again to the 1937-38 and 1938-39 NBC Symphony broadcasts when they were rebroadcast in 1963, one was struck by the extraordinary energy and fire of these early performances —which represented the energy and fire not only of Toscanini himself in those years but of his orchestra. Until then he had conducted orchestras made up mostly of middle-aged players; now he found himself conducting an orchestra which included a large number of young players—notably the brilliant young string-players who had been induced to leave the concert stage and string quartets for the part of the NBC staff orchestra that was to play with Toscanini as the NBC Symphony. Those early performances document their outstanding talent and their youthful vitality, which delighted and stimulated him, as they in turn were delighted and stimulated by his unique powers, magnetism and dedication. One of the youngest to join the orchestra in November 1937 was a cellist, Alan Shulman, who had been graduated from the Juilliard School only four months earlier, but had been playing in the Kreiner String Quartet since 1935. He was able to describe the Toscanini operation of those first NBC years; and since he remained with the orchestra until

24

the end, he was able also to speak of the tragic happenings of the last year.

What follows (like all except one of the subsequent monologues) is put together from the words spoken into a tape-recorder. I haven't used Shulman's every word; but the words I give are his.

SHULMAN:

For our first broadcast, on December 25, 1937, we had three or four rehearsals. We had been prepared by Rodzinski, who had started coaching us in September: four or five rehearsals a week, just going through the literature. We had a preview concert with him, then three or four concerts with Monteux; and then Maestro came. At his first rehearsal everyone was on tenterhooks until he came in, dressed in his black work jacket, and said "Brahms"—the First Symphony—and we went to work. It was electrifying: we were like racehorses that had been training for six months and suddenly were on the track for the race. You must realize that all I had had before this was training with Stoessel and Barzin, and that this was my first experience in a professional orchestra; and as the second youngest player I was in awe of the big shots: Mischa Mischakoff, our concertmaster; John Wummer, the first flute; Robert Bloom, the first oboe; Albert Stagliano, the first horn. So for me this first rehearsal was an overwhelming experience.

What struck all of us, and what we talked about, was Toscanini's total honesty, his total dedication, his subordination of himself to the composer's demands. Instead of the composer prostrating himself at the base of *his* pedestal, *he* prostrated himself at the base of the *composer's* pedestal—unlike many conductors around. And this continued through the years. He would say to us, "Be honest!"; and he himself had this honesty, this sincerity: he tried to get as close as one could to the truth in a piece of music.

There are a couple of incidents I remember that illustrate this honesty and humility in relation to the composer and his music. One occurred at a rehearsal of Beethoven's *Eroica*. So many artists—when they've reached the heights of success he reached—begin to take things for granted; and that's when they start slipping back. But this was where Maestro's unique integrity came into play—when he said: "I have been conducting the *Marcia funebre* for fifty years, and I conducted *male*. Please, may we repeat it—not for you but for me." He meant what he said—no question about that: he had studied the score again and found things that hadn't been revealed to him before; he felt he hadn't done justice to the music; therefore he felt he must repeat it. Not to be blinded by the glare from his own halo, but to be willing to look at a score again and find new perspectives—that was the greatness of Maestro.

The other incident occurred in October 1941. For reasons I'll tell you about later, he sat out the season of 1941-42, and NBC got Stokowski in to conduct us. At that time Emanuel Vardi was playing in the viola section of the orchestra and had quite a friendly relation with Maestro, who had come to Vardi's Town Hall concert. Vardi played my *Theme and Variations*; and Maestro came backstage and congratulated us. So one day in the fall of 1941 Vardi said, "Let's go up and pay Maestro a visit." I said, "Nonsense; we'll never get in." Vardi said, "What have we got to lose?" So we drove up to Riverdale on a sunny afternoon in October. We told Maestro we had come unofficially to pay our respects; and he was a most gracious host. We talked about a number of things; he played test pressings of the Beethoven Septet for us; and at one point he said: "Did you hear the Philharmonic broadcast yesterday?" We said no. And he said: "I listened, and heard the Franck Symphony. I was so angry I wrote a letter. I didn't mail it, of course. But the first sentence was 'Blessed are the arts which can survive without the aid of interpreters.' " This to me is a classic, because it represents his whole philosophy as a musician.

There was an honesty too in his dealing with us. As it happened he didn't blow up that first day: it was not until the second or third rehearsal that we got our first experience of the famous Toscanini temper. But that wasn't important: what *was* important was that he was fair: he knew his scores; he came prepared; he knew what he wanted and how to go about getting it; and he wasn't satisfied until he got it—he wouldn't compromise for half. But once he got it, that was it; and this made him the least demanding of any of the conductors we worked with—by which I mean that he believed in not wearing his orchestra out. We were scheduled for a two-and-a-half-hour rehearsal; and if after the two and a half hours he hadn't achieved what he wanted he had no qualms about keeping us overtime until he was satisfied; but if he was satisfied at the end of an hour he would dismiss us.

In contrast to this there was the incident of a well-known guest conductor's rehearsal of the *Eroica*. It was after we had done a Beethoven series with Maestro, including the *Eroica*; and at this rehearsal, after the first movement Harvey Shapiro and I put a sheet of paper alongside our music and marked on it every time the guest conductor stopped in the second movement. It was fifty-seven times! Maestro had come in after the first fifteen or twenty minutes and sat in the balcony of Studio 8H; and after a while he began to pace back and forth; but by the time we reached the end of the *Eroica* he was running—he was so angry. And we heard later that he went to the dressing room and gave the guest conductor hell for wearing out the orchestra needlessly.

It wasn't hard work if we could satisfy him: it was when we *didn't* satisfy him musically that it was hard. We'd turn a phrase, and it wasn't exactly right; so we'd do it again—and possibly a third and a fourth time—until we hit it; and then it was as though the clouds broke and the sun came through, and he'd smile, and with the tension broken the whole orchestra would relax and breathe again. Because when we didn't get it after two or three attempts we were building toward an explosion. And at such times he was capable of great cruelties—though I'm convinced he wasn't aware of them as such. His dedication to his art was so intense that he couldn't think of anything else, including human feelings; and so he rode roughshod over many musicians. When things went well it was heaven; when they went badly it was hell, and we ran scared. But one thing I must say: if we didn't deliver at a rehearsal there could be an explosion; but if there was a slip-up at a performance—this was the human factor, it could happen to anyone, and there never were any post-mortem recriminations, not even a mention of it. This to me was evidence of understanding and tolerance; and I point to it because all the public heard about was *in*tolerance and temper.

At the concerts there was electricity in the air. The man was supercharged; and it permeated the atmosphere, creating an aura of excitement that we didn't feel with other conductors. A concert can be a concert, or it can be a concert plus an event; and with Toscanini we had the double feature. But it was the dress rehearsals that were absolutely extraordinary: in that atmosphere of quiet and intense concentration we were hynotized, and the ninety-five men functioned as one. At the concert the presence of the audience made it impossible to have that quiet and concentration; and Maestro may even have felt subconsciously that some of the subtleties and the effort they cost would be wasted on the audience. In any case I felt that something was lost at the concerts; and this feeling was shared by many of us. Also, as you say, his movements were less energetic and expansive at concerts than at rehearsals, and the audience may have created a constraint that kept him from letting himself go all out as he did at rehearsals. And maybe it was easier to conduct in a work jacket than in formal clothes.

When you ask about the characteristics of his performances I think of the clarity he got—clarity of texture, clarity of architectural detail. I think too of his linear sense: his phrases were marvelous arcs, which added up to architecture on a grand scale that was commensurate with the concept of the creator of the work. I think of the flexibility—the forward motion, and yet the repose. The ability to milk every note of the phrase, with an Italian warmth, but also with intelligence and good taste. And the electrifying, incisive rhythm, which is something you don't hear today. I've heard musicians talk about Furtwängler; and I've heard his old recording of Tchaikovsky's *Pathétique* with the Berlin Philharmonic, which is very beautiful. But the tempi are a bit on the slow side; so I don't feel the excitement of the march in the third movement. Whereas my God, when Toscanini finished that movement you'd want to jump out of your seat, and the audience always broke out into applause—they couldn't help it: it was electrifying. And it didn't run away. That was another thing Maestro had: his remarkable sense for pace—for the judicious selection of tempi. We played Strauss with conductors whose way of achieving excitement was to take it at virtually unplayable speeds, in which we didn't play half the notes. Toscanini took it a third slower, in tempos in which we could play all the notes; and it sounded twice as fast because it was rhythmically alive. Then his ability to set up dynamics. He would say a *piano* in Verdi is not like a *piano* in Beethoven: you see four *p*'s in Verdi, and you play one; you see four *f*'s in Verdi, and you play one. And his sense for the different styles of music of different periods—though I must say I didn't feel he had it for Bach. We didn't do much Bach with him—only a couple of the suites and the Brandenburg Concerto No. 2, I believe; and I didn't get from it the feeling for the style that one would get from—well, possibly from Scherchen. But Beethoven —Brahms—Mozart!

His Mozart was dramatic: he played the G-minor Symphony differently from other conductors, and he was criticized for it; but I think he felt the G-minor was different from other Mozart symphonies—that it was the writing not of Mozart the symphonist but of Mozart the operatic composer. And it is: the opening phrase of the first movement is operatic: it's *Don Giovanni*. Before Maestro started it, his eyes flashed around so that he'd have contact—this was one of the remarkable things— so that he'd have contact with the entire orchestra before that baton came into play. And with the incisive up-beat we knew what the tempo was going to be: with that little movement it was impossible to go wrong. Also at the end of the slow introduction of Strauss's *Death and Transfiguration*, just before the *Allegro molto agitato* begins with the terrific whack on the tympani: he sustained the long chord while his eyes flashed from left to right so that he had complete communication with every member of the orchestra; and when we went into the boom! of the *agitato*, half the audience jumped out of their seats from the impact.

I've wondered how much schooling he had in music, and whether what he did wasn't the result of natural instinct that developed as he went along. Now that you remind me I remember he *was* a graduate of the Conservatory of Parma and did have a professional musical training; but I always had the feeling that he relied mostly on his innate musical sense, and that he could do no wrong because what he did was so perfectly natural. He used to say: "*Naturale*. Don't force. *Canta, canta*." He got every instrument in the orchestra to approximate the human voice—to sing. Once when he wanted something very soft he shouted: "*Lontano!* Far away! In Brooklyn!" Another time he said "Graceful! Graceful!" and then—this has been told many times—he pulled a silk handkerchief from his pocket and let it drift gently to earth like a parachute. Or he would say *"Una carezza"* and caress his cheek. And when he couldn't get what he wanted he would say: "Why couldn't they have been *farmacisti?* Why couldn't they have been shoemakers? Why did they have to be musicians?"

What performances stand out in my memory? The Wagner. Wagner programs were physically exhausting; but there was a *Stimmung* he achieved that was just beyond description. And of course the Beethoven. And the Brahms—the Debussy—actually *all* the standard repertory.

I don't think he had any appreciation of modern or contemporary music. He played it because he felt he had to; but with all due deference to his magnificent control of the orchestra, when we did something like the suite from *Petrushka* he was not at his best. A tricky rhythm could throw him off; and with the 5/8 and 7/8 and so on at the beginning of *Petrushka* he occasionally threw us a curve. Since you say the performance of *Petrushka* sounds perfectly secure, I may be imagining things; but I'd like you to check with other members of the orchestra. My feeling was that although his integrity compelled him to try to play this music he wasn't a hundred percent sold on it in his own mind, and so it didn't come off. If Cantelli had lived he would have done with contemporary music what Toscanini did with the standard repertory. When Cantelli did Bartók's *Music for Strings, Celesta and Percussion,* with its many parts in the opening fugue, it was with a feeling for balance and clarity of detail that made it nothing short of fantastic. Toscanini had this feeling for Beethoven, Brahms, Tchaikovsky, Debussy—but not for contemporary music; and so he played only a handful of things—the Shostakovich First, the Kabalevsky Second and *Colas Breugnon* Overture, Roy Harris's Third. The Shostakovich Fifth was offered to him: he took one look at the score and threw it down. But during the war he did the Shostakovich

Seventh—which was not as good a work as the Fifth—because he was emotionally affected by the siege of Leningrad. And a remarkable thing happened, which left us flabbergasted, and which I've never forgotten. He probably didn't care for the work as a piece of music, and played it for emotional reasons; but at our first reading of our parts he stopped us in a huge tutti and said: "*Contrafagotto*, what are you playing?" And it turned out that the contrabassoon was playing a B-natural in his part instead of the B-flat in Toscanini's score. Maestro's ear was one of the three great ears I've encountered in my years of playing under conductors: the others were Monteux's and Cantelli's.

That reminds me of an incident with Rodzinski. I don't know what we were rehearsing—it may have been a modern work—whatever it was, Rodzinski began to ride Robert Bloom's tail, and Bloom didn't like it. So at one point, when Rodzinski said, "Out of tune," Bloom put him on the spot by asking: "Maestro, what is it—sharp or flat?"; and all Rodzinski could answer was "Adjust yourself."

When I talk about Maestro I may sound like a bobbysoxer on Sinatra; but the fact is that I have yet to see his equal. If Cantelli had lived he might have attained that stature; for he certainly was well on the way, as his few records make evident. That was why Maestro sat in the hall during Cantelli's rehearsals beaming like a proud father: if he had had a son who was musically endowed, this was what he would have wanted him to be. You know, Cantelli was sent to a concentration camp because he refused to be conscripted into the Italian army; and he said: "The Germans took my stomach," so that he could only drink milk, and he weighed only ninety-five pounds. It was sheer dedication and will power that enabled him to carry on. He would work from 8 until noon in his hotel room, have a glass of milk, start again at 12:30, and go on till 5; and by that time he had memorized Stravinsky's *Rossignol* or Bartók's *Concerto for Orchestra*. He was accused of choreography on the podium, as another conductor is today; but with Cantelli there was nothing premeditated or stagy about it: he felt the music that intensely, and his bodily movements were an integral part of what he was doing. He was very remarkable; and his death is one of the great tragedies of our time.

To get back to Maestro, actually there were things he did occasionally that I took exception to. For example, the Trio of the Scherzo of Beethoven's Seventh: taken in the same tempo as the Scherzo it felt a little hard-driven. You're right: it *was* *meno*; but for me it wasn't *meno* enough. Then the occasional tampering with scores. True, it was mostly in the whipped cream stuff: I think he made some emendations in the *Skaters Waltz*, and I don't think the orchestration was the original. Also, I was shocked by what he allowed Harry Glantz to do at the end of *Stars and Stripes Forever*. I love Harry and he's a magnificent trumpet-player; but at one performance on the 1950 tour he took us all by surprise by standing up, with the rest of the brass following suit, in the grand finale, as if it were a performance in Radio City Music Hall; and the Old Man was amused and smiled and let Glantz do it every time after that. The Old Man also let Vito change the harp cadenza at the beginning of the *Waltz of the Flowers* in the *Nutcracker Suite*, improving on Tchaikovsky's harmonies. And I'll tell you one thing that disturbed me terribly as a composer: the completely out-of-character cadenza that Maestro wrote for Mozart's Bassoon Concerto. You didn't know it was Maestro's cadenza? Well, now you know. It wasn't good, and had absolutely nothing to do with the work, but just ambled on and on. Incidentally, Leonard Sharrow was upset too by the fact that he was allowed only one 'take' for the recording. After they recorded the Mozart Divertimento there was about three quarters of an hour of the session left—time enough for one take; and so there was only one take.

This attitude was the thing that bothered me in recording, and I believe was responsible for Toscanini's hating recording.

He felt it never did justice to his tonal palette and balances; and he was right; because when it came to balancing the orchestra I remember that Charles O'Connell, the recording director, was concerned with only one thing—that the session didn't go over-time. So everything was great: "Sounds fine, Maestro." Then the Old Man would listen to the playback and say: "I don't hear the oboe; I don't hear the second bassoon"; and they'd say: "Oh, but it sounds different upstairs. It's wonderful, Maestro." But when he got the test pressing he still didn't hear the second bassoon; and so he came to detest recording. For us, of course, even if the bassoon can't be heard there is the nobility of con-cept, the rhythmic force, the tremendous drive.

Another thing that disturbed me very much on the tour was the playing of *Dixie* in the South. Maestro was criticized for this by some of the press; but it really wasn't his fault: a man-agement executive had the idea of doing it and talked Maestro into it; and after the rebel yells it got the first time in Richmond he persuaded Maestro to do it in the other cities.

That tour was fabulous: the ovations we got all over the country! We played in some horrible barns: in Austin we played in the university gymnasium, which seats 6,500 and didn't offer the best acoustics. But in a few places—the Lyric Theater in Baltimore, which is an old hall but has damned good acoustics, the War Memorial Opera House in San Francisco, the Opera House in Chicago—we gave outstanding concerts. There were many incidents, and the visit to Sun Valley, a promotional thing on the part of the Union Pacific Railroad, where they took that marvelous picture of the Old Man in the ski-lift.

The South American tour of 1940 also was fabulous: the ovations there—for example when we played in the Teatro Colón in Buenos Aires and the Teatro Municipal in Rio de Janeiro—were simply unbelievable. An interesting thing hap-pened in San Paulo: the boxes were conspicuously empty, be-cause there was a large pro-Mussolini group of Italians in San

Paulo, and they stayed away. But the rest of the house went crazy. And there were amusing incidents. After a concert on July 3 in Montevideo some of us went to a night spot and didn't get to bed until 3 in the morning. A rehearsal was scheduled for 10; and Edgar Lustgarten and I, who shared a room, left a call at the switchboard, but they didn't call us. When we awoke it was a quarter of 11; and we were horrified. We dressed and rushed downstairs, and found the men of the orchestra coming back into the lobby. We said, "What happened?" And they said: "Maestro called us to play *The Star-Spangled Banner* on July 4 and then dismissed us."

Just before we got back to New York Chotzinoff read us a letter Maestro had written to us in his own hand. A little of it was printed in *The Times*; and I'll read it to you from the clipping, which is dated July 24, 1940: "You have never played so well, so inspired. We have never been so linked before. We must be proud of what we have done. While writing I feel sad at heart, and it will be always so when beautiful things come to an end." The rest was just as warm; and he told us he was looking forward to conducting us again in November.

But it was soon after he resumed work with us that the incident occurred that caused him to leave us for a year. It took him some time to discover that the orchestra NBC said it created for him played in other programs under other conductors; and it made him angry because it affected our work with him. On a Friday in December 1940 we were scheduled to rehearse from 5 to 7:30 in Carnegie Hall for a performance of the *Missa Solemnis* the next night. There was a concert of the Chicago Symphony in Carnegie Hall that afternoon, after which the platform had to be set up on the stage for the chorus in the *Missa*; so the rehearsal didn't start until 5:30, which meant it would go on to 8. But thirty-five men of the orchestra had to play with Frank Black in the Cities Service program in Studio 8H at 8; and they had to leave at 7:30 if they were to pack their instruments, get to 8H, change their clothes and be ready for the broadcast at 8. And since this was the first time we were doing the *Missa* with Maestro he was really out to work. So 7:30 came, and he kept right on working; then it was 7:32, and 7:33; and at that point the personnel manager stood behind Maestro and signaled to the men one by one to sneak out. I saw Carlton Cooley, right under Maestro's nose, get down on his hands and knees and crawl out; and it was only after a number of men had done this that the Old Man's eye caught the movement of the bassoon that one of the men was holding as he crawled out, and he discovered what had been going on. He was so infuriated that he threw down his stand and walked out. He conducted the performance the next night and finished the season; but a couple of months later when the conductors for 1941-42 were announced he was not among them, and we learned that Stokowski was going to conduct us instead.[1]

Were we aware of any change in his work in later years? Certain things were played faster; and I think the reason was that he was afraid of being accused of growing old. Yes, the *Tristan* Prelude did get slower and broader; and this was true also of the Prelude to *Lohengrin:* it got so broad that the violins ran out of bow. But in the Beethoven symphonies the tempi picked up—in the scherzi especially: you probably know that from comparing the recordings. As for whether we felt any lessened energy in the later performances, I would say he may have been so absorbed in his thoughts that he forgot he was conducting; because as time went on he stopped less frequently for corrections. No doubt the orchestra was better-trained and able to satisfy his demands; but time must have taken its toll. And yet when I think of that last broadcast—it was a traumatic experience I'll never forget—when he faltered in the *Tannhäuser* Bacchanale and Frank Miller began to conduct from the first

[1]All superior numbers refer to Mr. Haggin's comments in his Notes, beginning on page 209.

cello chair, and then Maestro began to beat again[2] and took us through the Prelude to *Die Meistersinger*, but as though something in him had snapped and he was saying: "I don't really care anymore; let's get through with this"—I find it hard to understand, because a couple of months later we did some remakes for Victor, and he came in like a house afire. It was incredible; and we said: "My God, he's a rejuvenated man!" Yes, there had been disturbing incidents throughout the season; and it may be that his mind was beginning to waver. But I wonder whether all through that last concert the thought that this was the grand finale wasn't preying on his mind. And I wonder too: *did* he resign? did he do it of his own volition? did *he* write that letter of resignation? These are things we don't know.[3]

A day or two after those last recording sessions we were invited to his home in Riverdale for a party. We got there at 5; and there was the usual abundance of food and liquor—but no Maestro to greet us as he always did. He was in his room upstairs; and at about 6:30 one of the men went up to investigate, and reported that Maestro was crying and saying: "How can I face my poor orchestra?" And we never did get to see him.

The other day I happened to hear our recording of the Brahms *Haydn Variations* on the air; and looking back the fifteen years to when we made it I marveled at it. We hear wonderful orchestras; but their playing doesn't have that added dimension Toscanini gave—that electrifying rhythm, that dynamic quality.

I would sum it up by saying that he drove a hard bargain with himself and with his musicians; but when it came off—which was ninety-nine times out of a hundred—it was Utopia.

Fred Zimmermann

HAGGIN:

I wanted, of course, to get to musicians who could talk about the Toscanini of the New York Philharmonic years. And as it happened, David Walter said to me: "The man you must talk to is my teacher, Fred Zimmermann. When I was studying with him in the thirties, he was playing bass in the Philharmonic with Toscanini, and was raving about him. He's a first-rate musician—and, by the way, also a fine painter—and very articulate." Zimmermann did prove to be an impressive musician, who had a great deal to tell—some of it surprising after Walter's introduction.

ZIMMERMANN:

I remember my first Philharmonic rehearsal with Toscanini in 1930 very clearly. We were all seated, practicing and tuning up, when the orchestra manager, Van Praag, came on stage, clapped his hands, and disappeared again backstage. Everyone stopped playing and talking, and we all sat in absolute silence until Van Praag reappeared, pointed toward the podium, and Toscanini walked on in his black rehearsal jacket, his head bent and his stick at his side. He hopped onto the podium, nodded to the orchestra, slapped the stick on his stand—and my first rehearsal with the Old Man began.

I remember how surprised I was that he was so short. And we hadn't played five minutes when he began to shout instructions and criticisms, and I was surprised again by his voice: it was so hoarse and loud. The shouting continued throughout the rehearsal; and I dismissed it from my mind that day as something unusual and temporary; but I soon learned that it was part of Toscanini's behavior at rehearsals. He didn't break any sticks that first day; but I found later that this also was part of the pattern.

It was my first symphonic experience: before that I had played in the Barrère Little Symphony; and it was quite a change from Georges Barrère, a soft-spoken, gentle man, to this volcano, this hurricane, whom no one could control, and who couldn't control himself. What Toscanini wanted, he wanted forcefully; he expressed himself forcefully to get it; and any failure to realize the ideal in his mind aroused impatience and anger.

What he demanded wasn't anything trivial, and yet it wasn't anything extraordinary. It was really very simple, what he asked for: that we play what was in the score—an eighth-note that was an eighth-note, a *pianissimo* that remained *pianissimo* to the end of the phrase—and that we watch him. And he was easy to follow: his beat was very clear and precise. We knew that 'one' was here, and 'two' was here, and 'three' was here, and 'four' was up here; when he subdivided we knew where he was and we were at every point; we knew when he was going to go into a circular movement and out of it; we knew that when he reversed the circle the phrase had ended and a new phrase was beginning. It was all very clear, very precise; and it was very beautiful: he had the most elegant way of holding and moving that stick. So it was almost impossible to make a mistake if one watched him. Also he was consistent: the way he rehearsed the

39

work was the way he played it every time that week. He came to the first rehearsal with a conception of the work complete to the last detail; and it didn't change.

This didn't mean it was the same two years later. A great thing about the Old Man was that he kept thinking about what he had done, questioning it, changing it. When we played Beethoven's *Missa Solemnis* there was a place where the basses couldn't produce the *pianissimo* he wanted. It got to the point where we were playing with only a few hairs of the bow, so that it was hard for me to hear myself or the man next to me, and we were sure we couldn't be heard out front. Some years later Toscanini came back to the Philharmonic and did the *Missa Solemnis* again; and when he came to this *pianissimo* passage he turned to the basses and said: "*Bassi*, I remember. I am sorry. I make mistake: no one could hear you. Now play *your pianissimo.*" It was wonderful that he had questioned his judgment in this place when he had taken up the score again—that he questioned his conception of the form of a piece, and studied the score all over again as though it were a new piece. Once during Beethoven's Fifth he shouted: "Don't you study this symphony? I study for weeks: every night I study this score!" This was part of his power: the drive he had to penetrate further and further into the score.

It was unfortunate that he was so volatile and volcanic: it often got in his way. *He* knew exactly what he wanted, and assumed that *we* also knew. But sometimes we didn't know; and when he lost control of himself he became inarticulate and communication stopped: there was no longer direction, but only cries of "No! No! No!" and the breaking of the baton. I remember our playing the first measure of the finale of Brahms's Second, and his beating the stick on the stand and shouting: "No! No! No! Again!" So we played it again. "No! No! No! Again!" So we played it again; but we still didn't know what was wrong—whether it was the half-note or the eighth-rest, too long or too short. And it went on and on. Another time he glared at the basses and said: "You are stupid, eh? You are stupid? Answer me!"; and we nodded our heads. "You are jackasses? Answer me!"; and we nodded our heads again. Many embarrassing and painful minutes were wasted, instead of the correction that could have been made immediately. What had happened was a slight oversight: in a *decrescendo* passage in the *Bartered Bride* Overture one of the notes had an accent that none of us had ever noticed or played. When we played the passage Toscanini stopped us. "*Bassi,* you play what? *Come è scritto?* What is written?" "Yes." "Ah, so play again." We played it again—and again; and after several playings he said: "Is not accent on this note?" And then he stormed at us for not noticing the accent ourselves. That was thirty years ago; and every time I play those two bars I have a trauma—I hear the Old Man shouting.

But what I liked about Toscanini was the fact that he made the same demand of himself as he made of us. And he was as angry when *he* made a mistake as when *we* failed to observe something printed in the part. When we were doing D'Indy's *Istar* he got lost almost every time in the transition to the 5/4 section: he worried about it when he came on stage, and worried himself into not getting into the 5/4 section correctly. This happened the night of a performance; and he was so distraught that he dug his fingers into his thigh violently, never looked at the orchestra, and at the end of the performance ran off the stage and didn't return for a bow. On several occasions when things didn't go well he turned to each section, saying "*Primi violini:* stupid! *Celli:* stupid! *Bassi:* stupid!"—but also "Toscanini: stupid!" And it was the same when things went exceedingly well: he blew kisses to the sections and said "Bravo, *primi violini!* Bravo, *secundi violini!*" and so on, finally patting his cheek and adding "Bravo, Toscanini!" I remember too, after the slow movement of Beethoven's Ninth, his putting his score to his lips and saying "Bravo, Beethoven!"

Another thing I liked about him was that there were no recriminations, ever. I remember hearing one of the men say to him after a concert: "Maestro, I'm sorry about the mistake I made this evening"—and Toscanini answering: "Oh, this evening is past; it doesn't mean anything anymore. But tomorrow morning . . ." Tomorrow morning everything would have to be exactly as it was printed in the score.

That was the great thing in the Old Man. He said: "We have an obligation. *I* have it; *you* have it." It was an obligation to the composer, to the music; they were of primary importance; only they mattered. And this obligation must be fulfilled always. I remember someone getting impatient and saying: "But this is only a rehearsal!" "Only a rehearsal!" said Toscanini. "This is where we play for ourselves! *Now* we play, not tomorrow night!" And at the concert too it was all for us and all for the music; and that made it wonderful to play with him. We felt his love for the music, his excitement; and we not only conformed to his view of the music—*his* Bach, *his* Wagner—but we reacted to his excitement with our own excitement about the music and the performance.

And there were marvelous performances. The one that stands out in my memory is the Schubert Ninth: it was a heavenly experience. After the concert I just couldn't bear to go into the subway; and so I walked for blocks and blocks to my home with the sounds of the performance ringing in my mind. Wagner too: it was deeply stirring, deeply spiritual; and being a part of it was a transcendent experience.

But we paid for it! Playing for Toscanini was a most rewarding musical experience; but it was also terribly trying. He created tension, apprehension, anxiety and fear in the players; and this kept them from functioning at the maximum of their capacities. It was difficult for them to have full control of those capacities when he was constantly shouting at them; and I feel certain that the performances would have been even greater in an atmosphere more conducive to maximum achievement.

But one thing I can say is that in this trying behavior there was no personal animosity. In all the time he was there he never fired anyone, never showed any personal dislikes, any personal favoritisms. This sort of integrity was wonderful to see: it was only the music he was interested in. And he was an easy man to play for if you had the skill to conform to his demands. If you could do this you received enormously valuable orchestral training—in discipline, in attention, in observing every detail of the printed score. It was training in playing with strict accuracy and restraint—in a classical style that represented Toscanini's great musical integrity.

He had this musical integrity to a degree that I would almost say inhibited him. That is, I felt sometimes that his classical style prevented him from letting himself go in ways called for by the music. Strauss's *Ein Heldenleben,* for instance: there are human voices talking in parts of it—the tubas' "Doctor Barta", for example. This is music for someone with the freedom to bring poetic imagery into play—the way Kleiber did with Berlioz's *Fantastique*—with the voices of the witches in the last movement and the March to the Scaffold. I couldn't imagine Toscanini getting into the metaphors of such program music, which he probably didn't like (maybe that was why he never played the *Fantastique*). It is true, as you say, that he did play some program music; but he played it purely as music: he gave it a classical shape and form. And I didn't think he was happy with *Ein Heldenleben;* because when we rehearsed it he didn't stop and yell: we played straight through it from start to finish, and then he put down his stick and walked away without a word. When he loved something he had a lot to say.

But on the other hand there was his Wagner: this was expressive, imaginative, poetic music; and in it the Old Man was a great poet. He played Wagner with an understanding of the mood, the situation, the problems of the characters, their reac-

43

tions to these problems. And he controlled the singers, keeping their expressiveness within the limits of good musicianship, good taste. It was intense, but within the boundaries of good taste.

But of course Wagner was nineteenth-century music, and Toscanini was a nineteenth-century man. He was so deeply involved with the music of his own generation that he was incapable—esthetically or emotionally—of stepping into the twentieth century. Yes, he did play some twentieth-century music: his *Petrushka* was marvelous; and his Debussy—I've never heard the end of the first movement of *La Mer* sound as he made it sound; and we always looked forward to playing it with him. But I'm thinking beyond Debussy and Stravinsky—of very modern works: he didn't play Bartók, for instance. Yes, he played Shostakovich; but some of the avant-garde composers he didn't touch: I doubt that he ever even looked at a score of Webern.

But everything we did with him was a great experience that I will always cherish; and I'm glad it came at a time when I was young enough to take what it involved. It was difficult—very difficult at times. He made it difficult for us, and difficult for himself; but it was more difficult for us because he could express himself and we couldn't. I remember a solo wind-player getting exasperated by Toscanini's prolonged shouting at the man next to him, and saying to the Old Man: "Oh, be quiet!" Toscanini turned to him and said: "I wasn't talking to you, you jackass!" The player answered: "Yes, I am a jackass—*I* am a young jackass, and *you* are an old jackass. *I* can still learn; *you* cannot"; and he packed his instrument and walked out. Afterwards Toscanini sent for him, and there was a reconciliation. Then there was the incident with the harpist Cella, whom Toscanini ordered out after an argument. "I will get *another* harpist!" Toscanini called after him; and Cella, at the door, turned and shot back: "He'll be one of my pupils!"—and slammed the the door behind him. Toscanini stood hitting his leg with his stick angrily at first, then more slowly as he continued to reflect on Cella's retort; then he rested the point of his stick on his forehead as he thought; and you could see on his face what was going through his mind: he was not going to have a pupil of Cella replacing Cella. And Cella was back the next day. On the other hand there was the incident with a solo wind-player who got angry and walked out. At the door he turned and said: "*Good-by!*" "Good-by!" said Toscanini, adding: "When the Pope dies they elect a new one." This time it was not Toscanini but the player who was given something to think about (he was back the next day).

As for my personal impressions of Toscanini, he never came through to me as a person. He was kept insulated; and we never had a chance to talk to him as the NBC men did later on. What I knew was that he came to work, worked hard, and left; that he made enormous demands, which we had to learn to satisfy; that he was very severe; and that he was great. I'd love to be able to play one more rehearsal with him, and one more concert with him.

HAGGIN:

When I told David Walter about Zimmermann's anger over Toscanini's misbehavior, he said: "Interesting. He must have changed his mind. In those days he used to say: 'It's too bad he behaves that way; but if that's the way he has to behave to get those performances, okay." At the end of our session Zimmermann had said he would continue to think back and see if he could recall anything further about Toscanini, and asked me to telephone him in a couple of weeks. When I did, he said he wanted to correct his over-emphasis of certain unpleasant but essentially unimportant aspects of Toscanini's work with the orchestra. So I went to see him again; and this time he pushed aside the tape-recorder, and I had to make notes, from which I wrote up what follows.

Fred Zimmermann

ZIMMERMANN:

What I said last time was what first came to mind when I began to think back to those years with Toscanini in the thirties. But as I continued to think back I realized that those first recollections had been concerned far too much with something of minor importance. He called us stupid; but the important thing was that this man who called us stupid was a great musician— one with a genius for re-creation. He was a man with unique equipment who could look at a score and imagine the final realization in sound of all those little dots, and who knew the difference between *these* dots that were Schubert and *those* that were Rossini. He was a man who had an ideal in his mind and was intensely serious about it, completely involved, obsessed, as he had to be. And he wanted the same complete involvement from us. But it wasn't *always* possible for us to put our personal problems and worries out of our minds and be as completely involved with Beethoven as he was; and this was something he didn't realize and take into account. All he was aware of was the sublime ideal in his mind; he had no awareness of the human factors that kept us from producing it for him; and so he didn't understand our not producing it, and became impatient. Also he was very quick, and expected us to be quick too. "You are late!" he would say. "I was seven-month baby: I couldn't wait." And when we weren't quick, *that* made him impatient. When he became impatient he made us tense and anxious, and therefore less able to produce what he wanted; but this too was something he didn't realize; and he became more impatient and angry.

He was impatient also because what he asked for was, he thought, very little: only that we do what was marked on the printed page—observe every marking of durational and dynamic value; make the *crescendo* that was marked, without an acceleration that was not marked, and the *decrescendo* that was marked, without a retard that was not marked; make only the

46

accents that were marked, and make no accent when playing up-bow on a secondary beat; keep a prolonged *pianissimo* at a constant dynamic level. But all this was for him a truth to which we had a moral obligation: he demanded of us the truth that was on the printed page. And any failure to produce it was a moral transgression which called forth his fury and statements like "You are lazy!" and "You are *anti-musicale!*" (Another statement I remember, when he couldn't get what he wanted, was "You conspire against the music!" And when a scale passage wasn't cleanly executed he would say: "You eat the notes!")

Not only the musical phrase that came out different from what he expected upset him: *anything* that wasn't as he expected it to be upset him. Once, in a temper, he dug his hands into the pockets of his jacket so violently that he tore them away. He made a tremendous effort to control himself, turning his back to us and saying: "No, Toscanini, no! *Calmo—calmo —calmo!*" Then he began to conduct again; but the passage went no better; and in renewed anger he started to dig his hands into his pockets again, but found they weren't there, since he had torn them away. This new frustration made him so furious that he began to tear the jacket itself to pieces. Another time he attempted to break his stick; but this one only bent and wouldn't break; and this made him so angry that he began to bite it. A musical phrase that wouldn't come out as it should; pockets that weren't where they should be; a stick that wouldn't break as it should—all these were things that upset him.

This was an inability to accommodate himself to the external realities that were different from what was in his mind; and it resulted from the intensity of his involvement with what was in his mind. Serious involvement is essential in an artist; and I'm not saying Toscanini was the only one who had it: Kleiber also had it; and Beecham (even though he began the rehearsal with a joke); and others. But in Toscanini it had an extreme intensity. I used to be fascinated by his intense con-

47

centration as he stood on the podium before a performance, with the point of his stick resting on his forehead or his chin, never moving, until suddenly and quickly the stick snapped into the air, his eyes gathered in the players, and the performance began. And before a rehearsal sometimes he would stand motionless for a moment in intense absorption, and then hit the stand violently with his stick before raising his arm to begin.

It was the same with his ability to balance the orchestra in a chord—by having the clarinet play this much louder, the bassoon this much softer—and to get the chord to be in tune and precise in ensemble (for this there was the frequent injunction "Together!"). Again I'm not saying or implying he was the only one who could balance the orchestra, but merely that in this he was extraordinary, even uncanny. I've never encountered an ear like his.

His beat too was the most beautiful I've ever seen, and functionally the most explicit and efficient (I remember his saying: "I conduct *so*" as he made a big movement, and "You play *so*" as he made a small movement). Those circular movements that were unique with him—a creative act in conducting —were a wonderful way of conveying the continuity in the music: they kept going the way the music did. This *going* all the time was what one felt in his performance—a going *toward* something—toward the end, where the whole thing was wrapped up and tied up in a package, a completed shape.

As I said last time, he was a great teacher, to whom I owe a great part of my orchestral training. But of course I learned from others too. When we played *Till Eulenspiegel* with Toscanini it was a piece of music with a coherent shape; but when we played it with Kleiber I discovered that there was also a human story in it: this wasn't just music; it was Till encountering a pilgrims' march; and this was Till's hanging. Right at the start of my experience as an orchestral musician I found myself in two different worlds; and I learned from both. Later I learned things from other conductors; and with them I had important musical experiences that I didn't have with Toscanini. For instance, with Kleiber I learned to know the music of Alban Berg, which Toscanini didn't play. I don't mean this as a criticism of Toscanini: it was enough that he understood and performed the music of his own time; others could perform Berg.

And in some things Toscanini was ahead of his time. I mean the early days when he was a young man conducting in Italian opera houses where the audience was accustomed to get arias repeated, and he defied the audience and refused to repeat the aria and walked out. From the beginning he was different from the others—a man of great musical integrity and great courage.

William Carboni

HAGGIN:

I asked Zimmermann to find out if any other New York Philharmonic musicians would tell me what they remembered about Toscanini; and he reported that William Carboni would. I called him up; we arranged time and place; and when he arrived he turned out to be another musician I had seen for years at the NBC Symphony rehearsals.

CARBONI:

I first knew about Toscanini from my father, who used to go to all the operas in Philadelphia and New York and took me as a kid to hear Titta Ruffo and Caruso. He talked about Toscanini and music; and that's how I got to play the fiddle. I remember the last concert Toscanini gave with the Philharmonic in 1936: I hitch-hiked to New York and stood all day to hear it in the gallery; and I never thought I would play with him. I came to New York; and in 1940 I played in the substitute orchestra at NBC while the NBC Symphony was in South America with Toscanini; and when they came back I had an audition with the Old Man—the best audition I ever had. I played in Studio 3B—with my wife—a Brahms sonata for viola

—and that was all. Spitalny, who was sitting next to Toscanini, asked him if he wanted to hear me play any Strauss or Wagner; and Toscanini said no: if a man could play a Brahms sonata alone he certainly could play in an orchestra. Then he came over to me and patted me on the shoulder and said, *"Bene, bene,"* and put his arm around my wife; and she said it was the most exciting thing—she just found herself in his arms—you know? An old man! Seventy-something! And so I was in: I was in the orchestra. The best audition I ever had: I didn't have to read a lot of stuff.

Then I remember the rehearsals with the Old Man: two and a half hours—and they seemed like nothing. You know what the two and a half hours can be with some conductors: you go crazy; it never ends! But with Toscanini it was as though you had just sat down and played a few notes—and it was time to go home! Because you were never bored. And it was as though he had a built-in time clock that told him when the two and a half hours were at an end. He would pull out his watch—you remember?—but he didn't have to. He rarely was off; and if he did keep us five minutes overtime he was apologetic about it. It was because he knew how to apportion time in a rehearsal— knew what he could do in the time, and never began something he wouldn't be able to finish within the time available.

You got a beat—you watched him—and you followed him. When he looked in your direction you just *had* to play—you couldn't just sit there. Did we feel the force of his presence? Always—always! As soon as he walked in it was just like a magnet: you could feel the magnetic lines pulling you.

Others may have had finer stick techniques—meticulous stuff, dividing everything; but I don't think the Old Man was interested in that. He was interested in the line of the music; and it would come out by singing: he was singing all the time, and he made you sing on your instrument. Of course his beat was always clear in its placing of everything in the measure:

within the meter it was delineative. Sometimes in big climaxes
it would go round in circles; but you still knew where you were.
And he could make a beat last forever when he was prolonging
something: you'd think his arm was a mile long. He didn't have
to stop and talk when he came to a change of tempo or change
of meter: he was prepared; he knew *before* what he wanted to
do; he didn't have to talk about it; he *did* it; and you watched
him and followed him. There are conductors—Cantelli was another—who don't *have* to speak; and very few like the Old Man
in that respect. You watched his arms and made the *crescendos*
where *they* made them. *He* was excited; so *you* would get excited: in the Verdi *Requiem* your hair stood up.

I remember that many times we went through a slow movement, and he wasn't satisfied with it and said, "*Da capo*"; and
we did the whole thing through again; and this time we began
to get a feeling of line, of continuity—instead of stopping every
two bars, with some conductors, and never getting to play the
thing through. And I remember once, during a Brahms cycle,
we went through a symphony from beginning to end at the first
rehearsal. The Old Man stood there like a child: we had done
what he wanted; he had nothing to say; and we still had two
more rehearsals. So he said: "*You* know it; *I* know it: go home—
I'll see you at the concert."

What he stopped for was little things—to get them exactly
the way he wanted them. And it was when things didn't go
that the tantrums came—especially when he was excited. If he
knew something was difficult, he was patient—*very* patient. But
something wrong that was stupid or careless infuriated him. He
couldn't stand any sloppiness or casualness, because *he* wasn't
that way. I remember his saying *he* was sweating and wet, and
we had to be too: *he* was giving everything he had, and *we* had
to give it.

I loved him even when he yelled, because he never yelled at
me, after all: he yelled at the whole viola section; and when

you're taking only one twelfth of it that's all right. But when you're a solo clarinet or English horn taking all of it, then it's hard; and it was very hard on some of the men.

As for what the Old Man had that made you give everything—and what Cantelli had—a lot of conductors you don't look at: they don't have the personality or the magnetism to hold your attention; so you play with your head buried in the music, you see only by peripheral vision the beat going up and down, and as a result you fall in where you shouldn't, or you don't make the retards where they are wanted. But the Old Man and Cantelli got what they wanted because you were always watching them; you had to look at them; and when you looked you saw what they wanted and you had to do it.

In an orchestra there are always some men who don't care and don't give their utmost—who give just the bare minimum, just enough to get by. The Old Man got more out of most of the men than they would ordinarily give to a conductor; and they gave it because they looked at what was up there and they *had* to. That red face—that violence—it could kill anyone! It was like nature—like a raging sea, or a thunderstorm: it's bigger than you, and you don't buck it—you have to go along with it. You couldn't hold back with the Old Man: he made you do what he wanted. So he got more out of most players than they were willing to give; and they didn't like it: they complained that he was a tyrant, that he worked us too hard; but if they had given at the beginning, he wouldn't have had to. The Old Man knew he had to; he knew that if he allowed the men an inch they would take a yard. He told Cantelli: "Never say *bene, bravo*—never, never! Always say it's not good enough, and maybe you'll get something." Once in a while he might say, *"Non c'è male*—not bad"—once in a while. Generally it was "All right, but it could be better." But after the rehearsal—or when you'd go out to his home—he was sweet, like a child. I loved the Old Man; and I think everybody did.

53

You knew that as a man he had principle and character: what he felt was right was right; and you could kill him but it would still be right. It was like a cat: you can't make a cat do anything; he's got courage and guts. A dog will try to win your affection; the Old Man wouldn't—with anybody. He was a man; and I think he had the feeling that Beethoven was the same kind of man: I remember his saying once, "Beethoven was real man"—meaning no fooling around there: solid; and that's the way *he* was. You knew he couldn't be pulled or swayed by management—that if NBC didn't do what he liked he'd stay home: for $6,000 a concert he'd tell them to go to hell.[1] Someone else would be influenced by the money; but it didn't influence him; and so you had respect for him—great respect for the Old Man. At rehearsal breaks he would talk to everybody, and get carried away and talk about programs he did long ago—always friendly, sweet and kind; but you knew flattery would get you nowhere. And I think he was hardest on himself. Were you there when he slapped himself in the face? We had played something; and he said: "I listen to this performance; and I was *stupido!*" and boom! he knocked himself in the face. It would have knocked anybody else over.

You knew when he came in to do a work that he had studied it and really worked it over—that he knew it and knew what he wanted. He was not like the conductors who let the orchestra carry the ball, and remember by what it does: he was always *leading* the orchestra; he knew what he wanted, and you knew that he knew. He never came to a rehearsal unprepared—never. Everything was prepared thoroughly—including new works he didn't know. He got the score of the Shostakovich Seventh on Wednesday, and by Friday he had the whole thing memorized. (By the way, did you hear the story about that symphony? Just before the Old Man died his son was playing records for him; and one of the things he played was the Shostakovich Seventh. The Old Man asked what it was; and when Walter told him, he said: "Did I play that?" Walter said yes; and the Old Man said: "I must have been crazy." He was a little intolerant of modern stuff; but he was old. He always said let a young guy like Cantelli do new music: *he* did enough of it when *he* was young.)

Another thing you knew about him was that no matter what happened at a performance he would never bat an eye—never; never show anything to the public or on his face. But when he played the piece the next time, two or three years later, he'd say: "You remember when you played . . . ?" (That was when he was in good humor.) And he had no favorites: he would bawl out anybody; because the only thing he cared about was the music. One of the men came from the same town as the Old Man, Parma; and they were friends; but once when he played badly the Old Man said: "If I see you on the street in Parma I go on other side!"

What I remember about his performances? The way he looked when he walked out on the stage—his meticulous appearance, with his shoes and pants and everything just perfect. Even before he came out, everybody's eyes were watching that corner for his entrance; and when he walked out he was ready, set, and all extraneous things had to be forgotten. You could tell what the music was doing by his face. I often think of the start of the Brahms Second or the Brahms Fourth: how quietly and peacefully the Old Man would begin it, letting the music play itself; and here his face—his skin—was white. Then, when the music became excited, his blood went up, his face got red, and he was singing away, yelling at the top of his lungs, his whole being 'gone'. That's when, if anything went wrong, everything was at the top, and the top blew off. What happened in quiet music was all right—nothing to get excited about.

The beginning of the Brahms Second was an example of his repose—his letting the music flow, instead of pushing it. And there was also the clarity. I remember a thing like Strauss's

Heldenleben, where there are passages of sixteenth-notes that go on for bar after bar after bar; and with some conductors you get time to play only fifteen and a half sixteenths, and you lose the rhythm and begin to fish for the notes and can't find them. With the Old Man the tempo was exactly straight, and there always seemed to be room for the last sixteenth: you could play all of them. It was always possible to play more notes with him than with anybody else. Other conductors, when they come to the concert, get excited and play the music faster, thinking that way it is more brilliant. But when the Old Man took a tempo at a rehearsal you knew that when you played the piece at the concert it would be that tempo.

I don't think the concerts were as good as the rehearsals, in many cases. I remember I'd feel sorry for the Old Man: I knew the way he worked at things at rehearsals; and many times they didn't go that way at the broadcast. He tried and gave his utmost; but I remember his saying it never went off at the concerts the way it did at rehearsal; and I think this hurt him inside, and I felt sorry for him. One reason for the difference was the strain and tension on everybody's part at the broadcast, because at NBC we played a program only once, whereas other orchestras would have played it two or three times. Also I think he was basically a shy man and may have been bothered by the audience, even though he didn't have much respect for it, judging by the remark he'd make once in a while: "Anything you do is good enough for them."

The performances I remember? The *Otello*: it was immense! Also the *Aida*—and the *Requiem.* And I'll tell you a performance that stands out in my memory—the *Skaters Waltz:* beautiful! And other things like that: the Boccherini Minuet, the *Zampa* Overture—the so-called junk stuff. When we went through the *Zampa* Overture the first time in '43 he said he hadn't done it in years and it was fun—let's do it again; so we repeated it! Could he play the *Blue Danube Waltz?!* And how!

He knew all that stuff. Maybe it was at the rehearsal of *Zampa* that Mitropoulos was present; and when some of the men asked him how he liked the music, he said: "There is no bad music, only bad conductors."

Yes, the Old Man's performances did change: toward the end he knew he was getting old, and he was afraid of their getting draggy and heavy like Bruno Walter's. As for the greater energy you speak of in the performances of the first NBC years, *he* was younger, and everybody in the orchestra was trying and working like crazy. Also it was a better orchestra in those years— with some of the woodwinds and those strings. Some of the old boys in the Philharmonic still talk about the Old Man and are convinced he was much better when he was there than when he was at NBC; but I suspect these things grow in people's imaginations.

He hated recording. He would hate it even more the way it's done today; but in the 78-rpm days he hated it because of the business of stopping at the end of a side. He felt that he should conduct the performance and the engineers should worry about getting it on the record; that when he couldn't just think about the performance but had to think about stopping, it spoiled the performance. And besides, it never did sound right on the record. When tape came in, the difficulty was that once he started what was intended as a short test passage, he might keep going to the end of a movement and find out then that it hadn't been recorded.

He gave no interviews, accepted no honors: he felt he was merely doing his job of serving the composer, and nothing was owed him—everything was owed the composer. That was why he could conduct a Strauss waltz. He did nothing for show, nothing for himself; and that was why we worked. *He* was working like crazy for the composer; so *we* worked like crazy with him.

I remember when we did the *Grand Canyon Suite* he kept

57

asking Grofé if the tempo was right and so on: after all, Grofé was the composer, and the Old Man always felt the composer was much more important than the conductor. Every time he asked Grofé anything he called him 'Maestro'; and Grofé was just in heaven. When it was all over the Old Man called him up to the podium to ask him if everything was all right; and Grofé said yes and was so overcome as he backed away that he backed into the chairs and fell over them.

The Old Man just seemed more sincere than anyone else—trying to find what a man like Beethoven had put into his music. I remember what Hindemith said once: "Music has a face: leave it alone. If you don't like it, don't play it, but don't change it." The Old Man felt like that.

Alexander Kipnis

HAGGIN:

I wanted also to get to the singers who had sung with Toscanini. The record-reviewers who specialized in opera disapproved of his performances of Verdi's operas on records, in which he didn't permit the self-indulgent singing that distorted tempo and phrase. These reviewers objected to his "fast and rigid tempos" that "thwarted" the singers' attempts to sing "expressively"; and contended that he used only the inexperienced and inferior singers who would submit to his tyranny. What I heard was a beautifully and coherently plastic flow, created by a beat which was never anything but flexible in relation to the music, and was unyielding, in relation to the singer, only in compelling him to operate within that plastic flow. Moreover, Milanov, Albanese, Nelli, Peerce, Warren, Vinay, Valdengo and others were not inferior singers, but some of the best available to him at the time, and sang expressively with him. So did the famous singers of the past whom he conducted—Destinn, Fremstad, Hempel, Matzenauer, Rethberg, Kipnis. Had he conducted differently for these singers? Or had they accepted his tyranny? I couldn't ask Destinn, Fremstad, Hempel and Matzenauer, who were dead, or Rethberg, who didn't reply to my letter asking if I might see her; but I was able to ask Kipnis. A friend reported having met him at a party, where he had talked about Toscanini, mostly with admiration, but with strong objections to the 1937 Salzburg Magic Flute. These were something I decidedly wanted to hear; and luckily Kipnis was willing to tell me about them.

KIPNIS:

I sang for the first time with Toscanini in Bayreuth in 1930. I was one of the last singers to arrive for the rehearsals. Most of the singers came six or eight weeks before the beginning of the festival; but I had already sung in Bayreuth, and was allowed to come only two weeks before the beginning. Toscanini was very impatient; and I had a rehearsal with him as soon as I arrived. It was perfectly pleasant, and I was not nervous at all—perhaps because I knew my part well and had sung it at Bayreuth before. Yes, of course I knew Toscanini's formidable reputation; but I also knew what I could offer, and there was no reason for me to be nervous. One of the assistant-conductors played the piano, and I sang the entire monologue of King Marke from *Tristan*. Toscanini walked back and forth in the room; he didn't interrupt—he just listened; and once in a while he made a gesture as if he were going to conduct. When I finished he didn't say a word, but only grabbed me by my hand and took me down to where Siegfried Wagner was sitting in the *Festspielhaus*, and said: "Why don't *all* the singers sing like that? Your father wrote '*Muss es sein*'; but on your stage they sing '*Mussssss es sein*' with six s's." He was objecting to the fact that the singers gave more importance and emphasis to pronouncing the word than to singing the music.

No, I don't recall any further rehearsals. The rehearsals of *Tristan* were very long; and I didn't stay for all of them because King Marke has only two scenes. But I can say that Toscanini's manner of rehearsing was more or less routine, though a very painstaking routine. A singer, if he knows his responsibility, surely is nervous before each performance; but after he has sung several pages and knows that his voice is in good condition, all the nervousness disappears. And so it was with Toscanini: we all knew what he expected of us; and after the first fifteen or twenty minutes of rehearsing with him it became absolutely natural and we were colleagues: he was not Maestro Toscanini in the sense that he was someone we had to fear. And it was very pleasant. (The only time in my experience that he was not very pleasant was in Buenos Aires, when he was suffering from a terribly painful bursitis, which made it difficult for him to conduct, and he conducted with both hands, holding one hand with the other in order to be able to lift his baton.) Also, Toscanini could be a diplomat in his own way—or a realist. We had heard many stories about his calling in the manager of La Scala and demanding *"un altro baritono"* or *"un altro tenore"* because the baritone or tenor didn't sing well; but when I was with him in Bayreuth we didn't have *un altro tenore*; we had Melchior to sing Tristan, and Melchior was the best; so Toscanini was calm—he didn't break any batons or throw any scores.

In his working with singers Toscanini was very expressive; and he demonstrated how a phrase should be sung with his hoarse voice and with his piano-playing, which was definitely not the playing of a pianist. I remember in Salzburg when he demonstrated to Milanov how to take certain phrases in Verdi's *Requiem*, and I wondered how she would do them; because even with his hoarse voice and his piano-playing the music sounded as if it were created at that moment. Milanov said: "I cannot do it because I haven't the breath support"; and Toscanini was very kind and smiled. I don't remember him being irritable or shouting at any time: in Salzburg he was as though in his own home. There was no excitement there; and I think he felt happier than in Bayreuth. I don't know what it was in

Bayreuth—maybe the atmosphere, the spirit, or the feeling that this was Wagner's place. There was still, written in chalk on the door of one of the dressing rooms, Wagner's invitation to the soloists to have tea that afternoon after the rehearsal; so you had the feeling that the spirit of old Wagner was still there (the Germans say, *"Der spukt herum."*). Also, though it never came out in public, there was the unpleasant situation with Muck and Toscanini on the same stage, in the same theater, in the same town: you could feel the jealousy of Muck. Until Toscanini came, Muck was the principal conductor and the king—the musical Amfortas of Bayreuth. When Toscanini came, they built a room for him—the so-called conductor's room; and it was embarrassing when Muck, with a bitter expression on his Mephistophelian face, shouted: "So many years we have been in Bayreuth without a conductor's room; but now we have to have a conductor's room for Mr. Toscanini!" That summer Siegfried Wagner passed away; and a few days after his burial we had a concert in the *Festspielhaus*. On the program was the *Siegfried-Idyll* conducted by Toscanini: it was the most beautiful *Siegfried-Idyll* I have ever heard in my life; and everyone in the audience had tears in his eyes from the sound of this music, and the thought that the Siegfried for whom it was written was no more. Then old Muck conducted the Funeral March from *Die Götterdämmerung*: it was so old, like a piece of parchment, a piece of dusty old scenery—in comparison with the unbelievably beautiful *Siegfried-Idyll*. A few days after that we had a benefit concert for retired elderly singers who were in need. Maria Müller and I were the soloists; and the concert was in a little old and beautiful theater, the *Markgrafentheater*. Toscanini and his family sat on the right side of the theater, Muck with his—I don't know if it was a family—on the left side; and they didn't look at each other. Oh yes, definitely, Muck started it. Toscanini had no reason to be jealous: he had his operas to conduct, and he was concerned only about his artists and rehearsing them so they knew their parts.[1]

You ask about the hypnotic power which some have spoken about—which they say caused musicians to exceed their capacities. I would say every singer tries to do his best in any case. The inspiration comes, of course; but we singers always felt great responsibility, and gave our best, with Toscanini or without Toscanini. I cannot say that when I sang with him I gave a hundred percent, and when I sang with another conductor I gave sixty percent or eighty percent.

I remember that singing a part with Toscanini—Sarastro, Rocco, the Landgraf—very often I made accents which Toscanini had not heard from other singers; and at such moments he would look up, but he didn't say anything—he didn't say, "Don't do that." For instance, in *Tristan,* when King Marke says: *"MIR dies? Dies, Tristan, MIR?"*—in this quasi-*parlando* outcry I diminished the tone on *mir,* going over to a slightly breathy quality; and Toscanini looked up, but he didn't say anything. He insisted on the *rhythm* being the way he wanted it; but he never told me anything about phrasing, and he never said anything about the phrasing or accents which represented my feeling. I remember one thing he insisted on: in Bayreuth the melodic turns in *Tannhäuser* were done in the German way, as part of the rhythm of the measure; but Toscanini insisted on the more graceful Italian way, in which they were delayed and sung as a quick introduction to the next beat.

Other examples of such Italian style or taste? I would say his *Tristan* was like an Italian opera; and curiously enough, some time before Toscanini came to Bayreuth, Siegfried Wagner said *Tristan* should be sung like an Italian opera. So when some of the singers and critics found fault with Toscanini's *Tristan,* saying: "It is like an Italian opera," I answered: "But Siegfried Wagner said very clearly that it should be sung like an Italian opera." And once, when Koussevitzky, who didn't care very much for Toscanini, said to me: "I heard *Tristan* with

you in Bayreuth. Don't you think it was like an Italian opera?",
I told him the same thing, and said that was the way *Tristan*
should be sung, because it was not a Teutonic opera.

The chief characteristic of Toscanini's Tristan was its lyricism, which the typical German conductor doesn't bring to this
work. The heavy staccato style in which Kurwenal sings in the
first act is suitable for the music of Kurwenal, but not for what
Isolde or Tristan or Marke sings, which has nothing Teutonic
whatsoever. I always loved the lyrical approach to *Tristan*,
which I heard many times from other conductors, but never
in such a degree as from Toscanini. We had a conductor in
Berlin named Leo Blech, who had a lyrical approach almost to
anything. And I sang in *Tristan* very often with Furtwängler,
who in this work was definitely not one of the Teutonic conductors.

Toscanini's *Tannhäuser* was different. Though the work is
not late Wagner, still it is a German opera, in a German style.
But Elisabeth, Venus, Wolfram, the March, the Hymn are
based on a lyrical approach: the only characters who are a little
dramatic are the Landgraf and Biterolf. And Toscanini's approach to every phrase was very soft. Of course he made the
ensemble of the knights, when Tannhäuser is sent away to
Rome, very dramatic, and also Tannhäuser's aria when he returns from Rome; but they were dramatic in the frame of a
lyrical picture. It was not Italian; it had its German character;
but in this character it was lyrical. Toscanini always insisted:
"Sing. Sing. I would like to hear a singing tone." Also it was
the first *Tannhäuser* in which the Hymn sounded like a hymn.
Usually it was taken so fast that what should be heroic praise of
Venus sounded like a little ditty. In Toscanini's slower tempo it
was a real hymn. Later, other conductors took over his tempo;
but they made it *too* slow.

Die Meistersinger I didn't sing with Toscanini; and I didn't
hear the whole opera from him in Salzburg, only scenes; but I

was very much impressed. My feeling in general was that Toscanini was a dramatic conductor—that his real element was the drama of Beethoven's symphonies, *Fidelio, Tristan, Tannhäuser, Parsifal;* although being a great musician he could also conduct a comedy or a purely lyrical opera. In performing *Die Meistersinger* he was concerned with the music, not with the comedy; and being guided purely by the music he, for example, avoided all exaggerated caricature—with Beckmesser, or with Kothner. He didn't want the usual exaggerated *"DER— SAENGER—SITZT!!!";* he wanted *"Der Sänger sitzt!"*—sung, as it is written in the score. And the same with *"Fanget an!"*

Somebody said that it's not difficult to conduct Wagner; that it's more difficult to conduct Donizetti or early Verdi, because it doesn't guide you, it doesn't tell you much, whereas Wagner tells you clearly everything you need to know. Still, in spite of his clarity, a lot of good conductors make mistakes in Wagner. Whereas with Toscanini, something like the changes in rhythm—from three beats to four, and four to five—just before Isolde's entrance in the last act of *Tristan*—such a headache for the tenors!—with Toscanini it went just like that . . . As for his performance of *Die Meistersinger*, and the German criticisms you mention—that it was too transparent, too lyrical, not solid and German—I feel that its lyrical character was justified. Surely, it is a German opera; but it is not a Teutonic opera like *Die Walküre* or *Die Götterdämmerung.*

I come now to *The Magic Flute* in Salzburg. As I said before, in spite of his *Falstaff* my feeling was that Toscanini's real element was drama, not comedy. And we had the impression that he wanted to make of *The Magic Flute* something different from what he used to hear. He thought the German conductors had such respect and devotion for Mozart that they tried to make of *The Magic Flute* a bombastic opera, by making everything too slow: *Andante* was made *Larghetto*, *Larghetto* was made *Adagio*, *Allegro* was made *Andantino*. And he decided

65

this was wrong—this was why *The Magic Flute* was not as successful as *The Marriage of Figaro* and *Don Giovanni*. That was in his mind when he came to the rehearsals. He knew the music well, and also the libretto: in spite of not being very fluent in German he knew every sentence, every word of the opera by heart. And his idea seemed to be that everyone in the opera had a little song to sing, which should be delivered in a fast tempo —except the service of Sarastro and the priests. Possibly he was right in some places; but the impression we singers received at that time was that the entire opera was upside down. He spent a great deal of rehearsal time with the Three Ladies—with their first entrance, which sounded magnificent, as I never heard it sound before. Even now, on a bad tape, it sounds good. But Papageno's entrance, *"Der Vogelfänger bin ich"*, was too fast; Tamino's *"Dies Bildnis"* was definitely too fast; the Queen of the Night's first aria, *"Zum Leiden bin ich auserkoren"*, was taken at such a speed that she could not follow the beat with her fast runs, and the orchestra and the singer were often far apart.[2] Then the presentation of Tamino's flute, the recitatives of his approach to the temple, his conversation with the Speaker —all were too fast. At the beginning of the second act, the entrance of the priests, Mozart wrote *Adagio*; and this was the slowest *adagio* I have ever heard. Sarastro's *"O Isis und Osiris"* was very slow: this was considered to be a service in the temple, not a little song. The Queen of the Night's second aria, *"Der Hölle Rache"*, was too fast. Sarastro's *"In diesen heiligen Hallen"*, which is marked *Larghetto*, was not very satisfactory—too fast. Pamina's *"Ach, ich fühl's"* also was a little too fast; the trio of Pamina, Tamino and Sarastro was much too fast; Papageno's *"Ein Mädchen oder Weibchen"* also went much too fast. The desire to drive this opera, to make it faster and faster, was felt all the way through; and it was not satisfactory. It's a heavenly, beautiful opera; and it cannot be changed. In spite of the fact that it is Mozart, it is a typical German opera—more

66

German, I would say, than *Die Entführung*.

After the first rehearsal we singers had a meeting. We realized that the opera might be a fiasco; and it was not only Toscanini's performance: it was everybody's performance. We had a fine cast, of singers who were well equipped and acquainted with the music; each of us had a position, and none of us was a 'prima donna' singer: we were all pulling together and in the same direction, and wanted a success not for this one or that one but for all. We realized that this might not happen; and we didn't know what to do. So we went to Dr. Graf, who was staging the opera, and asked him to speak to Toscanini. He said: "It is more possible to move the mountain behind the *Festspielhaus* than to change Toscanini's mind. If you want to sing the performance, and if you want us to *have* a performance, sing the way he conducts. If you want to change him, the best thing would be to quit." We had another meeting; and we decided to sing. The opera did not turn out as badly as we expected; but it was not a success. People don't talk about *The Magic Flute* with Toscanini as they talk about his *Tristan* or Verdi *Requiem* or *Missa Solemnis*. *The Magic Flute* is a forgotten thing: when one speaks with people who were in Salzburg *The Magic Flute* doesn't come up. You tell me you remember the audiences' enthusiasm;[3] but how could a performance with Toscanini *not* be received with enthusiasm, even if it were a *bad* performance? That is something to keep clearly in mind. No, *The Magic Flute* didn't have the Toscanini touch, the Toscanini fire. Also, not one word was cut in the dialogue; and I believe that with so much dialogue the music lost some of its impact. (Speaking of the dialogue reminds me of something I never experienced with any other conductor. Toscanini asked us to modulate the dialogue into the key of the aria which followed it. He asked me, for instance, to modulate into F major for the aria "*O Isis und Osiris*", and into E major for "*In diesen heiligen Hallen*".)

Fidelio also has a great deal of dialogue; but it has drama, which *The Magic Flute* doesn't have. And it doesn't need a sense of humor. So *Fidelio* in Salzburg was a different thing, because here Toscanini was in his element. We speak of a dramatic tenor or a dramatic soprano; and Toscanini was a dramatic conductor. No, we weren't aware that the tempos were faster than usual here too—or rather, we knew it was faster, but we didn't *feel* it, possibly because the drive of the drama was so strong, so immense. I was struck only by Toscanini's faster tempo in the finale of the first act, when the prisoners go back into the prison. The tempo in the score is very indicative —*alla breve*, very fast—but nobody does it in that tempo. Toscanini did, and he was right: in his tempo the drama came out very strong—even when the singing ended and the orchestra went on, and Rocco and Fidelio, loaded with their tools, started down to the dungeon.

Toscanini was completely absorbed in the music of *Fidelio*: I think he was not *there*, actually. He was like a high priest of this work: in what he did, it was as if he felt Beethoven was present; and we had a beautiful performance. At the first rehearsal with piano we started from the very beginning; and after each number we stopped and waited for corrections from Toscanini. He was brief and to the point; and we understood him very well, speaking some Italian, some German, and also some English. After Florestan's aria at the beginning of the second act there is the famous digging duet; and when the Fidelio and I finished it, we waited for corrections. Toscanini sat with his head bent down deep in his hands, and didn't say a word. After a few minutes he looked up at us and said, "What music!" At that moment the Fidelio—since you heard it you know who she was—went over to Toscanini and embraced him and kissed him on the mouth; and he was so embarrassed that he said loudly: "If you do that again I will not transpose your aria!"

68

In Salzburg one morning, after a rehearsal that had gone very well, I came out of the *Festspielhaus* and saw Toscanini sitting in his car. When he saw me he beckoned to me; and when I came to him he didn't say a word, but only patted my cheek! And I can tell you another story like that, about his kindness. In 1936 he came to Vienna to conduct the *Missa Solemnis* with the Vienna Philharmonic, the chorus of the Opera, and good soloists. In the *Benedictus* the long violin solo is played by the concertmaster of the orchestra; and this time it was played by old Rosé, who had been concertmaster for a generation—under Mahler, Strauss, and several others. At the rehearsal this little old man, with lots of white hair, stood up and stepped up in front near Toscanini, and seemingly was so afraid he might not please Toscanini that his face was pale and his hands trembled as he lifted his violin and started the long high note before the main theme of the solo. His performance wasn't bad, but it wasn't very good; and when he finished Toscanini bent down to him and patted him on the back!

I also remember something amusing that happened at the first orchestral rehearsal. After twenty years of service a member of the Vienna Philharmonic automatically acquired the title of Professor, just as a singer, who after twenty years might have a voice like the bark of a dog, acquired the title of *Kammersänger*. At Toscanini's first orchestral rehearsal the manager of the orchestra presented several players to him: this oboist was Professor A, this clarinettist was Professor B, this trumpet-player was Professor Z, and so on. Then the rehearsal began; and Toscanini corrected this and that, controlling his impatience for a long time; but finally he burst out: "*Tutti sono professori, ma non possano suonare!*" ["They are all professors, but cannot play!"]

I was not engaged originally for this performance of the *Missa Solemnis*. Toscanini didn't pick the soloists; and the bass, who was from Berlin, couldn't come for the first rehearsal. It was my first year in the Vienna Opera; and I was rehearsing in some opera when the Director came in and told me that the bass for the *Missa Solemnis* couldn't come, and would I be so kind as to help out only for this rehearsal. I said, "Surely." The rehearsal was to begin in about fifteen minutes in the *Grosser Musikvereinsaal*, which was very near the Opera; and I went there and greeted Toscanini, whom I knew from Bayreuth. He was very quiet and didn't say anything; then he started the rehearsal, which was with piano. Everything was all right; here and there he corrected a tempo; and I remember that he was very dramatic about the *Crucifixus*: he said he wanted it to be like hammering—"CRU - CI - FI - XUS!"—as if Christ were being nailed to the cross. After the rehearsal, as soon as I got to my hotel, I received a telephone call from the Director of the Opera: "Toscanini wants you to sing in the performance; he doesn't want the other man. Could you do it?" I said, "*Could I?!*" This was a renewal of our activities; but I sang with him in Vienna only in this *Missa Solemnis*.

I had sung in the *Missa* two years before in Vienna with Fritz Busch. He was a good, reliable conductor, but of an entirely different caliber from Toscanini: the burning of a volcano that there was always in Toscanini—there was no trace of this in Busch. And so the real feeling of the *Missa Solemnis* came to me only when I sang in it with Toscanini. This was an entirely different conception, an entirely different fanaticism—burning—expression—drama. The powerful rhythm of the opening chords of the *Kyrie!* And later, the *crescendo* to the *Christe:* the drive of this *Christe* I never experienced with any other conductor. I have on a tape the *Missa Solemnis* in which I sang with Toscanini in New York in 1940; and I think it is one of the greatest things he did.

But listening to this tape, I wonder why Toscanini allowed the soprano sometimes to dominate the solo quartet. It would be different if the soprano had the melody and the other voices were subordinate; but in a passage where everybody is supposed to sing *piano*, Toscanini allowed the soprano to sing so much louder than the others. In the *Agnus Dei* too the mezzo-soprano sometimes shouts so loud. I hear the beautiful voice of Bjoerling, and I have a good voice, and we could sing loud; but always Toscanini would hold up his hand to us, and the mezzo-soprano would come out too loud. I hear the same thing in the Victor recording of Verdi's *Requiem*. If somebody has the melody, surely he should come out. But in the *Lacrymosa*, after the mezzo-soprano sings her solo, the bass sings the same thing while she sings only "ah - ah - ah - ah"; and though he has the solo her "ah" comes out with such force that you can almost not hear his melody. The same thing happens again when the soprano sings the "ah".

I sang in the *Missa Solemnis* again with Toscanini in 1942 —with different soloists whose names I don't remember, including a young lady whose presence could be explained only by Toscanini's eye for feminine beauty. Everybody was depressed by that singer; and it wasn't possible to say anything: none of us was on such terms with Toscanini that he could go to him and simply say: "Maestro, you cannot let her sing." I never tried to get close to Toscanini. Once we visited him in the Hotel Astor; and he asked us why we didn't come to see him more often, complaining that so many people came and bothered him, while the people he would like to see didn't come.

No, the *Fidelio* was not the revelation to me that the *Missa* was. I had had so many performances—good, poor, mediocre. And when you sing in opera you are not in such contact with the conductor as in a concert: the orchestra and the prompter's box are in between. Also you are performing a character—which is not like just standing there and getting the music in your face. So I can say the *Fidelio* was very good, and very strong, and made a strong impression during the rehearsals; but it didn't affect me as the *Missa Solemnis* did.

71

The Ninth Symphony was, in a way, a surprise for me. I expected Toscanini to take the recitative in tempo; but he made it very flexible, and didn't insist on having it go one, two, three, one, two, three. It was very simple; and it was easy to sing. The last phrase on the word *"freudenvollere"* is written to be sung in one breath; and when I sang it once with Bruno Walter he said: "Do me a favor and don't sing it in one breath." I asked why; and he said: "Because most of the people, instead of listening to the music, sit there wondering, 'Will he make it?'" At the first rehearsal with Toscanini I again broke the phrase—and he didn't say anything: I sang it that way. As for my impression of his performance, certainly it was different from others: it had more drive, more fire, more fanaticism; it was not what we used to call *sehr gemütlich*. And I remember the last section of the finale, which begins *Poco allegro* and accelerates *sempre più allegro*: if it is too fast it is banal; but in the tempo in which Toscanini began it and accelerated it, it was extraordinary.

In Oslo once the wife of a conductor there asked me: "What is it about Toscanini—what is it he does that my husband cannot do? Does he do something with his hands? Or with his eyes? Does he conduct faster? Or slower?" I answered what Gurnemanz answers Parsifal. Parsifal asks him: *"Wer ist der Gral?"*; and Gurnemanz says: *"Das sagt sich nicht. Doch bist du selbst zu ihm erkoren, bleibt dir die Kunde unverloren."* ["Who is the Grail?" "That may not be told. But if you are chosen for it, you will not fail to know."]

Even after Toscanini's death, when we hear a recording of his, the power of his conducting and of his conception of the music is still completely alive. The recordings of other conductors become mechanical transcriptions; a recording of Toscanini does not. When I hear the *Missa Solemnis* on the tape that I have, it is not mechanical music; it is to me as if he is standing there and still conducting. This kind of conducting, this kind of interpretation, is not a dead thing.

Nicolas Moldavan

HAGGIN:

More than one NBC player said that Nicolas Moldavan, who played viola in the Flonzaley and the Coolidge Quartets, was a distinguished musician who would undoubtedly have valuable things to say about Toscanini. When he opened the door of his apartment he turned out to be another of the NBC Symphony musicians I had said hello to at rehearsals without knowing their names.

MOLDAVAN:

I could hear Toscanini only occasionally while I was playing in the quartet, because I was always traveling. It was not until I went into the NBC Symphony that I began to know him really—to know what only a musician playing with him could know about him and about what made him great. In this transition from a quartet to an orchestra—particularly with a man like that—I was all ears. And I may say that had I played in quartets *after* playing with Toscanini—with what I learned in those twelve years with him—I would have understood much more about how to play quartets and how to approach music. In a quartet you have four individuals; and if I feel like playing

73

this passage a little broader I take my time; and the cellist takes *his* time; and so the music becomes distorted. What Toscanini taught me was that a piece of music has a frame, and you phrase and build within this frame—any piece of music, a quartet—and if I were starting now I would approach music in the way I learned from him. Most musicians distort: if you listen to a recording you hear this bar is a little longer and this one a little shorter; and Toscanini showed that it wasn't necessary to take such liberties to make a piece of music beautiful.

This conception of music was one of the important things in his conducting. Other conductors we played with—good conductors (they were all good: these days you may not be great, but you have to be good)—it took those conductors half a page to know what they wanted to do, what tempo they wanted to take. Toscanini had the piece of music there like in a frame— in the right tempo, and with whatever he wanted—before his eyes when he started the rehearsal; and if he stopped and started again, it was the same tempo. That was one of his great gifts; and it was something which only those who played with him knew about—those who were able to understand; because there are all sorts of people in the world and in orchestras; and I am speaking about the conscientious, sensitive musicians, who had played a great deal and knew music and would notice things.

That whole picture was always before him. Other conductors work out details here and details there; with him it was the whole: if he got that he was satisfied. Things like up-bow, down-bow, he didn't bother with: he expected you to take care of them. You produced every note clean; the phrasing was up to him. And he did the phrasing—of detail within the whole— with his stick. There were no words: we knew his stick. When he did this or did that with it we knew what it meant: he didn't have to say anything. The build-up of a *crescendo*, for example. Nobody could build up a *crescendo* as he did—by holding you

74

back—holding you—holding you. Other conductors don't know how to do that: they run away with you; and when it comes to the *forte* they haven't anything left. He knew how to build it up gradually. And he did it all with his stick. Other conductors use their tongue—which orchestra musicians hate, and which produces complete disruption and disintegration at a rehearsal. The musicians are used to being told with the stick; and the moment a conductor starts to explain things, they don't listen, and talk about their own business. Some conductors don't stop talking. Bernstein, for example: he can conduct anything—the 5/7 and 3/13 in the modern pieces is nothing for him; but when he comes to Brahms he doesn't stop talking. The musicians hate it: they have played the Brahms symphonies hundreds of times; what can he tell them about that music? Or Bruno Walter: he always talked; and Toscanini got furious and said: "He doesn't let them play!" With Toscanini it was "Watch my stick!", and he let you play. If you did it right he didn't bother you; if you did it wrong he would get angry and say: "Don't you see my hand?" Conductors talk because they don't have rehearsal technique: they know the music, they are good musicians, but they don't know what to do with an orchestra—how to handle it, how to get its attention, how to give it what they have in themselves. Whereas Toscanini knew all this. That was why a rehearsal with Ansermet, who was a fine musician and knew every detail but talked too much, was something you dreaded; but a rehearsal with Toscanini—or with Cantelli—was something you looked forward to. For certain players—the first oboe, the first clarinet, the first horn—who had very responsible and exposed parts, a rehearsal was a difficult time; but for most of us it was something to look forward to. Toscanini would accomplish in two and a half hours what the others with all their talking didn't accomplish in five; and sometimes his rehearsal would be finished in two hours.

Then another thing. An orchestra musician feels the person-

75

ality, the authority of a conductor the moment he steps on the podium and takes his stick and shows what he knows. With other conductors you hesitated. With Toscanini there could be no hesitation, no question: you knew this was a genius standing before you; and you had confidence and respect. It was not because you were afraid of him—because he was the boss and could fire you—which he never did in all the years that I was there—not even one clarinet-player who drove him crazy because his playing was so cold. No, it was because you felt that this man standing there was a superior human being.

Also, you were affected by his intensity. There were times, in the playing, when everybody felt like giving, like going with him: those were the great moments. Or if he tried two or three times and it didn't go—the tempo wasn't right for him, or something else—then it was *"Andiamo!"*; and something in it—the fire in him—would communicate itself to us; we would feel it with him, and would go all together. This happened many times; and the only explanation was just magnetism, electricity.

Then there was the knowledge he had. No matter what it was—the quartet literature, the violin literature, the cello literature, the piano literature—he knew everything. It was most amazing. Others have great knowledge too: I remember when I was with the quartet in Los Angeles once, we had an evening with musicians—Feuermann was there, and Szigeti, and Szell—and we played quartets for our pleasure. And Szell sat down at the piano afterwards and played not only the quartets but each part separately. Though Szell leaves me cold as a conductor, he has this great knowledge. But Toscanini surpassed them all. To remember so many things—it was fantastic.

And his integrity. He always rehearsed the orchestra's part in a concerto without the soloist. How many conductors do that? To them it is an accompaniment; to him it was a piece of music, which had to be rehearsed. When the soloist came to rehearse with the orchestra, Toscanini never said a word to him

if the playing was musical; and he followed one hundred percent. The last time Heifetz played the Mendelssohn Concerto
with us, he began the Allegro of the finale in a much faster
tempo at the concert than at the rehearsal; and the Old Man
didn't try to hold him back: he—and we all—followed Heifetz
through to perfection. With singers sometimes he had trouble:
they held the phrase, or they mispronounced a word. He stopped
Nan Merriman once because the Italian word had two r's and
she pronounced only one. It was always *"Parole!"* and "Don't
swallow the words!" and "Don't eat the music!" But he was
patient with singers—provided they were musical. He never had
trouble with Jan Peerce, or with any other musical singer.

For me his great gift, his genius, was that he kept the music
always alive, so that people didn't fall asleep, as they often do.
Particularly in a slow movement, where it's very easy to get
sluggish, and it gets slower and slower, until the trend of the
music is lost. When Toscanini felt that it was slowing down,
he was able—without giving any indication, without anybody
noticing it—to bring it alive. In a Haydn or Mozart symphony,
for instance, those long slow movements, which were made so
much longer by everybody else, and dragged out until they fell
apart and were dead: with him they were always alive. That is
the greatest test—not to conduct Strauss.

Speaking about Mozart, one year Bruno Walter, who was
considered a Mozart specialist, conducted the G-minor Symphony and made it very graceful and gay. Toscanini was at the
rehearsal; and we knew by the way he looked, and walked back
and forth, and left the hall, that he was angry. A month later,
or whenever it was that he came back to conduct us, he put on
this symphony; and at the rehearsal he started the first bars and
stopped: "No — NO — NO!!! Everybody imagines Mozart as a
little boy with short pants! No! He was a man! This music
must be *drammatica—molto drammatica! Arco! Arco!"* And the
symphony became another piece—not a tiny thing, graceful and

77

gay, but *molto drammatica*, with full bow. And it made sense, because it was done with conviction, as everything was by Toscanini.

You ask about his tempo in the Andante of the *Jupiter* Symphony, which was considered too fast. He felt that people played *andante* too slowly because they didn't understand that the word *andare* means to walk. And to emphasize the contrast he would exaggerate at the start; but then the tempo would settle down. As he got older he got a little faster: usually a man slows down with age; but with Toscanini it was always forward. And he would come to a rehearsal and begin by saying: "I listened to the record of our performance three years ago of this symphony. Shame on you!—and on me too! Was slow! Was no good!" And as a contrast, to show us, he would start with such a fast tempo—and then of course come down to the right tempo.

This illustrates that he was always listening to what he did before, and studying it, and thinking about it. He was full of music, and always searching in it.

There were great, great moments which I'll never forget as long as I live. One which moved me almost to tears was the *Götterdämmerung* Funeral March, because of the music itself, and because he particularly felt it. There was so much emotion, so much profundity—and power, yes—when he did it. This was one of the rare moments I'll never forget. I remember also Schubert's *Unfinished* Symphony—the rehearsal—not the performance. The performance was fifty percent less; and only the people who were at the rehearsal, who faced him there, could know this. At the performances he stood there and conducted and didn't give a damn—he even had a candy in his mouth: the real work was already done. His great moments were not at the concerts; they were at the rehearsals; and anybody who missed them, missed Toscanini. If you were there you were fortunate;

because that was where there were the moments of beauty and intensity that only Toscanini could achieve.

You ask about changes in the later years. I think he slowed down a great deal in his powers and his demands; and this caused the changes you ask about in the performances. Oh yes, I was aware of them—definitely. Particularly in recordings. With them he had the attitude that he didn't give a damn, because he could never get from the machine the sound which he had in his ears and his mind. Particularly with a piece like *La Mer*, which was a nemesis for him, because he couldn't get the color he thought Debussy meant. At a rehearsal he would somehow —but not on a record. And as you know, for many years he didn't accept the recordings of *La Mer*. It was in later years, when he was less demanding, that he said okay.

I'm a little man, talking about a great man, trying to say why he was great. There was his musicianship, plus a tremendous drive and force. And whatever he did, he did with conviction, with integrity—which was his greatest quality for me. He didn't compromise in anything: in dealing with music he was a man of one hundred percent soul, mind and integrity.

Robert Shaw

HAGGIN:

Robert Shaw didn't himself rehearse and perform under Toscanini; but as the one who prepared the chorus that did rehearse and sing under Toscanini, he could tell about anything of interest in that particular and special working relation. And what he recalled did add new and extraordinary details to the picture of the Toscanini powers and operation.

SHAW:

The first time I met Toscanini was in 1945, when the Collegiate Chorale was to sing in Beethoven's Ninth with him. I went up to check the tempo changes with him and to ask him about certain technical things. Because we were a little short of men's voices during the war years we'd been in the habit of using some altos occasionally in high tenor parts; and in the Ninth I thought it would be wise occasionally to use some tenors in low alto parts too. I asked Toscanini if this would be all right with him. He said: "Will it make the score sound?" I said: "Maestro, I think this is the only way it *can* be made to sound." And he said: "Anything which makes the score sound is right." Then he said: "You know, I have never had a good

80

performance of this work. Sometimes the chorus is bad; sometimes the orchestra is bad; many times the soloists are bad. And
many times *I* am terrible." It was this fantastic modesty that
was part of the way he moved people. And I also think it was
the thing that made his tantrums easy to take. They *were* child-
ish; but they weren't "You are crucifying *me*; you are being cruel
to *me*." It was "You're being cruel to Beethoven; you are being
cruel to Verdi."

Toscanini was to come and listen and take the final rehearsal of the chorus before the orchestral rehearsals. Everybody
was there an hour early for a brush-up. This was in the City
Center, up on the fourth floor; and I was rehearsing when
someone looked in through the doorway and said, "Maestro's
here." He walked in with that slow, deliberate walk, and saw us
and came over. We greeted each other, and I introduced him,
which was unnecessary of course; and assuming that he would
take the rehearsal, I said: "Maestro, where would you like to
begin?" And he said: "No, you conduct. I listen." So I began,
more than a little embarrassed; because although the group was
very well disciplined, and I felt it was prepared for what *he*
might do, I didn't know whether *I* could pull it off. What happened was that as I conducted he walked up and down in back
of me. It was a long walk—if you remember that City Center
rehearsal hall; and of course everybody's eyes followed him as
he walked. They told me later that when we would get to a
fermata or a change of tempo he would stop and stand still until
we went on. When we finished he came—and it sounds silly—
but he was crying, and he threw his arms around me and said:
"It's the first time that I hear it sung." Then he started to walk
away, and said: "I'll see you at Carnegie Hall." He didn't touch
it at all. And in Carnegie Hall we just ran through it with the
orchestra.

By the time we got to know him he was a legend, which
prepared the young people of the early Collegiate Chorale—

who didn't ever expect to see him alive anywhere, let alone be in the same room with him—it prepared them, if he said, "Jump off the twenty-seventh story," to do that. As for our impressions when we worked with him, for me there was his incredible purity of motive—no showing off of technique or anything: he seemed to be quite unconscious of his technical virtuosity. And another thing was that he was always after the emotional or dramatic meaning of the music, rather than simply the right notes at the right time—though of course he wanted them too. I can think of first-class craftsmen who might take care of the cosmetology of the music, so to speak, and figure that if there's any soul it will shine through. But it was as though Toscanini would say: "Let's have none of this skin business; let's get down to where the thing really happens." So much so that in the last years I felt sometimes he was inattentive to much of what was going on—not just wrong notes but wrong rhythms—because he was hearing and conducting not the performers and the performance before him but something in his mind. I recall particularly a performance of Beethoven's Ninth in which the recitative had obvious roughness that didn't disturb him, as though he didn't really hear it. But then, of course, other things he did pick up and seize on—like those trumpets in the *Dies Irae* at the dress rehearsal of the Verdi *Requiem*.

The Verdi *Requiems* were the great moments for me. It seemed to me as though Verdi was conducting a Toscanini score: such identification of composer and performer I've never experienced. The Elisabeth Schumann or Lotte Lehmann identification with Schubert or Schumann—or Bruno Walter with Mahler—I don't think even that was as white hot as Toscanini's with Verdi. I had grown up with a modern Protestant disaffection for operatic religious music; so it wasn't until we did the *Requiem* with him that I realized how incredibly great a work it was. It was the heat he brought to it. You remember the incident at the dress rehearsal in 1951, where he came down off the podium in fury at the singer who had repeatedly made a wrong entrance. Then, you remember, he got back on the podium and stood there shaken and silent for a moment; and then he said: *"Dies Irae!"* He had asked me to go upstairs to hear the balances up there; so I could look down and see what was happening; and what I saw at that moment was that the faces of the chorus, which had been very red with the exertion of singing, were suddenly white. And the sound when they began the *Dies Irae* was unlike any sound I ever have heard out of voices: they were screaming with hysteria.

There was one other incident of that kind—the other time when he changed the tone of a choir of mine. I think it was in *Mefistofele*: he made one of his gestures—remember, where he would go like this? [Shaw leaned forward, his arm pointing down, and propelled it powerfully from side to side]—and in immediate response to his gesture the tone of the choir got richer and deeper and broader—a staggering thing which never happened with another conductor. In general, vocal sound, when it's in blocks of sixty people, remains what it is: you can't get a college glee club to change this tone just by gesture; you can do it by exercises or by telling them what you want. But with Toscanini the tone changed in immediate response to his gesture.

Another performance I remember was the *Falstaff*. It was my first acquaintance with the work; and Toscanini did it so wittily and with so much enjoyment that it was as funny as Shakespeare. I couldn't believe anybody could be this funny in music.

As for my general impression of Toscanini's work, I remember writing in one of my first family-style letters to the Collegiate Chorale about our experiences, that I had the feeling Toscanini sought expressive quality through dynamics or texture, not through tempo, which was the constant. And while in terms of inner pulse the tempo might be enormously fast, he retained clearly before him the point toward which he was heading; and this made it possible for musicians to articulate and singers to follow him even in his fast tempi. There was every reason to believe that the two fugues in the *Credo* of the *Missa Solemnis* simply couldn't be sung by human voices in his recorded tempos —but they were!

There is one episode with Toscanini I must tell about, even though it isn't about him as a musician. A group of forty of us were to do a broadcast of a Monteverdi *Magnificat* with Cantelli on Christmas Eve; and I phoned Walter Toscanini the day before and asked if we could come up after we'd finished the broadcast and sing a few Christmas carols for Maestro. He said it was a wonderful idea. So we rehearsed some of the carols on the record I'd made years before; and we went up to Riverdale. It was rather cold; and we expected to stand out on the porch and sing a few carols and then go. But Walter Toscanini must have been looking out the window; because before we could begin he opened the door and asked us to come in. We filed very quietly into the big central hall and stood on the stairs in the middle there and began to sing the carols. Maestro was in the television room looking at wrestling or something as he used to; and he came out, tears rolling down his cheeks. We must have sung ten or twelve carols; and when we finished, suddenly he went around shaking hands with everybody. Then a door was opened; and there was a table full of Italian cheeses and pastries and wines and champagne. And he went around and talked to everybody in the group—asked where they'd come from and so on—*each one*—which each of those forty people has cherished greatly, of course—so that we didn't leave until 3:30 or 4 in the morning.

He was always incredibly sweet and kind and inspiring.

Remo Bolognini

HAGGIN:

Nobody had to tell me Remo Bolognini was a distinguished musician whom I should talk to about Toscanini. There remained in my memory the delicacy and purity of his style in a marvelously light and winged performance of Mendelssohn's Violin Concerto that Toscanini conducted in 1933, when Bolognini was assistant-concertmaster of the New York Philharmonic. And when I went to see him I learned some of the background of that style: after he had been playing professionally a few years, a wealthy person had sent him to Europe for two years of study with Ysaye. It was immediately after this that Toscanini engaged him for the New York Philharmonic.

BOLOGNINI:

My father was a cellist—as well as a pharmacist and a calligrapher—and played eighteen seasons with Toscanini at the Teatro Colón in Buenos Aires; and my mother sang in the chorus. So even when I was not yet born I heard about Toscanini. The first time I saw him was when I was twenty years old and my mother took me to the Colón, where he was rehearsing something—I think it was the Prologue of Boito's *Mefistofele.*

85

It made a great impression of course. Then I didn't see him for many years; and I really came in contact with him in 1931, in Bayreuth. I was there to hear the festival. Toscanini had chosen Mishel Piastro as concertmaster of the New York Philharmonic, and was looking for somebody to be assistant-concertmaster; and Alfred Wallenstein knew I was in Bayreuth and wanted me to play for Maestro; so he sent him a telegram. I didn't know anything about it; and one day somebody knocked on the door, and it was a chauffeur, who said: "Mr. Bolognini?" "Yes. Who are you?" "I am Maestro Toscanini's chauffeur. I have been looking all over Bayreuth for you; because Maestro wants to see you." You can imagine my surprise. I went to see Maestro the next day at the theater; and he was suffering tremendously from bursitis: he could hardly move his arm; and that day he had to conduct *Parsifal,* no less! He was in great pain; but he was very sweet to me. He said: "I have heard so much about you—that you play so well, and have been studying with Ysaye." And many other things: he really was very sweet. Then he said: "I would like to have you as assistant-concertmaster in the Philharmonic, if you will accept." I said: "Maestro, for me it would mean a tremendous thing to be under your baton. But for my satisfaction, Maestro, let me play for you." He said: "Yes, any time." "But Maestro, I don't have an accompanist." So he called the chorus master; and we had a rehearsal; and I played for Maestro in the Villa Wahnfried. I played a Locatelli sonata arranged by Ysaye—a beautiful piece and a gorgeous arrangement. Then I played the Chaconne of Bach. Maestro was raving about it; and he said: "Do you play the Mendelssohn Concerto?" "*Yes,* Maestro," "Can you play the last movement for me?" "*Yes,* Maestro." So I played it; and he said: "Well, did you decide? Would you like to play with me?" I said: "Maestro, just one second." And I *dared* to tell him: "Maestro, you are so demanding. I don't know if I would be able to satisfy you." He said: "Why? What's the matter? You know the music; you play well; there's nothing to worry about." So immediately he sent a telegram to Van Praag, the personnel manager; and that was my engagement with the Philharmonic.

I stayed with Maestro four seasons. Then one day I was doing an extra job at NBC; and Mr. Spitalny, who liked me, called me and said: "Would you like to be a house man here?" And I don't know for what reason, I said yes; and I left the Philharmonic without even one word to Maestro—which he resented. After I was at NBC two years, he came there; so I was together with Maestro twenty seasons—which is my pride. It is my pride also to have been in contact with two giants like Ysaye and Toscanini—though there was contrast in their ways of thinking musically, and their personalities also were so different. In music, Ysaye was *"Laissez aller"*—"Let go"—whereas Toscanini wanted everything in place. But even with this contrast, they were two geniuses.

I don't remember the first Philharmonic rehearsal with Maestro; but I do remember when I had to play the Mendelssohn Concerto. As you know, the conductor always listens to the soloist privately, to see what they are going to do; so I went to Maestro, who accompanied me at the piano; and we talked, and he said at one point: "I am going to give you an advice. I have been conducting the Fifth Symphony of Beethoven for fifty years; but every time that I have to conduct it I look at the score, and I always find something." He was right: I looked— and I found something!

So every time he conducted something he would say: "We must play this piece better this time. Because last time we played it *I* was bad, the orchestra was bad." And he knew the score so well that it was impossible to fool him. I remember in the Philharmonic, we were playing *fortissimo* in some piece; and he stopped and said to one player—the second clarinet or someone like that: "Did you play this note? Because I didn't hear you." And the man said: "No, I didn't play it." Maestro had a tremendous ear.

But first of all he had—I don't know what to call it—an electricity, a dynamic. Even when he was in the audience at a concert or an opera, and the orchestra and the artists knew he was there, it changed the atmosphere. When he left the podium happy, everybody was happy; and when a catastrophe happened, everybody was in bad humor. He had something that I never experienced with any other conductor. Yes, there was a magnetism also in the great conductors you mention—Nikisch, Furtwängler, Cantelli (he was something remarkable, that boy; he had *everything—every thing!*). But the authority of Maestro, nobody else had.

For me he was complete: perfect in the tempi, perfect in the expression. His tempo gave you the possibility to play every note. For example in the Overture to *The Flying Dutchman*, where there are difficult passages for the strings: other conductors take it so fast that it is impossible to play every note; but with Maestro we could. And I remember that when he conducted those operas by Wagner that are so long, the difference between two performances of an opera would be only one minute. In expression he made the right *coloriti*—dynamics, nuances, and everything that is written in the music. And what made him more angry to a player than anything else was if the player didn't sing. There was a wind-player who was very cold in his playing; and Maestro said to him: "My God, you're so cold, if I would be a woman I would never marry you. *Canta!* Put some blood in the notes!"

He had knowledge of things that were difficult for an instrument. But now I come to the peculiar psychology of this man. He hated—and fought—the musician who thought something in music is easy; and so when we had to play the *Traviata* Prelude, and he came to the podium already with the idea that the orchestra thought this was easy to play, he would make a tragedy, and then he would say: "You think it is easy to play, eh?"

One of the places that always produced a tragedy was the passage for the cellos in the first movement of *La Mer*. But the last few times that we played *La Mer* at NBC Frank Miller rehearsed the cellos apart; and these were the only times that Maestro was happy—or if not happy, he didn't make a tragedy about it. In general Debussy was very difficult: every note has a nuance or accent or something. And Berlioz's *Reine Mab* was one of the most difficult things—very, very delicate—difficult for the strings, the woodwinds, the French horn, everybody. And how beautiful it sounded with Maestro! And do you remember the rehearsals of the beginning of the *Pastoral* Symphony? So many conductors take it so easy; but for Maestro that entrance was something terrific. Before the rehearsal I would tell my colleagues what Maestro would say: "Remember, this is a boring symphony if you don't play it the right way. There are very long *crescendi*, very long *diminuendi*." Then Maestro came, and said: "*Pastorale!* Remember, there are very long *crescendi*, very long *diminuendi*. Watch the *coloriti*." And what do you say about the second movement—the turns in the melody, which were made so gracefully that they didn't disturb anything!

I remember that one of the performances that impressed me the most was the Prelude to *Tristan und Isolde*: that was really something remarkable. And also the Funeral March from *Götterdämmerung*. There he always had to fight for the exact rhythm:

Because if that last sixteenth-note was not exact it changed completely the effect of the phrase. He used to say: *"Son passi di giganti*—steps of a giant." And one unforgettable thing in my life is when we recorded Beethoven's Ninth in Carnegie Hall. It was very late—twelve or one o'clock in the morning; and at the end of the first movement the orchestra was completely silent—nobody could say a word. But Maestro said: *"Così!"* I will never forget it. Especially in the first movement of the Ninth, there was another thing with which he used to take much care: did you notice that with him it was never boring, because he knew the places that were a little weak and would fall, and in those places he started to move—to animate a little. He did this also in the second movement of the *Eroica*, where it goes into the major: a little faster. And certain places in the second movement of Schubert's C-major.

When you ask about changes in later years—changes in tempi—I remember that in 1955 or 56, when I was assistant-conductor in Baltimore with Mr. Freccia, he rehearsed one day Rossini's *Semiramide* Overture in such a fast tempo; and when he asked me afterwards about the tempo I said that in my opinion it was too fast. He said: "It's Toscanini's tempo." I said: "No, Maestro, I am sure not; because I played it with him at NBC." He insisted; I insisted; finally we bet a hundred dollars, and he said: "Let's have lunch at my home; and then I'll play the record for you." And my God, when he played the record, it was that fast tempo! I wanted to pay the hundred dollars; but he said: "No, only five dollars." But that isn't the end of the story. When I was in New York I had a call from Walter Toscanini, who said Maestro would like to see me; so I went there; and after dinner we talked, and I told Maestro how he made me lose five dollars. He said: "Ah, but there are two records. One I made with the NBC; and one I made with the Philharmonic, when I came back from Italy angry because the stupid shoemakers, my colleagues, played it so slow it was a shame. I wanted to show that it had to have life; that's why I played it so fast."

Another time Walter Toscanini called me and asked me to come because Maestro wanted to play something for me. Imagine—for me! I went; and after dinner Walter went downstairs in the basement where they had records and tapes, and I was sitting with Maestro—Maestro and myself, nobody else— and he said: "You know, Bolognini, I wanted you to hear these records." They were *Le Donne Curiose* Overture of Wolf-Ferrari, the whole *El Amor Brujo* of Falla, Salome's Dance and *Death and Transfiguration* of Strauss. Well, to hear that music in that silent house with Maestro, and to observe him standing there—it was something I will never forget. And in *Salome,* in which the instrumentation is so heavy, so muddy, to hear every instrument—*every instrument*—it was terrific. After *Death and Transfiguration* it was such an impression that I was crying. Unforgettable!

The last time I saw Maestro it was on a Sunday afternoon; and I had to go back to Baltimore that evening, because I had to conduct a rehearsal the next morning. He said: "Stay for dinner." And I said: "Maestro, I can't, because I have to rehearse tomorrow morning in Baltimore, and I must take the train." He took my hands and said: "Oh, but please stay. Stay." Such a plea from a man like that: it was cruel to refuse; but I had to go. "*Vieni a vederme. Vieni a vederme.* Come to see me more often." I said: "Maestro, I would like to see you more often, but I am afraid to bother you." He said: "You never bother me! I know who bothers me! Come here any time you want!" One of the most unforgettable memories of Maestro. How I miss him! He was very, very nice.

Jennie Tourel

HAGGIN:

When Toscanini performed Berlioz's Romeo and Juliet *in its entirety the first time—with the New York Philharmonic, in 1942—Jennie Tourel, then completely unknown, sang Strophes. In those performances, and in whatever I heard her do subsequently, she used her small but lovely voice with a musical taste and intelligence that I thought would make what she would have to say about her experience with Toscanini worth having. And I was interested also in how he treated a soloist who was not a celebrity.*

TOUREL:

My meeting with Toscanini—in August 1942—was very interesting. It was when I came to this country and was struggling to get an engagement. Although I came as a leading singer from Paris, nobody knew me, nobody knew what I could do. Two friends—Friede Rothe and Mieczyslaw Horszowski—heard me sing in my home some Debussy. They told me that Toscanini was looking for someone who sings French, because he has to do *Romeo and Juliet* by Berlioz. And Horszowski said that he would ask Toscanini if he would be interested to hear

92

me. Toscanini said: "The name Jennie Tourel strikes a bell"—
that was what Horszowski told me—"all right; I will hear her."
It was like manna from heaven, because Toscanini for me was
someone unbelievably unapproachable. I heard him in '37 in
Salzburg conduct *Falstaff* and *Die Meistersinger*—no, I couldn't
get to *The Magic Flute*; I heard just these two performances.
And they were for me something that I couldn't even discuss,
because I was very young—and I was overwhelmed. And all of a
sudden I hear that I have to go and sing for him!

I went with Horszowski, who played the piano for me.
Toscanini was marvelous when we arrived; and his wife was very
sweet and very hospitable. We were talking, and he said what
did I sing in Paris; and I told him that I made my debut in
Carmen. Then he said, "*Ma*—now we'll go to the studio and
I'll hear you." When I was going up to the studio, which was
on the second floor, Mme. Toscanini said: "Wait a minute;
I'll give you a glass of water, because you have to sing for Maestro, and maybe you are nervous." And you know, I was *so* sure
of being able to sing for this great man; because it's always
much better to be in contact with a great man than with a
mediocrity, who has a chip on his shoulder. So I said: "Mme.
Toscanini, I really don't need water, because I'm not nervous.
When I have to sing for a great man I'm not nervous."

I went into the studio, and I started to sing. The first
thing I did was the Letter Scene from *Werther*; and after I sang
it Toscanini said to me: "*Brava. E bella voce.*" You know, I
was so taken with this that I said to myself: "Even if I'm not
engaged it doesn't matter: this gives me courage. If Toscanini
finds that I have a good voice, that gives me reason not to feel
frustrated or disturbed." Then he said: "Would you like to
sing something else?"; and I said: "I'll sing for you *Jeanne d'Arc*
of Tchaikovsky, because I sing it in French." When I sang it
for him he liked it very much. He said, "*Merci*," and took me
down back to the living room.

Now I *knew*—in my head—that he was looking for someone to sing *Romeo and Juliet*; I *knew* that there was a mezzo-soprano solo, but I have never sung it before. Then I had to be very smart. So when we came downstairs and he said: "I am going to conduct *Romeo and Juliet* by Berlioz with the Philharmonic. Do you know it?" I said, "Yes." He said: "There is one mezzo-soprano solo. I will give you the music. Could you come on Monday"—this was on Friday—"could you come on Monday and sing it for me?" I said, "Certainly." He gave me the music; he sent me back in his car; and he asked me to come on Monday. But he didn't say he was going to engage me; and this was torture for me, in spite of being very happy that he said I have a beautiful voice.

Well, I went home. Saturday, Sunday, and Monday—I worked like a dog, and I learned the music by heart. Monday I came to sing for him again. He played the piano for me himself; and he said: "Very good! You know it by heart!" I said: "Yes, I know it by heart." And he said: "Fine. Thank you very much." And you can imagine what it is—for somebody who already has hope and anticipation—not to hear that he's going to engage me. It was a let-down; but it was again a hope. I went home; and when Friede Rothe asked me what happened, I said, "Nothing." Because he didn't say anything—only that it was fine that I knew it by heart. But really, I can tell you truly, I wasn't upset. I was as a matter of fact quite happy. I told her: "It means that I do have something, if he approved. If not with him, then with somebody else: something will have to come."

That was on Monday. On Tuesday morning I was awakened by a call from Mme. Toscanini, who told me: "Congratulations. Maestro has engaged you to sing with him." And I almost fainted at the telephone. She said: "Do you know Bruno Zirato?" I said, "Yes, I do." "He's manager of the Philharmonic; and you have to go to him today, and he will talk to you." And so I signed a contract; and Zirato said to me: "Do you know what has happened to you? It is a great thing for you to be chosen by Toscanini." I said: "*I* know . . . I don't even have to say it twice."

Now I was very excited. A few rehearsals were in Toscanini's home; and he sent his car for me. And for some rehearsals he took me in his car to Princeton—to the Westminster Choir. My solo begins with the orchestra, and then the chorus comes in; and there are some other things I had to sing with the chorus; so he had me all the time at the rehearsals with the Westminster Choir. He used to come at eight o'clock in the morning to take me with him to Princeton. And the first time he asked me: "How often would you like to rehearse?" I said, "Every day." He said: "That's very interesting. Most singers don't want to rehearse at all; they just learn, and then they come to sing." I said: "Not me! I want to rehearse every day." He also told me he didn't like singers who put something around their mouth when they rehearsed so that they shouldn't get cold air in their throat. *I* don't believe in that too; I don't believe in mumbling in rehearsal: I rehearse absolutely full voice. It's like with the piano: you have to make your fingers work; and you have to make the place in your voice; then you can sing. And when we rehearsed with the orchestra he didn't like anybody to sit down, because *he* was standing; so we all had to stand. I understand that: why should I sit down when the conductor is standing?

What did he do when he rehearsed with me? You know— very little: he just played and listened when I sang; and he didn't ask me to do anything. My solo is really not very much to sing; and probably the phrasing was right, so he didn't change anything. And he never said a harsh word to me. Really, I can only tell you that no matter what I heard about him—you know, Zirato said I must not say anything to anybody until the announcement in the papers on Sunday; and when the news broke out on Sunday everybody began to call me and to say: "Be careful with Toscanini; he's very difficult; he's going to rehearse you every day; he's going to break your voice"—you have no idea how many people warned me against him. And I didn't feel it; I just did—not—feel it. I was in such awe before him. First of all, he was so handsome, his face was so inspired, that I stared at him all the time. And I felt terrific dedication to music in him right from the beginning, without even talking to him. All right, he was yelling at rehearsals; but he was yelling for a reason. He was the kind of person I admire, if the goal is perfection. And as you say, with a good musician he was quiet and reasonable: between us there was a great harmony.

He was a most perfect musician; and I was fascinated to watch him conduct the orchestra, and to listen to what he could do with a phrase. I still remember when I watched him rehearse the chorus: he was so meticulous. He rehearsed very, very much—and *very* precise. He didn't want the chorus to sing with music; and he was absolutely right, because when you sing with music you only read. The same thing with me: he wanted me to know it by heart; and I knew it so well that he could have put me on my head and I could still sing it! I remember that at the performance—it was the hundredth anniversary of the Philharmonic, you remember, and nobody knew me—when the reporters came to ask me, "Are you nervous?" I said: "No! I'm *not* nervous—but I'm excited. Look: to stand in the middle of the stage of Carnegie Hall for the hundredth anniversary of the Philharmonic—in front Toscanini, in back 250 people of the Westminster Choir, and knowing my piece— I can't be nervous; I can be only excited and exalted." I was absolutely aware of everything I was doing; and Toscanini knew that: he had terrific faith in me. At the dress rehearsal—oh, I must tell you that for the dress rehearsal I was told by Zirato to come at ten o'clock, and I came about 10 to 10. When I was walking up the stairs to Carnegie Hall backstage, Toscanini and Zirato were standing at the top of the stairs, and Toscanini— with the face of a *lion*—said to me: "TOO LATE!" I said:

"Maestro, I was called for ten o'clock." He said: "I WAS HERE AT 9:30; and *you* should have been here at 9:30!" I felt as if my heart dropped down. And he was right; because at 10 to 10 it means I rush in like a musician just to take his violin from the case and sit down; and instead there must be a certain composure. But it was all right. At the dress rehearsal, when I finished singing my solo, Toscanini said, *"Brava!"* Piastro was then concertmaster, and Joseph Schuster was first cellist; and they told me afterwards that as long as they knew Toscanini they never heard him say this to anyone; so that I should build a pedestal and stand on it. Toscanini said, *"Canta con expressione!"* And he was following me just like an angel.

I must tell you that all the hardship I had to go through in '41—leaving Paris, leaving a career, and everything I have collected, and what I have worked up to a certain point—did not matter at this moment for me. I don't make a melodrama out of it: I just very honestly tell you that it was one of the greatest things in my life. When I saw my name on the poster with Toscanini's it was unbelievable for me; and I couldn't think of anything else but to do this thing perfectly so that I would be approved by *him*. It was not only one of the greatest things in my life; as a matter of fact it was *the* thing that started me. I was a nobody here at that time; when I came to this country nobody knew what I could do; Toscanini was the one who heard me first, and recognized me, and gave me an opportunity. *After* that I sang with Koussevitzky, and made the premiere of *Alexander Nevsky* with Stokowski and the NBC Symphony.

I remember one day—I think it was before the third performance of *Romeo*—Toscanini always rehearsed my solo in the greenroom before the performance; and this time after we rehearsed he was playing the piano, and I said to myself: "This is not *Romeo and Juliet*, what he's playing; it's something different." So I said: "Maestro, what are you playing now?" He said: "I conduct next week Shostakovich; so I play it." His

97

mind worked in perspective: when he was through with one thing he was already living further. My mind works that way too: when I finish a concert I am already thinking about something that I'm going to do next time. It's a marvelous thing, because you don't get stagnant in things that you repeat all the time. Hindemith, after he wrote a piece, wasn't interested in it anymore. He never came to hear my *Marienleben*; although he knew I do it very well, he said he's not interested to hear it— he's written it.

I had just that one contact with Toscanini: I never sang with him again, because when he conducted the operas I wasn't asked to sing, and when he asked me once to sing again *Romeo and Juliet* I was already busy. And I can't tell you very much about him because I wasn't one of those people who were in the entourage and always went and bothered him and asked him to do things for them—never! I only went when I was invited. I didn't even go to his rehearsals with the NBC because I just didn't want to bother him. I remember once during the rehearsals of *Romeo and Juliet* he took me out for lunch, because there was some free time; and I said to a friend: "At that lunch he was more a gentleman than any other man who took me out for lunch." He was such a—*chevalier*, to entertain me at this lunch: he was *Toscanini*, and he was seventy-five, and I was still a young woman! I adored his profile! I adored his hands! And I had a feeling of tremendous awe before this great man.

I once, though, did something after that. It was ten years after I sang with him, when he was eighty-five. I wrote him a letter; and I told him that I felt terribly nostalgic, because it was ten years since I first met him and since he opened wide horizons of my career: I called him the godfather of my career in this country. I would like so much to see him if it's possible, just to say hello to him. He called me immediately, as soon as he got the letter; and he said, "Would you like to come for dinner?"; and I said I would love to, naturally; and I went. He received me like a father, with open arms; and he said: "I'm so glad to see you, Tourel"—he always called me Tourel—and then he said, "How are you?" and I said, "I'm fine," and he said: "Oh, you're all right, I *know*; I always say to everybody, '*Canta con la testa.*' ['She sings with her head.']" When he offered me a cocktail I said: "Maestro, I drink for the ten years I know you, and for the next ten years that I'll see you again." And he said to me in French, "V*ous, surement; moi, peut-être.*" I felt so terrible when he said that; and as you know, a few years later he died. Even then, when he was eighty-five, he was handsome— and very *aware*, very *alert*, when he talked about things, about music. He asked me what I sing; and he wasn't in favor of my singing contemporary music: he said it's not very good for the voice. Whatever happened to him later—I wasn't here at the time—probably happened all of a sudden.

He was very nice, and very—human. In '44 and '45 I went to South America; and I called him, and he asked me to come to his home Sunday, when they had people. He said to me, "What are you going to do in South America?"; and I said: "I'm going to do operas; I'm going to do *Carmen* and *Mignon*; and then I'm going to do *Norma.*" And he said: "Give my regards to Gabriella Besanzoni; she was also a Carmen, and now she lives in Rio de Janeiro. O-o-h, she was a very, very vain singer; tell her that you know me." I said, "I will"; and he said, "She wears lots of diamonds." He was a marvelous *human being,* who talked about everything, not only about music. He always asked me how I was, am I happy, do I like my work, do I like what I do. This is so astonishing when you talk to a man who's so busy, so revered. You think such a man is unapproachable— but no! with Toscanini you could be just like I am with—with you, with anybody: he made you feel that way. He was a great man.

Did he say anything about composers and their works? The one he talked about with me was Bernstein. He heard him

conduct; he talked with him; he liked him; he was impressed
with him; as a matter of fact he said he was one of the greatest
talents that came right now; and he wrote very warmly on a
photograph that he gave him. He always sent me a photograph
for Christmas. I have his and Bernstein's—they are the only
photographs that I keep on the wall: these are my two conductors.

I remember at the time I sang with Toscanini he was trying
to do the *Rhapsody in Blue* of Gershwin; but you know he
somehow never had the flair for that kind of music; and also he
was already not a young man. But with me he didn't speak very
much about composers. Verdi, naturally; and Puccini: I remember him talking about them, but not what he said. He
was not a very talkative man, not one of the people who always
talk about themselves; he was much more a thinker than a man
who blah-blahs about "I did this and I did that." When I asked
a question, he answered in a short way. I do remember he loved
Debussy—he loved *Pelléas et Mélisande*; and he always talked
about a singer I knew in Paris, Fanny Heldy—that she was a
marvelous Mélisande. He also spoke about Claudia Muzio, who
sang with him. Actually he didn't speak about singers very much
—only about some of the people in the past. And also, as I said,
I wasn't hanging on his neck: he was too great a man for me to
bother him. The only time—yes, this will be interesting. When
I made *The Rake's Progress* in Venice, afterwards I took a
plane in Milan, and the plane wasn't starting, and I wondered
what happened. Then I found out that they were waiting for
Toscanini. I was sitting in the back, and I saw Maestro with
his son Walter coming on the plane; and they went to the
front. I waited until we were airborne, then I walked down
and said to Walter: "Hello, I saw you coming in, and I want
to say hello to Maestro." He was already seeing very badly; and I
said, "Maestro, this is Jennie Tourel." "Ah," he said, "wonderful!" I sat down next to him; and he said: "I heard you on the

radio. Ah, Stravinsky was wonderful when he wrote *The Fire-bird* and *Le Sacre du Printemps*"—yes, *Petrushka* too—"but after that, no more!" And he said: "You had very good diction— very good diction. But *musica—*"—*that* he couldn't understand. I guess he had his favorites in composers; and *you* know how he felt about contemporary composers—Copland and all those. He did play Copland and other Americans? I didn't know about that.

I wish I could tell you more about him. One thing I can say is like a red light—that he was a great gentleman, and very polite—in spite of all the talk about him that he was rude, that he yelled, that he cursed. All right, everybody knew about his rehearsals: he cursed because he wanted to get what he wanted— that was all. He demanded from everybody exactly as I demand from everybody—that it has to come to perfection. We don't know *what* is perfection, but we *go* after it. And when things were right he was the happiest man—and very nice, and very human. I will never say anything like—"Oh—Toscanini never thought about anybody, because he was such an egomaniac." I don't think so; I really don't think so—not for the time I knew him. I can only praise him; and I can only say that he was a great influence in my life just for that one thing—that he de-manded discipline from everybody. In art, without discipline there is no art. I learned that from him. I wish I had more to do with him; but I have to be grateful for what I had.

I have his picture on my map of the United States, where it is a symbol that he opened this country for me. He was the first man who recognized me; and I am very proud that I was recognized by a great man.

Mieczyslaw Horszowski

HAGGIN:

Horszowski was, like Jennie Tourel, a musician of taste and intelligence; and though he was not completely unknown here when he played Mozart's Piano Concerto K.595 with Toscanini and the NBC Symphony in 1943 (he was the pianist with whom Casals had recorded Beethoven's Cello Sonatas Op. 102 before the war) he was not a big-time celebrity. For these reasons I was interested in what he would have to tell about his experiences playing with Toscanini.

HORSZOWSKI:

The first time I heard Maestro Toscanini was in 1906 in Montevideo—a performance of *Tristan*, which of course made a great impression. During the first world war I was living in Milan, where he conducted a series of twelve concerts for the benefit of the orchestra players; and I heard all of these concerts, of course. And he also conducted a season of opera performances at the Teatro dal Verme, which started with *Falstaff*, which was unforgettable, then *Pagliacci* with Caruso (this was his last performance in Italy), then *Ballo in Maschera, Forza del Destino, Manon* (of Massenet) and *La Traviata*. Then, when La Scala started again after the war, I heard nearly all the important operas conducted by Maestro Toscanini. I didn't hear his *Don Giovanni*: he rehearsed it, but when the tenor became ill it was postponed to the next season, and someone else conducted it. But I heard *The Magic Flute*—yes, Maestro Toscanini conducted it at La Scala before he did it in Salzburg. And I heard *Parsifal* and *Fidelio*. Then after the opera season he conducted every year two symphony concerts, which I heard. Also, I came here in the winter of 1926 and 27, and again in 1934 or 35, and heard him with the New York Philharmonic. And when I left Italy before the last war I heard him with the NBC Symphony.

It was Maestro Toscanini who suggested the performance of Mozart's Concerto K.595. I had played it with other conductors; but he hadn't heard me. He loved this concerto; it was his favorite Mozart concerto; and he had a photostat of the manuscript, which was given to him by Serkin, who had great difficulty in obtaining it, because it was for Maestro Toscanini and the Germans didn't want him to have it. (The manuscript was in the State Library in Berlin; they don't know where it is now.) When Maestro Toscanini received this photostat he was very happy; because in the published complete works the slow movement was in 4/4, but the photostat showed that in the manuscript it was *alla breve*; and he said: "I always was sure the slow movement is *alla breve*." Also, in the photostat were seven bars in the first movement that were missing in the published edition.

It happened that I didn't have much rehearsal before the rehearsal with orchestra. Two weeks before, I became ill with bronchitis and had to go to the hospital. I told the doctor I had to play with the NBC Symphony; and he told me I would have high fever and he hoped for the best but didn't know how I would react to the sulfa drugs. The Tuesday before the broadcast, which was on Sunday, Maestro Toscanini came to the hospital to speak to me about the concerto. We went to a little room of the nurses, which had an upright piano; and he asked me to play my solo. So I started; and after listening a short time he said: "No, no. I don't need to hear you. We will find each other"; because he saw that I was not very strong at that moment. On Saturday I came to the rehearsal with the orchestra. Maestro Toscanini began with the orchestra's *ritornello,* in which he put all the details in order—this more *cantabile,* this more rhythmic; and this was at the same time a rehearsal for me, because in the *ritornello* were all the elements of the movement that I would play later just the way they were stated now. He had looked at the work from every side, to achieve his idea; and he was clear and firm about it. When *we* study something we have doubts; with him there was no doubt: everything was the way it had to be. So I could fit right in—into the tempo and everything else.

I remember one detail that will interest you. I know my weak points: I know I have a tendency to rush; and this worried me, because I knew Maestro Toscanini—I remembered his rehearsals of Rossini overtures: the strict tempi in the *crescendi* —no rushing. But when he arrived at this passage of rapid figuration—beginning here at bar 39—he said to the orchestra: *"Andiamo, andiamo! Non siamo a scuola!* More animated! We are not in school!" So I didn't have to worry about rushing the same passage when I would play it with the orchestra later, at bar 150.

I don't remember anything else at this rehearsal, which was short—just once through. But at the concert, just at the moment when we had to go out on the stage, Maestro Toscanini showed me this passage in the Larghetto, beginning at bar 100— a transition, a sort of cadenza, leading to the return of the principal theme—and said to me: "More animated, more lively; because in tempo it is dead. Then the theme in tempo again." He didn't say anything about it at the rehearsal: probably he thought of it afterwards. Or as you say, he may have read the score again that night, and decided the passage was too slow.

No, there was no special occasion for the Martucci Concerto. Maestro Toscanini always liked it; he performed it with Martucci several times; during the war he performed it with a pianist who came here; and he wanted to give it again. I heard this performance, and liked the work; so I didn't play it only because Maestro Toscanini asked me: it was something which appealed to me. The week before the performance I went to him three or four times to play it for him; and he showed me how he wanted many things; then we had at least two rehearsals with the orchestra.

At the rehearsal of the first movement he stopped here, and said he couldn't conduct with my tempo; and he was right. It's a dialogue; and the piano has to continue the same tempo as the orchestra, or the connection is lost; and I had played a little slower. Once this was corrected we went on until this second idea—a great solo for the piano, where he left me completely free. It's a very beautiful solo: people said it is music which comes from others; but it has the character of Martucci.

I did some things that were not to my own satisfaction: this passage, for example, didn't sound as full as I would have liked; but Maestro Toscanini didn't say anything, because the important theme is in the orchestra, and the piano is only reinforcement which is not to be heard as a virtuoso thing for itself. Then this beautiful big cadenza, where again Maestro Toscanini left me completely free. And this is very beautiful—a long cello solo, which was played so beautifully by Frank Miller. Look at the ornamentation for the cello with the piano. And in this recitative Maestro Toscanini made some correction; but would you believe it, I don't remember anymore what it was. Then the last movement: brilliant, as you can see. It reminds me of all the last movements of piano concertos.

Oh yes, his corrections and suggestions were always reasonable—always illuminating: something which I hadn't understood completely, but which now I saw clearly. And it was just more expression, and better form—these two things, always.

I couldn't see much of him when I played, because he was with the orchestra. When I had a long solo, he looked—he didn't conduct. I once saw the film, *Hymn of the Nations*, where you saw Maestro Toscanini's face; and it had a power you couldn't escape. This the audience didn't experience at a concert; and I didn't have this experience when I played. But I could feel that he was following every note in my playing—not as note but as part of the line of music; and that if I had made an unexpected retard or *rubato*—which of course was not possible in the Mozart —the orchestra would have been immediately with it. Sometimes playing with an orchestra—I must use a figure—is like playing with an overcoat: you are not quite at ease. Playing with Maestro Toscanini, you had wings.

Jan Peerce

As the tenor in the broadcast performances of Fidelio, La Bohème, Act 4 *of* Rigoletto, La Traviata *and* Un Ballo in Maschera *that were issued on records, Jan Peerce could say whether Toscanini's dealing with a good singer and good musician in these performances was different from his dealing with Kipnis in the Bayreuth performance of* Tristan und Isolde *in 1930.*

PEERCE:

Toscanini had heard me on the radio, and seemed to have liked my voice; and when he was going to do Beethoven's Ninth in 1938 he asked Chotzinoff if he knew me, and Chotzinoff said yes. So Toscanini said: "I'd like to hear this boy personally"; and Chotzinoff called me and asked if I'd like to audition for Toscanini. After I'd almost fainted and got up from the floor I said, "Of course!" Chotzinoff was supposed to play for me at the audition; and I waited in the lobby of the Hotel Astor, where Toscanini was living, but there was no Chotzinoff. (He later told me he was afraid because he didn't know how I would do; but I thought the truth was he didn't want his presence to

influence Toscanini's opinion of my singing.) Finally I called
the Toscanini apartment and was told to come up; and when
the door opened after I buzzed, lo and behold, there was Toscanini acting as his own valet. He greeted me very cordially and
shook hands; and he asked me if I had brought any music with
me. I said: "Only the tenor part of the Ninth Symphony." He
laughed and said: "Ah, I wanted to hear you sing something
more—" more singable, shall we say. I said: "I'm sorry, but I
don't have anything else with me." And he said: "Do you *know*
anything else?" I said I knew some arias; and he asked which
ones; and the first one that came to my mind was "*Una furtiva
lagrima*". "Oh," he said, "you know '*Una furtiva lagrima*'.
Come: I play for you." And he sat down at the piano—without
music, of course—and began to play; and believe it or not, he
made a mistake! One of the very rare mistakes that Toscanini
made! As you know, the two stanzas of "*Una furtiva*" begin
the same but continue differently; and in the first stanza Toscanini played the continuation of the second. He stopped; but
I went on with the first stanza; and after cussing himself out he
resumed playing, and we finished together. At the end, exclama-
tions of "*bella voce!*"—he liked it very much—and he said:
"Would you like to sing in the Ninth Symphony with me?" I
said: "It would be the greatest moment of my life!" And he said:
"All right, you sing with me," and told me the date. And that
was how my association with him started.

Oh yes, I was at ease at the audition. The challenge was a
challenge; but there's the animal instinct of self-preservation:
you fight back. The first moment was what I had expected; but
when we shook hands I found he was a human being who smiled
and was very cordial and very sweet and very fatherly. I remember it began to snow as we were talking; and when I sang I was
concentrated on what I had to sing—and on the snowflakes I
could see through the window: Toscanini didn't matter at the
moment. Till he made the mistake; and I guess he was im-

pressed by the fact that I could keep going no matter what happened: it meant I was *some*what musical.

Leinsdorf prepared the singers; and by the time I came to the first piano rehearsal with Toscanini I knew the tenor part pretty well. What struck me was Toscanini's self-discipline, and the fact that when he sat at the piano the most important thing in the world for him was what was happening at that moment. If you pleased him by just doing the music—no matter what it was—*as written*; if you gave the notes the right values and the words their right pronunciation and flavor, he was the happiest man in the world; and every time you sang a phrase he liked you'd think he was finding a thousand dollars. And yet, I can tell you a story: in one performance of the Ninth Symphony—I don't remember which one and who the soprano was—he changed the music for the soprano. This man who kept saying, "*Canta come è scritto*" and "Is written this way; sing it the way is written"—this man changed the B-naturals in the last quartet for the soprano! Yes, I heard about his transposing "*Abscheu-licher*" for Lehmann in Salzburg; but to change *notes!* I said to myself, "What's this?" And that was one time when I realized: "Look, he's a human being."

With him it wasn't just a piano rehearsal and then "Let's do the performance." You saw him for weeks—three times, four times a week, as often as he felt; and the day you had a rehearsal with him, that was it: you made no other appointments. If he called you for a three o'clock rehearsal, he might keep you till 4 — 6 — 7 — there was no telling. When we were through we used to love it when he was happy after a good rehearsal and would offer us a cup of tea or coffee and a piece of cake and we'd sit around; and Moscona, who sang with him many times, or Nan Merriman would know how to get him to talk: it was fabulous, the way he would give you his opinions on everybody and everything. I'll never forget: once the subject of coloratura sopranos came up, and he said: "Coloratura sopranos! If I had a daughter who wanted to be a coloratura soprano I would cut her throat!" Or someone mentioned a guy who said he had been Toscanini's assistant at La Scala. "That pig?! I wouldn't let him into my room!" He remembered—everything he remembered. With me he remembered tenors. Once he mentioned Paul Alt- house: "Was very good—ve-e-e-ry good—good musician—good, good. Knew how to sing." Then he mentioned a tenor who wound up badly—the poor fellow died on stage—Aroldo Lindi, who toured with the San Carlo Company for years: Toscanini spoke in glowing terms of this boy in his early days. And that Italian, Pertile: he was musical—he knew what to do with a phrase. And of course, sometimes you'd mention a name to him, and it was "That pig!"

At the orchestral rehearsals he was so dynamic, so forceful, so fiery, that I couldn't take my eyes off him ever—and this was true even after fifteen years: I had to watch the expression on his face as he conducted, which conveyed his innermost feeling. And because he had this drive, this power, you just responded as if you had known exactly what he wanted. He had it not only over singers but over instrumentalists—the men in the orchestra. It was a great orchestra, and these boys had played with every- body and knew everything backwards and forwards; but the way they responded to this man was something! They *wanted* to please him: they knew he was so sincere in what he asked for that they were anxious to do the right thing. It's been said that musicians played or sang over their heads for him; but I don't think he made me do the impossible: that would be pushing the point a little too far. What I would say is that he got as much out of you as he could, and as much as you *should have given.* Though he didn't ask for anything but what was there in the score: in fact, I'm sure that if you had tried to *overdo* something he would have said it was overdone and don't do it that way. He wanted passion, but passion from within; he wanted warmth, but not manufactured warmth. And he wanted you to know what you were singing. He always said: "Say the words correctly: the tone will come." And it's true: if you know what you're saying, the meaning of the words will bring out the quality of the tone—provided you have the tone in your voice.

People ask, was he acting or was he sincere; and my answer is, he was *he*. Once he got on that stage he was a different person —he was just the musician. He was an actor; but he acted what he felt. When we did *Bohème*, tears were coming down his face; and it wasn't put on: nobody saw it, just us. We singers were more fortunate than the public; because all they could see was his back and his arms waving, but we could see the man, and what the music meant to him, whether it was the Ninth Symphony or an opera.

That performance of the Ninth went off very well, and Toscanini was very happy. Of course, between you and me, what is there in the Ninth Symphony for the tenor? It's no aria: you sing sixteen bars, then the tenors of the chorus join you, and you're inundated—you're a thwarted man. I did it for the association: it was my moment of discovery, which led to other things with Toscanini. Also, it's a trying experience to sit there for those three movements, knowing you're going to have to open your mouth and sing. I'll never forget Pinza that first time: he kept clearing his throat, and finally he said to me: "I always promise myself I will never sing with that man the Ninth Symphony; but when he calls me I can't resist him." I said: "What's the matter?" And he said: "You have to sit for forty-five minutes, and then you have to start with '*O Freunde*'." He was afraid of that frog in the throat—which never happened, incidentally.

I sang Verdi with Toscanini the first time in a Verdi program in January 1943: the Trio from *I Lombardi* and *Hymn of the Nations*. What he liked especially was my pronunciation of Italian; in fact, he found fault with the pronunciation of certain Italians, and asked me to demonstrate to one of them. I felt terrible, because this was someone who spoke a beautiful Italian, but for some reason didn't sing it well. No, there was no special problem with the musical style. You see, when you came to Toscanini it wasn't to learn something from the start: you were prepared by Trucco, and had a pretty good idea of what you were doing; so Toscanini didn't have to tell you much. He'd sit at the piano, and if there was something to tell you he'd say: "This is the meaning of this phrase." Or he'd ask, "You know the meaning of this?" and you'd tell him, and if you were right he'd say: "Yes. Now do it a little darker," or "Do it warmer," or "Do it with more heart." He had ideas for everything; and everything he wanted seemed right. They say he didn't let you hold high notes; but if you listen to the records you find you *held* high notes—you didn't *over*hold them and make the thing ridiculous. When I did *Bohème* with him I reveled in the sound, and he let me; and in *Rigoletto*—just the other day I listened to the Quartet, and I hold those B-flats—just enough—but I hold them.

The *Hymn of the Nations* was something Toscanini felt very close to, because he was a warmly patriotic Italian, very proud of his background, and the piece was by Verdi, and it was tied up with Garibaldi—it was written for a Garibaldi Day celebration. These things made Toscanini feel this was his piece of music—especially when he changed the words from "my beautiful country" to "my betrayed country"—"*mia patria tradita*". He made sure that when "*tradita*" came along you said it and meant it.

In another Verdi program in July 1943 we did the fourth act of *Rigoletto*, which we did again at the Red Cross concert in Madison Square Garden in 1944. I had already sung *Rigoletto*—I started singing it about 1940, before I was at the Met—but of course Toscanini's tempos and interpretation were different. I like the people who tell you he played something faster because he knew it had to fit on a record! He played it faster because he felt it *should* be faster. I'll never forget when we did *Traviata*—the fast tempos in some places. The *"Libiamo,"* for instance. He said: "This is a drinking song on a festive occasion; you can't go to sleep." Or the gambling scene. He explained what's going on—what's happening with the girl and the boy— he doesn't really want to gamble, but is jealous. Toscanini said: "Verdi meant it to be exciting; and [here Peerce imitated Toscanini's burlesquing of the usual tempo] *that's* not exciting." And he sang it as it should go [Peerce demonstrated Toscanini's faster tempo], singing everybody's part, getting the meaning, and making it live.

In the *Fidelio* of 1944 he worked us very hard. Mind you, he didn't speak German well, but he knew every word and corrected our German and made us enunciate it clearly. His tempos were fast; but he could explain every one of them. Some of the singers had done *Fidelio* at the Met; and everybody had ideas and feelings in the matter; and you could talk to him. "Maestro, is there any special reason for this? Don't you think we could do it a little slower?" And he told you why you couldn't—what would happen if you did. He said: "How should this man act? If you sing it slowly you will lose the intensity." But he listened to you: he wasn't the ogre he was painted. The only time he was a tough guy was when he got angry; and when would he get angry? When he thought you were betraying the composer— weren't doing what the composer wanted. If you made a mistake once, it was *nischt gefährlich*: he'd look at you; but if you made it again, or made more mistakes, then there was hell to pay. In *Fidelio* one day he lost his temper with a singer who made a mistake he had made the day before; and it was terrible: the man stood there crying because of the things Toscanini called him.

No, it was my first *Fidelio*: I learned it for Toscanini. He made me learn it; because I didn't want to: why should I learn a part I might never do again. He said: "You learn the part.

You please me." There were other things he wanted me to do which I wouldn't do. He wanted me to sing a Wagner program with him once; and I'm sorry to this day that I didn't. He wanted me to do the second half of the first act of *Die Walküre*. That was the first thing he heard me sing on the air when I was at Radio City; and what appealed to him, he told me later, was the fact that he was hearing a Siegmund who was not yelling— who was singing. I have a letter in which he wrote me, when I told him I was sorry but I couldn't do it: "Who told you that in order to sing Wagner you must not know how to sing?" That was his argument; but I refused; and even afterwards he said to me: "You should have done it." The other thing I refused to do was *Aida*. I was careful about my choice of repertoire, because I wanted to be able to sing for a long time, and if you give too much—especially in your early years, when you don't know as much about vocal technique as you do later— you can't last: by the time the technique is part of you, you say: "Where's the voice?" This is where the critics can be of service to a young singer: they can tell him he's on the wrong track. Instead of only saying "Great performance", they should question whether the guy should have done the part at all. I remember listening to a Toscanini broadcast of an opera while I was getting dressed for a concert in Cleveland, and saying to my accompanist about two of the singers: "They never sang like this before, and I predict they'll never sing like this again." They were fantastic; but they gave too much, and got into vocal trouble afterwards. Singing is like charity: you give—but you don't give everything, so that you have nothing left for yourself; you have to be a little selfish. So I refused to do *Aida*.

In *La Bohème*, in order to satisfy Toscanini, we had to undo a lot of things we'd learned from others. And I remember how he spent hours with the baritone who tells Marcello, at the end, that Mimi has died—"*Marcello, è spirata*"—how Toscanini spent hours to get this baritone, who was a great artist, a great

actor, to speak the words the particular way he wanted—with a
breathless quality that Cehanovsky just didn't dig at the beginning. "No—no—Cehanovsky, no—*caro:* 'Marcello [Peerce imitated Toscanini's croaking whisper]—Marcello'—" until he got
Cehanovsky to do exactly what he wanted. The same with
everybody: he had something to say to everybody, to give him
the feeling for the interpretation of his part. The notes, he said
—everybody knows the notes: the thing is to make the notes
mean something. And even when he didn't say anything, when
you just listened to the beginning as he zipped into it [Peerce
sang the orchestral passage] you had to sing [Peerce sang the
vocal phrase]: there was no other way of answering when your
cue came. Or before *"Mimi è tanto malata"*: just with the expression on his face this guy was giving you a message [Peerce
sang the phrase].

In the broadcast of *La Bohème* he sang along with me—in
the aria especially; and in the third act, my God, he helped me
cry. You can hear it on the record; and there are some people
who say, "It spoils the record." And I tell them: "Isn't that
funny; for me it makes the record." Imagine hearing Toscanini
—not planning it, just naturally singing faintly in the background [Peerce imitated Toscanini's croaking]—and knowing
this guy's blood is on that record; and some shmo says, "That
spoils it." They don't know what inspires people.

I suppose you know what happened at the end of the broadcast? No? Well, after Mimi's death there is one beat of rest,
and it's a tradition that the conductor doesn't beat that rest.
Toscanini had explained to the orchestra that he wouldn't beat
the rest; but at the broadcast he was affected by the drama of
the moment and was crying, and his hand made some sort of
movement. Some of the brass thought he was giving them their
first beat, and came in, but others didn't; and there was bedlam.
Of course it didn't take Toscanini more than three beats to
straighten them out; but for him the heavens fell; the world

went black; he wouldn't take a bow; he cried; he carried on; he sent for the brass section: "What did you do? What did you do? You're sorry! What, sorry? *You* go home now with your wife and have dinner; what do *I* do?"

You asked whether it was true that the next time I sang *Bohème* at the Met I was told to forget some of the things I had done with Toscanini. Sure. *You* know: those petty jealousies. I antagonized some people at the Met once when I was interviewed on the air—I think by Tex McCrary—and he said: "Your association with Toscanini was marvelous, of course. But who do you think—at this time—is rising to take his place?" And I said: "No one!" He said: "You mean to say that of all the people—" And I said: "No! No one!" And I was very vehement about my no ones. And of course there were five different conductors at the Met who thought, "Why no one?" There was only one conductor—I mean it: if I were questioned today I would say it—only one, and the poor fellow died—Cantelli— who showed signs of that kind of greatness. Who else? Do *you* know anyone else? In another interview I said: "A lot of his imitators think that if they speak with a hoarse voice and cuss out musicians, that will make them Toscaninis. No, *that's* not Toscanini: you have to be a genius." So some of the conductors *don't* like me so much!

I've already told you a few things about the *Traviata*. I remember another example there of Toscanini's insistence that the notes must mean something. Merrill has a great voice, the greatest baritone around; but Toscanini wanted him to get a certain softness, a certain mellowness; and finally he said: "Merrill—Merrill—please—please, Merrill—be a father—don't be a baritone." He never yelled at me; but once I came near it—in a *Traviata* rehearsal. I made a mistake—I mispronounced a word. He looked at me and his hands dropped from the piano: *"Un altra volta.* Again." So I did the phrase again; and again—I didn't think of it; it was a small thing—I made the mistake. And he dropped his hands: "Peerce! You too?!" I said to myself: "There has to be a first time"; and I tell you, my heart sank: it would have killed me, to be the butt of his anger.

At one *Traviata* rehearsal he gave the orchestra a *Geschichte*. My wife Alice had never come to a rehearsal; and I told her: "You're missing a lot if you don't come to the rehearsals. They're better than the performances." So she said: "All right, I'd like to come." But she couldn't come any day but Friday. "Oh, come on!" I said. "Friday is the dress rehearsal— just a final run-through. Can't you—" No, it had to be Friday; So I arranged it for Friday; and at the rehearsal on Friday Albanese said to me: "Oh, I see Alice." All week there had been fireworks: Toscanini had really carried on; and I said to Albanese: "Today she comes, when he'll just run through it." So he starts the orchestra in the Prelude to Act 3; and he stops them: "*Piano!*" He starts them again, and stops them: "*Piano!!!*" And the third time: "*Io voglio PIANO!!! PIANO!!!*" And *he* broke his stick; *he* threw the score; *he* knocked over the stand; *he* stamped his feet. I saw my wife looking at me; and afterwards she said: "I *shouldn't* come Friday?" But the beautiful thing was that finally he cooled off and began to play with his mustache and said: "Next season, anybody in this orchestra who wants to play with me must have audition. Nobody can play next year without audition." At that point he saw Mischakoff, the concertmaster, looking up at him with that smile on his face like a little cherub's; and he looked down at Mischakoff and said: "You too!" Mischakoff had been with him ten years at that time!

There was one broadcast in there that he wanted me for; but I was booked for two concerts at some college that just wouldn't release me; and I think that time he wanted to do *Lucia*. He loved *Lucia*. Most people: you mention *Lucia*, and they say, "Aaah—*Lucia!* Kukuraku, kukuraku [a term of ridicule for coloratura singing]!" But when you mentioned *Lucia* to Toscanini he'd say: *"Lucia!* [Peerce imitated Toscanini's intake of breath] *Che bell' opera!";* and if he was near a piano he sat down and played it for you. I said to him once: "You know, Maestro, I'd love to do *Lucia* with you—at least the Tomb Scene"; and he said: "Yes, yes, some day." And I think he wanted to do it at that broadcast.

About *Un Ballo in Maschera* I had a whole thing with him, which of course I didn't publicize at the time. I had been promised that *Ballo* originally—oh, yes, I had been promised it; but there was some management political business, and all of a sudden I *heard* that my friend Bjoerling was to do it. When I inquired, "Oh, yes, there was a change." "What do you mean, there was a change? I was *promised* this thing!" "Well, he had a change of mind." "*Who* had a change of mind?" And right away the people around him began to guard him: before that I could get to him any minute of the day; now I couldn't. I was heartbroken, because I worshipped this man: for me he was someone on a pedestal who could do no wrong; and when this happened I said: "I don't ever want to see this guy or talk to him, great as he is." And if it weren't for my wife I would never have done it—which would have been terrible, because *Un Ballo* is one of the best things I ever did with Toscanini, and one of the greatest things that ever happened to me. Walter Toscanini called my wife to ask her if I would talk to his father; and I refused at first; but she said to me: "What are you, crazy? Are you going to cut off your nose to spite your face?" So finally I said: "All right, I'll talk to him." So he got on the phone: "Peerce—Peerce—believe me, is not my fault." And I felt miserable; because I knew he had been victimized; and to have him, a man like that, whom I loved so, apologizing—I felt so miserable, I cried. I said to him: "But Maestro, I haven't done *Un Ballo in Maschera* in six or seven years, and I don't remember it." "Peerce, you will know it—you will know it." This was just a week before the broadcast; I had a concert on Sunday and a performance at the Met on Tuesday; and he wanted me

Wednesday for rehearsal with the orchestra. No piano rehearsal: I couldn't *give* him a piano rehearsal. He said: "You don't have to memorize it: you can hold the book." Well, I got to work with my accompanist and coach, and got the thing back in my system. When I came into Carnegie Hall for the rehearsal there was electricity in the air, with people who knew about all this wondering what was going to happen. I'd seen Toscanini upstairs for a minute; and he'd said to me: "Just sing. I follow." "I'll follow *you*, Maestro." "No, no, you just sing." We went through the first act without a mistake; and he called an intermission; but before that he jumped off the podium and threw his arms around me and kissed me. This was the side of Toscanini that seldom came out; and I felt just like a kid. And upstairs he said to me: "You afraid? You afraid? I told you: you just sing." I said: "But Maestro, I was worried about not satisfying you." He said: "Don't worry. Just sing." And it was a fabulous success. The fire he gave to it![1]

About a year ago a friend called me and said: "They've just announced they're going to do the Toscanini *Bohème* on WOR." So I turned it on and sat listening to it; and what it made me think was that at this late date—with the new sound, and stereo, and shmereo—this was still the greatest recording and made the greatest sound—greater than what you have on all the new ones. You get the quality of that extemporaneous performance: you know you're listening to a real show. You didn't walk into a studio where someone said: "We'll start at letter D and make twelve bars; then we'll cut and make fourteen bars after letter K"; you didn't make one note here and one note there—*you* know the way they make records these days. No—you went in and did a show. So you had to remake an ending or something; but it was a living thing; and that's the greatness of the performance. And I can feel proud of my singing in it; because it isn't a patching together of one note here and another note there in the recording studio: it's the real singing I did that day.

Sol Schoenbach

In addition to the recollections of the musicians who played with Toscanini for years in the New York Philharmonic and the NBC Symphony, I wanted those of musicians who played with him only a few times, when he made guest appearances with their orchestras—specifically musicians of the Philadelphia Orchestra, which he conducted in three of its Friday-Saturday pairs during the season of 1941-42, another pair in November 1942, and a pension fund concert in February 1944. I was unable to talk to Marcel Tabuteau, the orchestra's first oboe in that period, and one of its great personages, who after retiring went back to France; or to William Kincaid, its first flute and another great personage, who I was told was ill. The first horn, Mason Jones, whom I did see, claimed to have nothing to tell. But the first bassoon, Sol Schoenbach, was able to tell me a great deal that he remembered.

As the men of the orchestra had stood smiling behind Toscanini after the performance of Schubert's C-major, at the concert of November 15, 1941, their smiles had seemed to me evidence of how much it meant to them to be playing again under a great conductor (Stokowski had just left the orchestra), and one who was in addition a great musician. But I now discovered that it had meant less to them than I had thought. Schoenbach—who, I gathered, could be taken as speaking for his fellow-musicians in the orchestra—recognized, certainly, that Toscanini was an extraordinary conductor and musician; but had reservations and criticisms concerning objectives and methods that the Philharmonic and NBC Symphony musicians did not have.

SCHOENBACH:

I was raised in New York; and my teachers were Benjamin Kohon, first bassoon of the New York Philharmonic, and for the major portion of my studies Simon Kovar, the second bassoon. And so all I heard about was Toscanini, and from the inside: they used to bring home the music and discuss it; and I was very well steeped in that tradition. Also, my sister gave me a subscription to the Saturday night Philharmonic concerts, which I heard from the top balcony from the time I was a little boy. So when I got to the point where I myself played with Toscanini, I had enough background; and at the first rehearsal I was full of respect and awe.

I found that Toscanini never quite explained himself. He would make all kinds of remarks and shout; but it wasn't clear what he was driving at, unless you yourself knew what the problem was. The conductors I had worked with were quite articulate; but though Toscanini was voluble he wasn't articulate. (I guess the language was a problem.[1]) So when he was dissatisfied he couldn't say exactly what to do about it. He would say "Sing!"—which was a wonderful suggestion; but when you 'sang' and it didn't quite fit into his idea of the phrase, he just got furious. Oh yes, he did sing it for you; but that didn't help, because he sang in this half-voice that was out of tune, and when you listened to it, you couldn't relate it to what he said he wanted. He had something in his mind; and he did the passage over and over until he got it as he wanted it; but he couldn't tell you specifically what he wanted. So it wasn't just being in an exposed position that kept me from feeling at ease, but not knowing what was going to happen, when he was going to erupt. Fortunately Marcel Tabuteau had had his previous experience with Toscanini at the Metropolitan, and could relay to us in the woodwind section what the problem was— which prevented some shouting. Also, I had this background through my teachers, which was helpful. And the Schubert C-major doesn't have a very exposed bassoon part. So I escaped his wrath.

Another thing that caused trouble was that we had an approach to the music down there, best presented by Tabuteau. In addition to being an instrumentalist he was a very great musician, who had made an analysis of all that goes to make music—how rhythm is put together, and how the line of music is derived from the harmony, and so on. He gave this to all his students at the Curtis Institute, and not just his oboe students, because he had the woodwind class. I went to Juilliard, where Barrère was our woodwind teacher; and when I came to the Philadelphia Orchestra I noticed that there was something special going on. I set about analyzing it, and asking Tabuteau questions; and I began to participate in it. Toscanini wasn't acquainted with this approach; and many times we got into trouble because he thought of music as starting from beat 'one', where we thought of it as starting with the preparation for beat 'one'.

I don't think he made any such theoretic studies: he was concerned with preparing the piece that had to be played. An orchestra was just an instrument for him: as a pianist would say: "Deliver me a Steinway," Toscanini would say: "Deliver me an orchestra." Whether it was French or German or American or the BBC, he set out to make the music come from that orchestra the way he heard it from the score: he wouldn't

change it by one iota to suit the players he found in the particular orchestra. Every player was—not an enemy, but someone who had to be taught to do the thing right. Toscanini was in full possession of the facts; and we were all just instrumentalists who had to be beaten into shape so that we played the music right. And he never gave us much credit for brains. He seemed to regard orchestra players as inferior; and *he* had to get them up to a professional level. But I will say that he wasn't like some conductors who, when they're not satisfied, try to get rid of the man and get someone else. He worked with what he had, whether it was the greatest or not so great. He wasn't the most patient man; but he didn't say to the player: "Go home, and we'll get someone else."

As for what he wanted in the playing of a wind instrument, his first consideration was the singing quality: he kept shouting *"Cantare! Cantare!"*; and he wanted the instrument to sing out. Another thing he cared a lot about was intonation. Then rhythm; and here I'll say there was another thing I observed with Toscanini, for what it's worth (it's easy to sit here and talk about the giant he was!): he was so preoccupied with rhythm all the time that very often he made a rhythmic problem terribly complicated when it wasn't. Anything that involved a dotted figure—for example the beginning of the Allegro in the first movement of the Schubert C-major:

almost before anyone even played it he'd say the eighth-note was too early, and he'd begin to carry on. All these common little rhythmic things that musicians are familiar with seemed like an obsession with him: you hardly had played before he'd stop and say it was wrong; and then it usually did get wrong, because it wasn't clear to us exactly what he wanted. We did the Mendelssohn *Midsummer Night's Dream* music—you know what transparent music that is—and he fussed so much about the tempo and the rhythm, the tempo and the rhythm, that after a while you had trouble with something you never had trouble with before. We began to feel that he had a complex about this—that he was so afraid *he* might be wrong, that he assumed *we* were wrong—though many of us didn't find any problem. And I remember once when there *was* a problem he didn't settle it. Knowing how fussy he was about everything like that, I went to him and asked about a triplet figure in the first movement of the Beethoven *Pastoral*, which in the exposition came to an eighth-note, but in the recapitulation came to a quarter-note, with no logical reason for the difference. He went into a long discussion about the original manuscript that he had seen in the British Museum or some other library; but he never answered the question—because I don't think there *was* an answer.[2]

To get back to that first rehearsal: I remember the Schubert C-major vividly. He was concerned with the movement of it, the flow of it; and he tried to make everything clear—he didn't want anything muddy. One of the other pieces on the first program was Debussy's *Ibéria*; and there is a bridge passage from the slow movement to the last movement—a distant-sounding passage in which the bassoon plays with the flute and violin. I played it all the time; but he sent word that he didn't want me to play it for the recording; and when I asked him why, he said *his* score—a revised version suggested by Caplet—didn't have it. I don't remember whether I did play it or not for the recording, which I never heard: those recordings never came out; they were supposed to have been damaged.[3]

I'll never forget the Tchaikovsky Sixth on one of the later programs. It starts with a bassoon passage; and because of Stokowski's and Ormandy's training, it was my custom to play this opening passage in one breath—which took a lot of doing. At the first rehearsal with Toscanini I presented him with my great accomplishment—and he didn't like it! He didn't say anything at the time; but I could see that he wasn't really in accord. Either he sent for me or I went to him; and in his dressing room he asked me why I played the passage all in one breath; and I told him this was what I had been trained to do. He said no, he preferred that it be segmented; and he proceeded to sing in that voice of his: "I-ee love you; I-ee love you—" this mournful Tchaikovsky Sixth in that voice! I had all I could do to keep from laughing; but I played it his way. Then, later in the movement, just before the development section, there's a passage that traditionally is begun by the clarinet and ended by the bass clarinet, although the last notes are scored for the bassoon. He absolutely refused to have those last four notes played by the bass clarinet. He said: "It's in the bassoon part; and you must play it," And I—*tell*—*you*: to play that! I think it's marked six *p*'s; and with Toscanini it became twenty-six *p*'s; and it became the biggest feat in the world: I filled my bassoon with absorbent cotton and handkerchiefs and socks!

As a wind-player I can say it was a privilege to play with Toscanini. All the conductors I've played with were fascinating; but he was one of the greatest. You ask how he differed from the others. One difference was that whereas Stokowski was engrossed in colors—he'd even ask you to change your reed, because he thought your instrument was too bright for the gray he wanted—Toscanini was more interested in the lines: all he saw was this melody moving like that; and it had to move just right: he wouldn't permit one note to get in the way of another. But the chief difference was Toscanini's drive, his intensity. Everything was intensely felt; and he burned with white incandescence. When you started the piece you knew you were going to the end, and you felt swept along. He never dawdled, never went on any side excursions: it was unrelenting. Sometimes the music didn't lend itself to this: his strict observance of tempos didn't help the Tchaikovsky Sixth, which I felt needed a little more expansion in space and time. You thought it was marvelous? Well, one gets used to certain conceptions: Stokowski and Ormandy used to give it more space.

With Toscanini it's the drive and intensity that I keep coming back to. Though he didn't have the greatest technique with the stick, it certainly was adequate for everything that had to be done. But I think it was his personality more than his technique that enabled him to hold huge forces together in concentration. A conductor has to be a personality, has to have something in him that's dynamic, that makes him a leader whom men are willing to follow even if they hate him. And Toscanini had that.

I would say a concert with Toscanini was not as exciting as the rehearsals. There *was* excitement, of course, at the concert, and the feeling that everything had to go or else; but you also knew there wasn't much he could do if something went wrong except show you his displeasure; and mostly it went off like a preconceived affair: he never did anything but what he had asked for at the rehearsal. However it didn't have, for me, the excitement that the rehearsal had, where I didn't know what was going to happen to whom, and where he was going to blow up.

I don't think this complete autocracy, and these tantrums, could happen today—that the union and all the other forces today would put up with it. I don't think it could even get started. Toscanini was an established figure; and the situation was very different in the thirties; so the men in the New York Philharmonic were living in terror when he was putting the orchestra together; and when he took it to Europe with programs that were already studied and well rehearsed, I remember the fear that my teacher exhibited, which was shared by all the other men in the orchestra. Or take the Philadelphia Orchestra.

When Stokowski comes back now to conduct it he's mellow and it's "Dear Old Stokie"; but in the days when I first came to the orchestra the men used to sit on the edge of their chairs and go absolutely white when he came on the stage. People will not put up with that kind of abuse today. When Cantelli came to the Philadelphia Orchestra and started to throw some abuse—yes, in Italian—someone who understood got up and said he wouldn't have him talk like that in front of the ladies in the orchestra.[4] I don't see how those fellows in the NBC Symphony can say Toscanini was sweet and wonderful after the way he demolished people. Of course a conductor should have the right to have things done his way; but he should also say what his way is, not call people names.

But to get back to Toscanini's work: I remember one incident that showed something very extraordinary about him. You remember that during the war he did the Shostakovich Seventh with the NBC Symphony. Well, a couple of years later, at a reception after a pension fund concert he conducted for us—which I'll tell you about in a minute—there was a secretary of the Russian Embassy present who said to Toscanini: "You played Shostakovich's Seventh; and we in Russia are very grateful. But how is it you never have played the Fifth Symphony of Shostakovich?" Well, it was a fantastic experience for me when Toscanini told him why he hadn't done the Fifth; because it turned out that he had studied it just as much as if he *had* played it. The average person knows what he has to know; and what he doesn't have to know he doesn't bother with. But Toscanini had made a thorough study of the Fifth; and he explained to us that if you observed the metronome markings in the score, you arrived at the exposition at a certain tempo, and that played this way the music was boring, and he wouldn't play it. Other conductors ignored those metronome markings; but not Toscanini: what was printed was like from God; and if that's what it said, that was what he would do. The man from the Russian Embassy said: "Maybe the markings are wrong. I happen to live in the same apartment house as Shosta-kovich; and I will ask him personally." Some months passed; and back came a recording of the Shostakovich Fifth conducted by Shostakovich and played exactly as the score had it, with a statement by Shostakovich that the score was correct. This proved to Toscanini that he had been right to think it was boring and not to play it. I found out that there were other scores that he had studied and absorbed even though he hadn't played them; so that when you asked him why he didn't do them, he knew why, and could tell you why.

About that pension fund concert in February 1944, which was the last time Toscanini conducted us. I guess it was in 1943 that I was elected to a small committee to organize a pension plan for the men; and I came up with the plan that is now in operation, called the Pension Foundation. One important part of it was to raise money through concerts; and we had a mar-velous beginning with Piatigorsky and Milstein; then we had Lily Pons and Kostelanetz; but we weren't getting the kind of money we needed to really establish the plan. Someone sug-gested getting Toscanini—which was a challenge, and which I thought was a good idea. I got in touch with Walter Toscanini, and found that the family would be delighted to have me come over and talk with Toscanini; because the dynamic Maestro wanted to conduct more than his season with the NBC Sym-phony. So I saw him at NBC, and he consented to put on a Beethoven concert. It was quite a program: the *Egmont* Over-ture, the Sixth, the Septet, and the *Leonore* No. 2. I couldn't say to him that we didn't want such a wonderful program; so I tried to intimate that it was well above the union limitations on the length of a concert. He flew into a fury in which he denounced all the officials of the union, living and dead, and carried on like a maniac; and I thought I'd leave it alone. But he kept on fighting: "People think that I'm old, that I'm sick!

I'll show them! I'll conduct more than two men!" So we ended up with an enormous program.

When he came for the rehearsals we put in a supply of champagne; and at the first rehearsal Tabuteau made a speech in French and Toscanini answered in his bad French. Every rehearsal was just wonderful—a love feast—until the last one, when he blew his top. It was in the Septet. When I had asked him why he wanted to do the Septet, he had said it was the first score he had bought with his own money: he hadn't eaten lunch for a week to save up the money for it; and it was still his favorite piece. In the last movement the violins have a passage—a series of triplets ending in two eighth-notes—which is very difficult because the two eighth-notes are high E-flats, which are followed by a huge leap down to a low B-natural; and because of that leap the violins rushed the two eighth-notes. As I said before, rhythmic exactness was an obsession with Toscanini; and the rushing of those two eighth-notes irritated him. His irritation used to start at his feet and rise from there; and by the time it reached his mouth it was like a volcano erupting. And on that Sunday morning he just blew up completely. I had been a hero for the orchestra because I had persuaded him to come and conduct for nothing for our pension plan; but now after he insulted everybody, they were angry with me.[5]

The concert was fantastic, all of it: the usual Toscanini treatment of everything showed up. After the concert there was the reception I mentioned before; and I came in late. Toscanini was sitting and eating by himself—he hadn't eaten before the concert, and was quite hungry—and he insisted that I sit down and talk with him, which consisted mostly of listening to him. He was very happy, and was already making plans to come back the following season, when he would do the Beethoven Ninth. It never took place; and I don't know what the reasons were, because I went into the army. But I'll never forget: in the course of the conversation he told me how he was at the

Metropolitan and got fed up with just conducting opera and went to Gatti-Casazza and said he wanted to do the Beethoven Ninth. Gatti-Casazza put him off, until it got to the point where Toscanini said: "Either I conduct the Ninth or I quit"; so Gatti-Casazza said o.k. Toscanini told me the soloists he had— those great voices, the golden voices you hear about—and the fine chorus, and the orchestra; and he said that before the performance he took his pulse, and it was just right; so everything was just right. But, he said, "the next day the *critica* wrote in the papers: 'Who does this man think he is, conducting Beethoven? He should stick to Verdi and Puccini.'" Gatti-Casazza said: "You see?"; and Toscanini was furious. Then, years later when he was conducting the New York Philharmonic he performed the Ninth; and the soloists weren't up to it, the chorus wasn't up to it, the orchestra wasn't just so, and, he said, "before the performance I took my pulse, and it was terrible—I must have had a fever. But the next day the *critica* wrote: 'At last we have heard the Beethoven Ninth as it should be.'" This was to show me how little it all meant; because, he said, the Metropolitan performance the critics had condemned was much better than the Philharmonic performance they raved about.[6]

As he was entertaining me and telling me this and that, all of a sudden he began to tell me about a performance of *Carmen* he had conducted, and about a chord which involved an oboe and three trombones, and how the oboe in those days had an almost trumpet-like sound so that it matched those brass instruments. And while telling me this story he got angry all over again about something that had happened in that performance thirty years before: he blew his top and banged the table and knocked over the dishes. Everybody came running up and asked: "What did you say to him?"; and I said: "I didn't say a word."

But that Beethoven concert! I'll never forget Tabuteau after it was over: he said, "Now I can die." That program was absolutely the end as far as every detail was concerned. It was prepared with great heat, and presented with great illumination; and everything went right. Sometimes, no matter what you do, something goes wrong; but not this time: this one was incredible. I think this was the greatest performance he did with us. The others I don't remember as being special, though they were very good. The Mendelssohn *Midsummer Night's Dream?* Yes, that was marvelous. It had such transparency: he really worked on that; and of course he wouldn't settle for less. Somebody else would get tired and say "What's the use?" or "Let's go on"; but not he: he'd go over and over and over it. Also, I'll never forget his correcting the English of the singers: he had a fantastic ear for that sort of thing. The *La Mer?* Terrific! I remember in the first movement how he worked that cello passage over. Also in the last movement, where the flute and oboe play the theme over the harmonics in the violins—how carefully he had that whole thing worked out to get the feeling of the long shadow, and that sound almost like the wind up there above the sea. I was carried away almost to the point where I'd forget to come in and play.

Well, it was a great privilege for us, hm?

Josef Gingold

One of the young violinists who gave up a concert career to join the NBC Symphony in 1937 was Josef Gingold. Two years later he played in a quartet of NBC string virtuosos headed by William Primrose (Oscar Shumsky, Gingold, Primrose, Harvey Shapiro), which made an exciting first public appearance at a New Friends of Music concert with a dazzling performance of Mozart's Quintet K.614 (with William Carboni, second viola). When I began to attend Toscanini's rehearsals at NBC in 1942, Gingold was one of the musicians I enjoyed talking to about the things that happened—the one who spoke with the greatest enthusiasm and warmth. It was he who, after an extraordinary rehearsal of La Mer, *exclaimed: "You can quote me on this: we come here to go to school!" And he spoke about Toscanini with the same warmth and an additional fervor twenty-three years later.*

GINGOLD:

My first rehearsal with Toscanini—for the first NBC Symphony broadcast in 1937—I think was the greatest musical experience of my life. I had of course heard Toscanini many times

132

with the New York Philharmonic: he was my favorite conductor; and that was why I joined the NBC Symphony: I
wanted to make music with this giant. I was a little apprehensive
because of what I had heard about his temper; but I thought
I'd try it for a season and see what happened.

That Sunday afternoon in 1937, a week before the broadcast, when he raised his stick to begin the Brahms First, there
was electricity in the air; and the first chord gave me goose
flesh. I don't think I've ever been as thrilled as I was then; and
I'm still thrilled when I speak of it now, thirty years later. He
went through the entire Brahms symphony with very little
comment,[1] apparently pleased with the orchestra; and we responded to his conducting by not only playing our hearts out
for him but playing over our heads. After the Brahms we played
the Mozart G-minor; and it was a marvelous performance, a
marvelous experience. I have still to hear a Mozart G-minor as
great as Toscanini's: in it Mozart emerged in a new light.
Toscanini made it a great drama; and I will never forget the
opening phrase—the pathos it had with the inflection he gave it.
He kept saying to the violins: *"Molto arco! Molto arco! Non
tedescho! Italiano! Molto arco!"* [Gingold illustrated with big
movements of his bow arm as he sang the opening phrase in an
impassioned manner.] It was *his* Mozart; and it was wonderful![2]

We also did the Vivaldi Concerto Grosso in D minor,
which opened the broadcast on Christmas Eve; and I recall
that at the broadcast, I don't know what happened, but Toscanini's first beat in the Vivaldi was very indecisive, so that we
almost didn't get started together. For a moment the orchestra
was a little shaken; but somehow we did get into it, and then it
was all right. (I don't remember his making any mistakes—
though I did see him balled up once, in Copland's *El Salón
México*, by the constantly changing meter. Even so, I believe
Copland said it was one of the best performances he ever had.[3])

I remember in those first weeks a wonderful experience in

133

the two movements of Beethoven's Quartet Op. 135, which Toscanini played with string orchestra, and in which I've never heard any quartet approach him. The way he worked out every detail in the Largo! And the fire in the Scherzo! And those complicated string crossings that he worked out with the first violins alone! I wish he had done all the Beethoven quartets: for me they are the greatest masterpieces in the quartet litera- bture; and where can you find a first violinist who is a Toscanini? He also did the *Moto Perpetuo* of Paganini, which was a lot of fun for the violinists, who practiced their parts and were well prepared.

It was in our second season that we played Tchaikovsky's *Pathétique* the first time; and it was quite a revelation to us, and gave us a bad morning. He came to the rehearsal with the preconceived idea that the orchestra was set in its way of playing the symphony; and he was right. We came to the second subject, the D-major melody which traditionally—for I don't know how many years—we had all played with a *ritardando* on the first three notes. When Toscanini began to conduct the melody in tempo, the orchestra took it away from him and slowed down the first three notes. He stopped: "*Signori, perchè?* Why? Is written so, eh? *Ancora!*" We started again; and again we made the *ritardando*: it was so ingrained in us that we couldn't help it. And he threw a fit. "*Si, tradizione!* The first *asino*, the first jackass, did it that way, and everyone follow him!" Then he pointed to the score: "*This* is my *tradizione!* So play like this!" Toscanini's logic was unanswerable: if Tchaikovsky had wanted a *ritardando* he would have written it in the score: "Is very easy to write *ritardando*, no?" So we played the three notes in time; and from then on we played everything as Tchaikovsky wanted it. This was the way we played it at the broadcast; and for the first time musicians and music-lovers heard the music as Tchai- kovsky wrote it; but a great many of them didn't like it, because it was different. And today I hear the Tchaikovsky *Pathétique* played again in the "traditional" manner. I won't say by everybody: George Szell, for instance—who, incidentally, was a great admirer of Toscanini; oh yes, he had a tremendous admiration for him[4]—Szell, who treats the classics with the utmost respect, tries to follow in Toscanini's footsteps with a personality of his own. I never heard Cantelli, unfortunately; but except for him, Toscanini didn't have the great young disciples to continue what he achieved.

I remember marvelous performances we gave in Buenos Aires. We were having a beautiful trip; we were rested; we were playing nothing but symphonic music, and not one broadcast a week but a concert every other day; Maestro was in fine spirits. And one performance of the *Tristan* Prelude and Finale in the Teatro Colón was UN-FOR-GETTABLE!

Certain performances of Toscanini's I don't think will ever be equalled by anyone else. The *Enigma Variations*, for instance: I don't think anybody did it as well. I don't think there will ever be a *La Mer* like his. The time he spent with the cellos and violas in that passage in the first movement! Also the Beethoven Ninth. The first movement: it was classic; it wept; it was operatic! The slow movement! And the recitatives of the basses in the finale! Berlioz's *Queen Mab*: the magic of it! The Rossini overtures: impossible to duplicate! The Wagner: no one conducted Wagner like Toscanini—*no one!* And of course Verdi: who will ever hear Verdi played like that? Even the accompaniments in performances of the arias: never banal, always with dignity, grandeur. Nothing was too small; everything was important. A little miniature like *Queen Mab*: how he worked on it! Twenty batons must have been broken to achieve it! Or the little Martucci pieces: with what grace and charm he did them! And I played with him at that Chatham Square benefit—in that little orchestra in which Heifetz played, and Milstein and Adolf Busch and Feuermann, with a few NBC men; and Toscanini conducted the *Moment Musical* of Schubert, the *Musical Joke* of Mozart, the *Perpetual Motion* of Reis, and a piece called *Loin du Bal* by Gillet, which you hear on Muzak and used to hear in hotels. Even though it was supposed to be a jamboree, we had a rehearsal, and the Old Man conducted as if it were a concert or broadcast: everything was done perfectly. And what he did with this little piece, this trifle, *Loin du Bal!* It came out like a wonderful jewel! Whatever he played, he played as though it was the greatest work.

I think he was the greatest recreative artist of this era—certainly as a conductor; and the explanation of how he did what he did has to begin with the unexplainable—that he was a genius. One can say he was a masterful conductor, who knew what he wanted and knew how to get it; one can speak of his tremendous knowledge, his thorough preparation, his ear, his baton technique. But I think that in the final analysis it was his genius that really won out: he was a genius blessed with all these things he needed for realization. It was not just one of them, but the combination of all of them.

From a purely technical viewpoint he had the clearest beat of any; but it wasn't the beat of a specialist in virtuoso conducting; it was the beat of a musician who had a stick and could show whatever he wished with it. And he never did more than was needed. He once quoted Hamlet's directions to the actors: "Suit the action to the word, and the word to the action"; and he himself made the motion that was suited to a *forte*, a *piano*, or any dynamic. He once said to the violinists, in a *pianissimo* passage where we were using too much bow: "Watch my hand. If my motion is small, your bow must be small; if my motion is large, your bow must be large." And the marvelous way he could conduct a slow tempo—the control! He is the only conductor I know who conducted the *Parsifal* Prelude in four instead of the customary eight; and he didn't give the silent downbeat most conductors give to assure perfect unanimity at the very beginning. He said: "Is no cadenza *per me*: I start to beat when we start to play." And he did, and the violins came in together! Also, he beat it all in four, and with his superb stick control it was always together. (To say nothing of the mood, the magic that he got in this piece.) Also the second movement of *Ibéria*, which is written in two, but which everyone does in four. Toscanini said: "I know is conducted in four, but I cannot do it so"; and he did it in two—and the control was marvelous. He was like a human metronome: a *human* metronome, I say, because I mean that his sense of rhythm was so marvelous. We played the *Eroica* one year; and the next year he varied by five seconds in a work which takes forty-eight minutes.

And yet he was smarter than some conductors who are *Kapellmeister*—who always hold the reins: he would run with a running horse. We did a performance of the Haydn No. 88; and we heard later from the people who were backstage after the performance that the Old Man came up beaming and said: "Did you hear the beautiful tempo *primi violini* took in finale?" They laughed at the idea of the violins taking a tempo; and he said: "*Si,* they took the tempo." Of course it was his tempo; but within hairsbreadths it could be a tiny bit on the fast side; and once it started there was nothing he could do; so, smart man that he was, he took what he got—which happened to be perfect—and played along with it. And he was so delighted! So many times he walked off the stage cursing—disgusted with the orchestra or with himself. He was very tough on himself: many times he said: "*Stupidi—anch' io!*" Even when something was good he was sparing with his praise: when he said "*Non c'è male*—not too bad" that was a real compliment.

Which reminds me of an extraordinary incident the first time we played Wagner's *Faust Overture*. The piece starts with a solo for tuba; and when our tuba-player, William Bell, had played it, Toscanini stopped and said: "*Ancora.* Again." So Bell played it again; and this time Toscanini went on; and we in front heard him say under his breath as he conducted: "This is

137

first time in fifty-five years that I hear this solo played correct. Bravo, tuba, bravo, bravo." This was extraordinary; but so was the rest of the story. Since Toscanini said it so softly, only those of us around him heard it; and each of us assumed one of the others had told it to Bell, who sat too far away to hear it. Well, Bell and I now teach at Indiana University; and last year, when we were reminiscing about the Old Man, and I referred to Toscanini's terrific compliment to him, he didn't know what I was talking about. It turned out that no one had told him at the time; and when I told him what Toscanini had said, he was just as thrilled now as he would have been in 1938.

To get back to the other things about Toscanini's conducting: the score and parts of the Shostakovich Seventh arrived here at the last possible minute; and Toscanini had no more than two weeks' preparation before calling the first rehearsal. The work is about seventy-three minutes long; and when Toscanini began that first reading he knew the entire work by memory. Now we were playing from the parts of the Leningrad Philharmonic or whatever orchestra had played it in Russia—if not conducted by Shostakovich, certainly supervised by him—and not just one performance, but I believe twenty or more. When Toscanini had run through the first movement he said *"Da capo"*; and pretty soon he stopped and said, either to a trumpet- or a horn-player: "What you play there? You play *si bémol*, eh? I think should be *fa.*" The player said: "But Maestro, I have a B-flat in my part." "No, *caro*, I think should be *fa.*" And in his myopic way he peered at the score; and he was right. He was right the first time; he was right the second time; and I believe he must have found thirty-five or forty mistakes in the parts, that Shostakovich himself hadn't heard in twenty or more performances. The same thing happened when we played Roy Harris's Third Symphony. I think we had the parts from which the Boston Symphony had played it and recorded it under Koussevitzky. Roy Harris was at the rehearsals; and I imagine he must have been at the Boston Symphony rehearsals; and Toscanini kept finding wrong notes in the parts and turning to Harris: "Eh, Maestro, you don't think should be this note?" Poor Harris had to look at the music; and of course Toscanini was never wrong.[5] There was a contemporary piece—I can't remember what—that he programmed, tried once, and took off: he couldn't take it; it was too dissonant for him. He came to that rehearsal knowing the piece by memory; and as we were reading it we came to a terrific discord: it was so dissonant that we actually had to look at the fingerboard to see where our notes were. And he stopped: "Eh, *terzo corno!* Third horn! *Re!* I didn't hear!" The man had had a few bars' rest and had cleaned his horn, and hadn't been able to get it up again in time to come in. Toscanini couldn't see that far, and didn't see that the man wasn't playing; but he heard that the D was missing.

Then there was his knowledge—not just of symphony and opera, but of everything in music. I don't think he ever forgot anything. This background of all-round knowledge came into the playing, no matter what particular work he was doing. One felt it.

And then there was the spell which his genius cast over the men. My wife likes to tell the story about the day I had some bug and wasn't feeling well enough to go to a rehearsal, but there was something on the program that I wanted to play, so I said: "I'll bundle up and go, and I'll play that one piece and then come right home." I went there feverish and in no condition really to play; but once Maestro began the rehearsal, I became so absorbed in what we were doing that I forgot I was sick, I forgot about myself entirely; and at the end of the rehearsal I was feeling completely well. This was the effect Toscanini had: when you were playing with him your mind never wandered for one moment; you were completely absorbed in music-making and at one with him and with the composer. And also, no matter what you were playing, you were convinced, at that moment, that this was the only way it could be played.

It was the spell of his musical personality; but it was also what he gave of himself. From the moment he began the rehearsal it was music-making plus a workshop; and it was never "Let's take it easy and save ourselves for the concert": he never spared himself, and he expected his musicians never to spare themselves. How could we help responding to this man who worked harder than everybody else (there was a pool of water around him after a while), for whom music was a religion, and who made us feel the same way? We adored him; and we *tried* at least to give as much—and not only for him but for the music's sake. And let me say this: the concerts were of course a marvelous thing to have; BUT—THE REHEARSALS! As much public acclaim as he had in his sixty years as a conductor— and for me it wasn't enough; he should have had even more— only the musicians who were in the workshop with him really knew how great he was: they saw aspects of his art that one couldn't see at the concert. The concert was a finished thing; and sometimes one had a feeling, not that he didn't care, but that the work had already been done, the concert had to take place, so let's go through with it. *Sometimes*; I wouldn't say always. He was always inspired; but the rehearsals were incredible: he was as inspired at them as most conductors are at concerts. It was the wonder of wonders, the things you saw this man do, whereas you had difficulties playing just one line. You felt like a little nincompoop in the presence of a god.

A great, great genius—one in a lifetime: there will never be another one like him—not in our time. And the impact he had on all of us who played with him was such that our whole musical being was altered for the good—for the best. Music was a religion for him; and it rubbed off on all of us who came into contact with him. He instilled a love of work, a devotion and respect for music, for the composer. He taught us to look carefully at the composer's indications on the printed page—to see, for example, what he wrote *after Allegro*. He would say: "Is not *Allegro*. Is *Allegro ma—*" or "*Allegro con—*" Every word meant something. In *Allegro giusto* you had to pay attention to the *giusto*; in *Allegro vivace*, to the *vivace*. When we played an Andante he would say: "*Non marcia funebre! Andante!*"

But the statement one often hears—that one of the great things about him was that he played everything as it was written—those who say this are uttering a mere empty phrase. To play what's written is quite easy; what people don't realize is that Toscanini, being a great musician, read between the lines, and this was what gave the music the life it had in his performance. And very often he did change dynamics—because he had to. In a Beethoven symphony, for example, you will find that Beethoven wrote double-*forte* throughout a passage; and if you played it exactly as written it would sound poorly balanced and blurred. So Toscanini made certain changes in the dynamics for clarification, to enable certain voices to emerge. Where the violins had to fight against all the brass he changed the double-*forte* to *mezzo-forte* for the brass and left the double-*forte* for the violins, so the violins could be heard clearly without having to force.

His ideas of clarity, of voices always emerging clearly—there has never been anything like it. He would take just, let's say, the second clarinet and third horn and violas—inner voices—and make them play alone. And always "*Cantare! Cantare!* Sing! Sing!" He made these voices sing as if they were thematic, and then incorporated them with the rest of the orchestral texture. And how beautiful the whole thing became!

One thing he did that occurs to me is his beating in circles. Musicians I knew would ask me: "How do you know what he's doing?" The perspective was different for someone *in* the orchestra. He did the circular movement when he felt that the music called for expansion, for excitement, which he achieved

by getting away from the square one-two-three-four beat. He
always was making music; and as far as we were concerned the
beat had been established. It was difficult for an outsider to
understand; but we understood it perfectly.

As I said before, working with this man we felt that we
were in the presence of a god. That's why when he would throw
fits and would insult people—though it wasn't very pleasant, I
must say, and we wished he had acted differently—we understood and accepted it. Sometimes we accepted even when we
didn't understand. Chotzinoff once gave me the explanation of
an incident which baffled us at the time. He sometimes came
to a rehearsal with a preconceived idea about what was going
to happen. I told you about the first time we rehearsed Tchaikovsky's *Pathétique*; and in this case it was the first time we
were going to do the *Leonore* No. 3. At the end there is that
famous violin passage, which we prepared in advance: we practiced it individually, and together; and as you know we had a
marvelous violin section. The day of the first rehearsal, Chotzinoff told me, the Old Man was pacing back and forth, back and
forth, in his room. Chotzinoff asked him what was the matter.
"*Tutti violini di NBC son stupidi!*" "But Maestro, you seemed
satisfied at the concert on Saturday." "Eh, but you will hear
Leonore. They cannot play. Is *male, male!*" At the rehearsal,
we sensed that he was in an unusually bad mood; but it wasn't
the first time. When he came to the difficult violin passage he
stopped, pointed to the last four violins of the section, and
said: "Last four violins play alone." They played very well.
"Next four." They played very well. Down the line: everyone
played well. Then the whole section: it was marvelous. And he
was so angry that it went well, because it was contrary to what
he had expected, that he began to scream: "You are *dilettanti!*"
We just looked at him: there was no use trying to figure out
what this was all about.

But he could be very understanding and patient when

something was difficult. And he could be wonderful to people. When the orchestra manager once wanted to fire a musician, Toscanini said: "He stay." And when one of the men was killed in South America and Toscanini found out about it, he locked himself in his cabin and wept for hours, because he felt that if he hadn't made the tour this man would still be alive.

I myself had a wonderful experience with the Old Man. None of us ever approached him personally: we were asked to keep away from him when the orchestra was organized. So when I resigned from the orchestra in 1943 to become concert-master of the Detroit Symphony, I handed in my resignation to the personnel manager, not to Toscanini. But a notice appeared in *The Times* on the day of one of our Sunday afternoon broadcasts; and Maestro read it. After the broadcast Chotzinoff said: "Maestro wants to see you." I didn't associate it with the notice in the paper, and didn't know what it was about. For the moment I was stunned, and thought: "My God, what did I do?" I recapitulated the entire broadcast in my mind; but as far as I could remember I had played as well as I could, and hadn't spoiled anything. So I went in to see him; and he looked at me and said: "*Caro*, you don't like Maestro anymore?" I said: "Maestro, I adore you!" "Then why you leave?" "Well, Maestro, I've always wanted to be a concert-master; and of course one has to start in a smaller orchestra to realize this ambition." "*Ma*—is good orchestra here, and good maestro. Why you leave?" This was the first time he had shown any awareness of my existence: until then I had thought I was just another number—but not at all. He then invited me to visit him in Riverdale; and we spent a whole afternoon with him that was just terrific.

We debated whether to take our boy, who was then four years old. My wife didn't think we should; but I said he was old enough to be able to remember it and say he once shook hands with Toscanini; so we decided to take him along. Tosca-

nini was wonderful to him—gave him cookies, and took him out
to a swing or something in the yard. We were alone with the
Old Man the whole afternoon—four hours. He was sniffling
and sneezing, and said: "I have terrible cold"; but my wife
whispered that she thought it was hay fever, because *she* had it
and it was the season; and we found out later that he did have
hay fever. Well, he asked me about myself—with whom had I
studied? I said: "With Ysaye." "Ah, is great violinist. He play
with me innnnnn—Scala. Was innnnnn—April—eighteennnnnn
—ninety-six. *Mi-maggiore* Bach—and Mendelssohn." Just like
that; and if the Old Man said it was April 1896, it was so. "He
play beauuutifully. Beautiful *rubato e cantabile*. A beautiful
artist." And then he said: "You know, Sarasate play with me in
Italy first time Lalo *Symphonie Espagnole*. Is not very interesting, but beautiful technique. He play like—like lady."

It was lovely: he reminisced, and I asked him questions. I
asked him about the great days at the Metropolitan when he
was there. I said: "It must have been wonderful when they
had singers like Caruso and Scotti." He said: "When I am
young man I admire certain singers. And people say: 'You think
these are good. You should have heard *Rubini!* You should have
heard *Grisi!*' Is always so. Now in twenty-five years you will
say: 'Singers today are no good. You should have heard *Peerce!*'
Were not such golden years."

He spoke about Chaliapin, for whom he apparently at one
time had great admiration. He said that they were going to do
Mefistofele at La Scala and were looking for a suitable bass;
and it so happened that a very dear friend who went on a
business trip to Russia heard Chaliapin there. This friend was
not a musician, but he knew opera, he knew singers; and he
told Toscanini about this young Russian bass who he said was
wonderful. So Toscanini sent Gatti-Casazza on a special trip to
hear Chaliapin; and Gatti signed him up. It was the first time
that Chaliapin sang outside of Russia; and Toscanini said that

when he came to rehearse, "Was *molto bene, molto modesto*. He did some things not *perfetto*; but we worked. Everything I tell him, he say: '*Si, Maestro, si.*' And he did a wonderful Mefistofele. Correct! CORRRRECT!!!" You know what a compliment this was from Toscanini. Everything was done beautifully; and it was a great success. At last, Toscanini thought, he had a singer who not only had a marvelous voice and was a wonderful actor, but was modest and took direction. They engaged Chaliapin again for the following year; and meanwhile he was engaged elsewhere: he sang in London, he sang everywhere, and always with great success. Then reports came to Toscanini that Chaliapin had already had a fight with the conductor somewhere—that in the middle of a performance he signalled to the conductor—you know: "*Via, via, via!*" And Toscanini said: "No, no, you make mistake. Is *molto, molto modesto*. No, no." Then he had to go to Paris; and in Paris he saw in the newspaper that Chaliapin was singing in *Mefistofele*. So he went; and he said: "Was *porcheria! Male*—bad—bad taste—everything distorted! I went backstage, and I said to him: 'Chaliapin, you must restudy the whole thing when you come to La Scala! We must work again!' '*Si, Maestro, si.*' " Then, he said, about two weeks before Chaliapin was scheduled to return to La Scala, they got a telegram that he was sick, so they postponed the performance. Then they got another telegram that he couldn't come for some other reason. And finally it was evident that he didn't want to come. Toscanini said he was disappointed that this man didn't want to be corrected. To find a great artist like that, and not to be able to do anything with him! He was so disappointed in him!

Later that afternoon Toscanini played a recording of *Harold in Italy*, which Koussevitzky and the Boston Symphony had made with Primrose; and he listened, tugging at his moustache, and said: "Poor Primrose. *Poor Primrose!* Next year he come to play this piece with me again; and he must play correct!

This is not correct! This Koussevitzky play very good double bass, you know? *Molto bene*." And he said it was a wonderful orchestra, but Boston always had good orchestras. "I remember Karl Muck. He play the Beethoven First"; and the Old Man imitated Muck conducting the Allegro of the first movement in a dragging tempo. "He did not make the first repeat: *was boring also for him*, no?!" And we couldn't laugh as you and I are laughing now; because the Old Man couldn't take a joke, and to him this was serious: he didn't think it was funny at all.

He was in great form that day. He recalled that when he was at La Scala, Ricordi came to him and told him that a composer named Leoncavallo, who was associated with them in some way, had written an opera, and they wanted Toscanini to do the premiere. So he looked at the score of *I Pagliacci*, and said: "*E porcheria*." ["It's a mess."] And he said: "I didn't want to do it; but Ricordi, who was a good friend, begged me. He said: 'Do it just once. This man Leoncavallo is so poor.' And I don't know why, but I say: '*Bene, bene*. I do this *porcheria*.' And you know what success had this piece! It went all over the world for fifty years! But you know, *caro, anche* today is *porcheria!*"

It was a wonderful visit. A few years later—I don't remember exactly what year—I listened in Cleveland, over the radio, to an incredible performance; and I sat down and wrote a Christmas card to Toscanini. I wrote him: "I was just listening to your broadcast. It was absolutely sublime. Maestro, I wish you a Merry Christmas and a Happy New Year." That's all I wrote. On Christmas Day, at eight o'clock in the morning, a special delivery; and there was an envelope addressed in Toscanini's hand, with a bold "Special Delivery" at one side, and inside a card with a photograph of himself in it, and a handwritten inscription: "Thank you, my dear Gingold, for your very kind words. My very best wishes to you for a Merry Christmas and a Happy New Year." He went to the trouble—he probably went to the post office himself to send it! He never forgot a former musician.

And I had a lovely visit with him—it was the last time I saw him—when the orchestra played in Cleveland on the transcontinental tour. They played in the Public Auditorium, to 10,000 people. I went to the concert, and tried to get backstage afterwards; but there was a police guard at the stage door, and I couldn't get in. The next day some of the men came to my house for lunch; and I told them: "I tried to see the Old Man, but I couldn't get in. I feel so terrible: I wanted to tell him what a wonderful concert it was." And one of them said: "Call up Walter Toscanini; because the Old Man was expecting you, knowing you are here." So I called up Walter Toscanini; and he said: "But Father left word with Walker to let you in." I said: "I couldn't even get to Walker." He said: "Come to the train. We leave at midnight; and Father will be there about ten o'clock." I did, and had about two hours with the Old Man on the train—a beautiful visit. He wanted to know all about the concerts in Cleveland, and how I was doing. He told me I was getting too fat. And I must tell you this wonderful story. He was having trouble with his knee; and they had a railing around the conductor's podium, so that if his knee gave way he could hold on. In Cleveland he conducted the Brahms Fourth; and the Scherzo was as energetic as ever; but at the end of it, the three *forte* chords came out *forte—forte—pianissimo*. I was taken aback, but thought maybe because of the acoustics I didn't hear right. When I saw him he said: "You notice something in Scherzo of Brahms, eh?" And he looked at me with those eyes. I said: "Well, Maestro, I noticed the last chord was *piano*." "*Si, caro,* was *piano*. You know, I have trouble with my knee. And I start to make *energico* the last chord; but my knee is going to break, eh; and I could not make the last chord big as should be. I make *piano*; and the *stupidi musicisti*—they follow me!"

147

I had brought him a little present—a book containing the programs of the Bonn Festival of 1892, which included programs of the Joachim Quartet. It was a very rare book; and when I gave it to him he was very happy: he looked through it thoroughly; told me he had heard the Joachim Quartet play; and spoke about them. I also had brought along the memoirs of Arditi. He's the man who wrote *Il Bacio*; and he was a well-known conductor in his day. I brought the book because Arditi has in it a story of how Rossini once and for all settled the question of a note in the English horn solo in the *William Tell* Overture. Arditi asked Rossini which is it: E D B C B G or E D B C A G? And Rossini took out his visiting card and wrote on it E D B C A G and his signature. Arditi writes in his memoirs that now when English-horn-players ask him, he shows them Rossini's card; and he has a photograph of the card in the book. I showed it to the Old Man; and he said: "*Si*, is Rossini's writing. But is *banale* like this. Rossini sometimes write this way, sometimes another way. No, *caro*, is wrong—is *banale*. Is *banale* also for Rossini!"; and he shut the book *molto energico*.

It was a beautiful visit. And do you know what amazed me? When I left I embraced the Old Man; and he had the skin of a baby! I noticed also that he had all his teeth—and this was a man who was then over eighty! And the most beautiful eyes I've ever seen in my life! Incidentally, when he would look at the first-violin section, when he got angry, his eyes covered everybody: everyone thought he was looking at *him*—whereas he was looking at the whole section.

And that was the last time I saw the Old Man. He emerges today greater than ever—though I don't know whether his influence is very great now. The things he fought for are being distorted again—the tempi in Brahms's symphonies, for example: *allegros* are played as *andantes*, *andantes* as *adagios*—the very things Toscanini fought against. And if you question the conductors about this, their answer invariably is: "Well, that's the tradition." But there is hardly a day—when I am teaching, or practicing, or playing—that his image isn't before me, and that I don't recall some remark or idea or other reminder of his genius. I thank God for giving me those seven years of playing with him; because my whole life has been enriched by my contact with this great, great musician. And I am sorry that others didn't have this opportunity. In my twenty-five years of symphony playing I have played with great conductors and wonderful musicians; but there was only one Toscanini.

Hugo Burghauser

HAGGIN:

In addition to conducting the New York Philharmonic, in the thirties, Toscanini conducted in various places in Europe. Kipnis told a little about this; and a great deal was added by Hugo Burghauser, who after 1940 played bassoon in the Metropolitan Opera Orchestra for many years, but who before the war was the chairman of the Vienna Philharmonic during the several years that Toscanini conducted it in Vienna and Salzburg. Not only could he speak about what he experienced with Toscanini in those years, but as a member of the orchestra for fifteen years before that, he could place this experience in the context of what he had experienced with Nikisch, Weingartner, Richard Strauss, Furtwängler and Bruno Walter.

From Kipnis I had got the impression that the performance of Beethoven's Missa Solemnis *in which he sang in 1936 was Toscanini's very first performance with the Vienna Philharmonic. I said something about this to Burghauser; and he began by correcting my wrong impression.*

BURGHAUSER:

Before the *Missa Solemnis,* Toscanini conducted in Vienna the Verdi *Requiem,* which was important for very special and sensational reasons. After his very first appearances with the Vienna Philharmonic in Vienna, in the fall of 1933, he was—on my initiative as chairman of the Vienna Philharmonic—invited to appear for the first time at the festival in Salzburg in the middle of August 1934. Two weeks before he was to arrive, Dollfuss, the Chancellor, was murdered. Naturally all the foreigners left Salzburg; and in spite of the fact that Mussolini saved Austria politically, it was like after an earthquake, and everybody was in fear and despair. And then Toscanini—contrary to all expectation, and keeping his word courageously—did appear and conduct at the Salzburg Festival the two Philharmonic concerts which repeated the programs he had conducted in Vienna in '33. Because of this connection of the Philharmonic with Toscanini, the government of Austria asked me to ask him if he would conduct the Verdi *Requiem Mass* for the murdered Chancellor. To this—again to our surprise—Toscanini readily consented. And so in the fall of 1934—two years before Beethoven's *Missa Solemnis*—Toscanini conducted Verdi's *Requiem* in Vienna; and with his great reverence for Verdi it meant a great deal to him that he conducted it on the very same spot, in the Vienna State Opera, on which Verdi himself had conducted it sixty years before. Only, Toscanini conducted out of piety for the murdered Chancellor—which proved again how strongly Toscanini felt: he shunned official politics; but this was a political act against Fascist Germany and the Fascist murder. That obviously was his attitude and his reason for conducting the *Requiem.*

And when he conducted Beethoven's *Missa Solemnis* in '36, again politics got involved and made difficulties. We had engaged a great basso—I forget whom—from Germany; but on the very day before the first rehearsal he was forbidden by the Third Reich to come to Vienna. We were at that time with Toscanini in Budapest for a concert; and when I heard by phone that our German basso was forbidden to come to Vienna, I arranged with Kipnis, who was then the leading basso in Vienna, to be ready. When Toscanini first heard there was no basso, he realized there might be no *Missa Solemnis*; but when we both came from the airplane after the flight from Budapest to Vienna, Toscanini couldn't believe his eyes: there with my secretary was his trusted basso Kipnis ready for the rehearsal, which was to take place immediately.

But now I go back to the beginning. In 1933 Toscanini consented for the first time to conduct the Vienna Philharmonic. It happened that I was then the newly elected chairman of the orchestra; and Toscanini accepted my invitation. As a result there was a collaboration of five seasons in Vienna and Salzburg. Just last week, on the occasion of my seventieth birthday, the Vienna Philharmonic wrote me a congratulatory letter, in which they said that in connection with their wishes for my birthday they must mention that after 120 years of the orchestra's existence—from Nicolai to Hans Richter, Karl Muck, Mahler, Nikisch (I played in the Vienna Philharmonic with Nikisch fifty years ago: I was then, after the first world war, a newly engaged member, and had the great advantage of playing with this great man when he made his last appearances with the Vienna Philharmonic two years before his death)—in their letter the Philharmonic told me that—looking back, in historical perspective—they could now say this was the greatest, the real climax of the historical achievement of *any* European orchestra, but especially of the Vienna Philharmonic: to have had Toscanini those five consecutive years. And I can accept credit for it; because I had the initiative, and also very big luck. I quote now Napoleon, who when he promoted an officer—say from colonel to general—naturally because of his ability to be a general—always asked also the question "And does he have luck?" And I can say that I, as a sort of general of the Vienna Philharmonic, did have the most important, absolutely essential, mystical gift of luck. Because Toscanini—for ten, fifteen, twenty years—had been invited to Vienna, but had never accepted. He came once with La Scala for two evenings, and with the New York Philharmonic, and that was wonderful; but it was not what we wanted: we wanted him to lead *us,* if possible in a continuing and growing activity. And it so happened that to my invitation he accepted—which was sheer luck—though I did put in just a little diplomacy too, which my predecessors may not have done. In my letter to Toscanini, my very first letter as the elected chairman of the Vienna Philharmonic, I invited him as my predecessors and other people had done; only, I added that we as musicians realized his high standards and his inexorable demands; and as we were, besides the Vienna Philharmonic concertizing society, also the State Opera Orchestra, we had duties—rehearsals during the day, performances in the evening—which might, from his viewpoint and also in reality, limit our ability to rehearse with him; therefore, since whatever program he would choose—and he always chose chiefly what we call the Vienna *klassische Schule*: Haydn, Mozart, Beethoven, Schubert, Brahms; and then of course his beloved Debussy and Verdi—since this would be such an enormous task for him and for us, I suggested: if there was not enough time during the day, we were ready, after every performance at night, to have rehearsals with him after midnight as long and as arduous as he wanted. I suppose such a suggestion was never made to him; and later when I got to know him very well and intimately, I learned that such an appeal and such a suggestion psychologically overwhelmed him. When he saw such an ardent desire, such a zeal—it was a sacrifice, after all, for people who played opera every night till eleven or twelve o'clock, to be then ready to rehearse with him—then he was willing to come. This little piece of psychological diplomacy, so to speak—and of course I meant it seriously: after all it was our word, and it would have to be fulfilled—played a great role in Toscanini's decision: "This time I'm willing."

When he arrived, his first program was Beethoven's Seventh, the Brahms *Haydn Variations,* his most beloved Mozart *Haffner* Symphony, and the *Meistersinger* Prelude. I said: "Well, Maestro, we have four, five mornings, and of course nights." Toscanini, smiling as he looked at the program, said: "*Ma—per* Beethoven, Brahms and Mozart, *credo* we will not need more than possibly three, four sittings?" "All right, Maestro, we start. Whatever you want." After the first rehearsal—of Beethoven and Brahms—he said: "All right—not more than two more." And when he finished the second rehearsal, he said: "That's all we need"; and there was no third rehearsal. But although I had known the orchestra more than twenty years—fifteen years as a member, and many more as a young student—I never had lived through the phenomenon of such a superhuman concentration as it showed at these rehearsals. This was such a breathtaking experience: Toscanini was by then sixty-six years old—of course a mythical figure—I would say quite a bit mellowed, contrary to his awe-inspiring reputation, and with the utmost simplicity. And the orchestra, in my time from Nikisch to Richard Strauss—who was an extraordinary, not sufficiently recognized, grandiose conductor, one of the greatest, but so self-effacing in appearance that in spite of the greatest effect people were not aware how great a conductor he was—so, the orchestra, which had been day in, day out with Strauss, Weingartner, Bruno Walter, by then also Klemperer, with this ensemble of the greatest talent of the world, still unsurpassed in spite of all the Karajans!!!—the orchestra, with Toscanini, realized this was the climax of every musician's experience. Not only because he was superior to other conductors —which was taken for granted; but because he made us *superior to ourselves*—which was the phenomenon that was practically

unexplainable. This I call magic; and you can call it Indian fakir—hypnosis—telepathy—whatever you want—but a phenomenon clearly, realistically unheard of and unexperienced. This was the essence; and also that the effect with the old Beethoven Seventh, which every one of us knew in his sleep, and with the Brahms and the Mozart, was that they were *as newly created for us*. This was the greatest surprise; and it remained so for five years. And then again, while everybody was transported to some higher sphere, at the same time Toscanini was in educational method a sort of martinet of a country teacher—severe, inexorable, overlooking nothing, to the point of pedantry, yet with geniality.

From then on it was every year a matter of about a dozen concerts. Opera we played with him only in Salzburg; but in 1936 when Bruno Walter took over as artistic director of the Vienna State Opera after Weingartner—who was quite a great man in his time—Toscanini, as a gesture to his friend Walter, opened the season by conducting in Vienna a few performances of *Fidelio*—with Lotte Lehmann and others and the set from Salzburg. His first operas in Salzburg in '35 were *Fidelio* and *Falstaff*. It was what you call a *conditio sine qua non*: he said, "All right, *Fidelio*—but only on condition that I conduct also *Falstaff*." Now he would conduct *Falstaff* with an Italian ensemble, which was never done in Salzburg even with Mozart, whose operas were mostly written originally in Italian; and it was unheard of that in a German town like Salzburg, three miles from the border of the Third Reich, an Italian should come, an anti-Fascist, who publicly declares, "I make war on Mussolini, and I throw Bayreuth in the teeth of Hitler," and should establish there the first Italian performance of *Falstaff*. There were a lot of objections and difficulties;[1] but it was done— and of course done beautifully. And so *Fidelio* was done also; and this *Fidelio* was, so to speak, transplanted to the Vienna State Opera a year later, when Toscanini opened the season in

September 1936 as a courtesy to Bruno Walter.

He was also very often a listening guest in Vienna; because whenever he was going to conduct an opera in Salzburg—say *Magic Flute*, or *Meistersinger*, which was a dream—he listened before in Vienna to get acquainted with the style of the performance. Of course it turned out that he did it quite differently; and though we all believed ours was the highest standard, *his* standard afterwards made us realize ours was not always such a high standard until he took over. Fifteen or twenty years later, here in his house in Riverdale-on-Hudson, somebody played for him a recording made from the broadcast of his *Meistersinger* in Salzburg. It was by no means a perfect recording (there was never a regular recording of the performance); but when he heard the second act he was touched in just the same way as when he conducted it in Salzburg. He said then: "It's a heavenly dream." And here, when he heard it fifteen years later, he was moved to tears—this man who was hardly addicted to sentimentality, to show sentiment; he was moved to tears, such was the power of his own conducting. And of course for all of us also.

You ask how he achieved what he did, and how he differed from others. Speaking as a very old professional—a craftsman who has been playing now for fifty years—what I must say of Toscanini is that he was able to *project* whatever was in the score and in his mind. The *conceptions* of great interpretation, of what it should be, can quite often be found in fine artistic minds; but to *project* such ideas into the orchestra *unmistakably*, by technical means that are absolutely convincing—which Toscanini did—this is the sort of miracle which I can explain in part only as a result of a real capability of telepathic communication; and in fact he rarely used words to communicate what he wanted. Of course he exhibited the best conducting technique, an unfailing ear, gesture and facial expression which made so clear the intention of any dynamic nuance, that you knew—without his saying a word—that it meant not *piano* but *pianissimo,* not *forte* but *mezzo-forte.* This was perhaps, in the work situation, his greatest ability: to show unmistakably, unfailingly, even to a musician of medium-caliber mind, what is going to happen. And another almost unheard-of ability, which some of the *best* conductors did *not* possess: when he was conducting, especially in a performance, in a medium tempo, say an *Allegretto* or an *Andante*—about half a bar before the occurrence of a detail in the music you saw already on his face and in his gesture what he was coming to and would want. This was extraordinary: the parallel conducting of what was going on now and what was coming the next moment, so that the musician felt he was being guided through the polyphonic complexity of the music, like Theseus led by Ariadne's thread through the labyrinth. It was an entirely unheard-of ability, almost like the clairvoyance of a seer. And again it was a communication not with words.

Toscanini was in fact a poor linguist. Though he knew of course by heart the words of all the Wagner works, he wasn't able to pronounce one German word correctly. After five years of intimate acquaintance he still could not say 'Burghauser' but said 'BurgAHHHser'; and he could not say '*Meistersinger*', which he conducted in heavenly manner, but said '*Mashters-INNNger*'. Yet when a Hungarian chorus from Budapest sang with us—after Kodály's *Psalmus Hungaricus*—Beethoven's Ninth Symphony in German, and began to sing not "*Freude! Freude!*" but, being Hungarian, pronounced it "*Freide! Freide!*", Toscanini at once interrupted and shouted, "Not '*Freide!*' It is '*Freude!*' " So, although he was himself not able to speak fast correctly another language, he was aware of every wrong nuance in pronunciation—in *pronunciation, diction,* mind you—forget about the music. And of course again the psychological effect: a foreign-speaking chorus, standing here in Vienna and singing Beethoven's Ninth; and there is an Italian maestro who can only shout and curse in Italian, but who is all of a sudden a master in German pronunciation and diction! This creates such concentration and awe that people achieve beyond their usual capacity—not because they want to, but because they are elevated spiritually.

And another thing about Toscanini, in which he was different from others. Suppose a conductor makes a mistake—say when he is conducting variations, and by mistake jumps from the second variation to the fourth—which can happen. When he gives the down-beat or the up-beat for the fourth variation, then probably out of the hundred musicians, ten, maybe twenty, will begin with him this wrong variation. But Toscanini happened to conduct with us *Pictures at an Exhibition* by Musorgsky-Ravel in Budapest, after we had produced it in Vienna; and it happened that he started—instead of *Tuileries—Bydlo*. I say 'started': I mean he gave the down-beat for *Bydlo*. And a phenomenon occurred which not one of us, and hardly Toscanini himself, ever experienced: *not one musician started to play!* It was ghost-like, a little like a nightmare: Toscanini conducted in the air, and not one sound occurred! Toscanini, for a tenth of a second, was flabbergasted and stony-faced: how come nobody plays? But in another tenth of a second he realized that instead of *Tuileries* he had conducted the beginning of *Bydlo*, which was very different in dynamic character. And with an almost undiscernible nod, he gave the right dynamic sign for the beginning of *Tuileries*, and then the orchestra, most harmoniously, as if nothing had happened, started to play. Afterwards he said: "This is the greatest compliment an orchestra can pay me: I make a mistake, and the orchestra at once realizes I am wrong." Why? Because his *Zeichengebung*, his gesture for communication and conducting, is so unmistakable in its one possible meaning that you cannot take it as meaning anything else; and you say: "Sorry; he's mistaken; I don't play." But that a *hundred people* should have this immediate mental contact—this happened with no other conductor in my fifty years of playing.

Conductors make mistakes; but the orchestra usually goes with the conductor into the mistake; and of course they get out of the mess; but it is never entirely avoided. With Toscanini it was avoided—because of the magical power of this man. It's not enough to explain technically—to say his down-beat for *Bydlo* was clearly different from his down-beat for *Tuileries*. Because if another conductor gave this clearly wrong down-beat, ten or twenty musicians out of the hundred would make the wrong entrance. Consider that among the hundred people playing, say ten to fifteen were tired, not too bright, even if they were good technicians; how could you expect them to be alert like seers? Yet on that evening in Budapest everyone was; and that is what I call surpassing themselves.

Of course, usually conductors don't produce such miracles. Let's say the great Nikisch and Furtwängler, or even Bruno Walter and Klemperer, conducted a mediocre orchestra; then they were mentally, spiritually much better than the performance they produced, because the orchestra was not able to follow them in the higher sphere of art. This is quite understandable: how can a mediocre musician play better—with better intonation —than his physical equipment makes possible? And with other conductors even a bad orchestra plays better than the conductor conducts—which I say is the usual situation. After fifty years' experience I say truly and sincerely: in a good fifty percent of performances the orchestra plays better than the conductor deserves and *is able to do*. You can believe me: I have no axe to grind. Every evening, in the opera—any opera, from the Metropolitan to Vienna—the orchestra, on the average, plays essentially better than the conductor conducts. And this is a condemning shame for the conductors' profession. Unfortunately they are more phony than ever. What is phony? A wrong beating technique; no ear: sometimes an ear in the middle register, never in the high octave, rarely in the low octave: the contrabasses can play anything they want—wrong by inches on the string—

and the conductor's ear is utterly unaware of it. This means they are not gifted enough; but then they pretend to be maestros; and this I call phony. Contrary to all this phoniness going on in the realm of music, Toscanini was the outstanding rarity; and during his lifetime half a dozen—maybe a dozen—came near to him, and were gifted and sincere. But you have *hundreds* of conductors in the world; and they really depreciate and deprive and pervert the whole musical business—every day, every evening!

I tell you this to show what Toscanini really was. *Tja*—a deity! Not as a human being: he had all his faults and his shortcomings and his extravagances which were sometimes hard to bear. I talk about music, and the sense for music. After all, we know Beethoven threw a chair at his housekeeper, yet his Ninth Symphony was holy, and he even spoke about his feeling close to God. And Schopenhauer, the greatest philosopher of Buddhism and compassion, could be very cruel in life. So with Toscanini, we can say, we musicians, that among conductors within our fifty years' experience he was the nearest to a deity. And we can say—we are old enough—that before him the one predecessor of such quality was Nikisch. Though by far not so universal; because Nikisch would not have conducted Verdi and Bellini and Donizetti as he conducted Wagner's *Ring;* whereas Toscanini—with in-a-lifetime unheard-of universality—did conduct a *Meistersinger* as perfect as a *Butterfly,* and a *Götterdämmerung* as grandiose as any—almost you could say ascetic Brahms *Requiem.* Maybe Nikisch would have been able, but he did not have the opportunity; whereas Toscanini could prove his universality. I can say he did not make *The Magic Flute* as heavenly, as naive, as perfect-fairy-tale-like as Richard Strauss did: Strauss happened to love it like a child.[2] But from *Falstaff* to *Fidelio* to *Trovatore* to *Walküre* Toscanini achieved perfection. Strauss conducted a perfect Wagner, and a perfect Bizet, a perfect Boieldieu, mind you, and a *Barbier* not of *Seville* but of *Bagdad,* by Cornelius, to unheard-of subtlety: this was the greatest German master of my time. But Toscanini proved he could do the same, and also Verdi, Bellini and Donizetti. I did not find any other conductor who could do all this. And again a confession about the others: I found Italians who conducted Italian operas terribly; and Germans who mistreated their German music; and American boys who conduct terribly all the repertoire!

Toscanini, when we carelessly played just one phrase in routine manner—say in a Brahms symphony, which we thought we *possessed* (because many of my colleagues played with Brahms himself; and even in the thirties when Toscanini was in Vienna there were still a few violinists in the orchestra who had played with Brahms, who died in the nineties, and who was a good conductor)—Toscanini, when this happened, what did he say, what did he do? He did not correct us. He said: "*Ma, signori, è vostra musica!* It's your music! And you play it not right?" With Italian music it was different: it was *his* music; and "You are going to follow *me,* or I crucify you!" But when it was Brahms or Mozart or Beethoven, he said: "*Ma vergogna!* Shame! Your music! And it's not as good as it should be?" He was such a moralist, and he made such a moral appeal, that you were overwhelmed by the mere morality. Not intonation, not dynamics, not rhythm—which were of course all necessary; but like a Moses with the Ten Commandments he stood there and said: "This is the law, not of me: it is *Beethoven* who demands it!" So we found out what Beethoven is: nobody else made such an appeal to us. It was tragic; because after this we could never enjoy other conductors. I have clippings from Viennese papers which say: "It's now finished for good after this performance of the Verdi *Requiem;* because it never will be the same, and we never will be able to enjoy another performance, good as it will be. After this we are spoiled." You have an affair with Greta Garbo; what else can afterwards happen to you as a man?

I remember that Toscanini once said about a phrase in a love duet: "You play this as if you would say [Burghauser's voice dropped to a murmur] 'I love you.' Who ever believes you? In the first place not the girl! You must say [Burghauser's voice rose to a roar] 'I LOVE YOU FROM THE HEART!!!' " You can call it a gimmick; but he didn't do this often: he talked very, very little. When he conducted Beethoven's Seventh the first time—the second movement, which starts with an A-minor chord *fp*—we played "WHAmm: *FORTE—piano.*" He said [Burghauser's voice became reproachful]: "*Ma signori!*" And he put both hands to his heart: "BEE-THO-VEN!!!" Without another word he said "Again!" We played "Bai": the chord had a different quality.

What I tell you is for me like repeating a dream; but it was everyday reality. And it didn't need months or years: it was at the first rehearsal, from the very first hours. The contact was immediate. And with others too. I was with him once in Monte Carlo, in 1936: from an orchestra which played on the esplanade every day a little Bizet, a little Auber, you cannot expect much; but he conducted Debussy and Haydn's *Clock*; and it was amazing. I had never seen him conducting a poor what we call *Kur* orchestra, which played out of tune and had little technique, but usually played in the open air anyhow, so it didn't matter. Of course they were all trying hard; but you cannot change the basic ability in intonation and technique and bowing; yet after ten minutes it was amazing to hear what happened: the orchestra sounded what I would call galvanized; the playing had a coat of sheen and shimmer. He would not have been so patient earlier—when he was thirty or forty: then he was cold, and insisted, and was often brutal. But later he mellowed; even Bruno Walter then said: "*Er ist wie ein Heiliger.* He is like a saint." So you couldn't say anything against what he did. A saint can even curse and condemn people to hell—which he did occasionally; but the orientation, the direction, let us say, was heaven-like. Truly, it was out of this world, though we played on strings, we blew, we snorted, and we had the music before us, the Viennese classics with which we had a lifelong acquaintance—Beethoven, Schubert's Ninth—the great C-major, and we said: "But it's our old Schubert, with which we have grown up from the time when as children we sang the masses in the church; it's the oldest acquaintance of every schoolboy in Vienna, the choir boys, the singing boys. How come that with him it's entirely different?"

Do you know that when as an experienced opera conductor he conducted an orchestra in his very first symphony concert in Turin in 1894 he played the Schubert C-major? This shows how strongly it had impressed itself on his mind; because seventy years ago, in the middle of Italy, it was unheard of to play one of the longest, the "heavenly longest" of symphonies, which usually bores people because it is unending. It was only many decades later that they performed the *Missa Solemnis* in Italy, and *Fidelio*; and Schubert also was not known. And this little shaved conductor, as he was called—because among the bearded conductors at this time, in the 1880's and 90's, like Nikisch and Richter, Toscanini was the one who shaved—this little shaved conductor played the Schubert C-major—quite a daring thing to do. Well, what struck me when he played it with us in Vienna was the introduction of the first movement, before the transition to the Allegro. This is always what Toscanini called *pasticcio*— a sort of what we call *Brei*, like mashed potatoes or cereal; because it is not very discerningly, very discriminately instrumentated: the tender melodic instruments—oboe, bassoon in its highest register—are always covered by the big, thick sound of the strings. And what Toscanini did was to keep this beautiful, voluptuous sound of the strings down, so like little flowers which usually have been hidden in the deep grass, the oboe and bassoon flowered out. This introduction was miraculous. Then when the Allegro came it was clear sailing. And I can say that

we in Vienna, with our Schubert, the only one born in Vienna
—never before did we hear this symphony so discriminately,
with such finesse of different shades, projected into *Akustik*,
realized acoustically.

And the Andante with its oboe melody. Here there is the
great danger that it becomes unending; and Toscanini always
said—in *Magic Flute* also—he was desperate and in his exasperation he shouted: *"Ma signori, andante è caminare! Andante*
means walking. Maybe we Italians walk a little faster than a
heavy German; but I don't call *this* walking [Burghauser imitated Toscanini's plodding]! *This* is *andante* [Burghauser imitated Toscanini's brisk stride]!" So when he conducted the great
G-minor aria of Pamina, *"Ach, ich fühl's"*. The orchestra started
in six-eighth time: [slowly] ONE — two — THREE —
FOUR — five — SIX — ONE. And he said: "But this is
adagio, what you play. It says *Andante*: [briskly] ONE—two—
—THREE—FOUR—five—SIX—ONE. So you can put in the
expression, and you are sure there is enough breath." You could
call it simple to the point of primitive, yet so subtle that all the
Furtwänglers and Bruno Walters did it wrong.[3] Not Strauss:
Strauss in tempo and technique was in my lifetime's experience
the nearest to Toscanini; and to my great regret and sorrow this
was hardly realized, even among musicians.

So the Andante of the Schubert C-major was flowing, relaxed, not dragging—like a healthy, elastic man, instead of one
who is old and feeble: [Burghauser sang the oboe melody in
dragging tempo]. That way everything is lost. Toscanini, even
when he stepped up a staircase at eighty!—that was the way he
was able to realize even a slow tempo. Whereas other people
were boring even when they conducted fast! It's a tragedy I
lived through half my life. I had those five years of festivals with
Toscanini; and before that there were the years with Strauss.
But I played fifty years! And at the Metropolitan where I played
twenty-two years, the last ten I experienced the poorest musician-

ship in my life! Not because these young American conductors are not brilliantly gifted; but because they are utterly untrained and therefore unmatured. An old musician cannot consider them professionals: they are brilliant amateurs. An amateur can be trained to become a professional; but they are spoiled: instead of being trained they start at the top, as generals. And what musical perversities they commit, what technical shortcomings! It's a great pity!

You ask how Toscanini's Schubert C-major was received by Viennese musicians. We heard this symphony in Vienna, in the *Musikvereinsaal*, in the *Philharmonie*, at least every second year —from Furtwängler, Bruno Walter, Weingartner—one of the greatest in his time—Fritz Busch, Strauss and so on. It was conducted by these men with few differences; and of course it had the deep, genuine sentiment of Schubert melancholy and *Lebensfreude*. And now there came an Italian firebrand, who conducted it absolutely differently: with greater dynamic emphasis, greater *Steigerung*—which meant technically more *crescendo*, more *diminuendo*, more accentuation, the *sforzandi* more *marcato*, sharper, and immediately more *piano*, with greater contrast. No soft contrasts, like Bruno Walter's, which were very lovely and fine. Toscanini made in the *Plastik* stronger contrast: instead of half-relief—bas-relief, as you call it—he carved a little deeper and sharper, with the shadows blacker. You could say it didn't have the good old *gemütliche* Viennese sentimentality, which was true; but it was fascinating. Some critics said—quite rightly and to the point—Toscanini's Schubert C-major was nearer to Beethoven than to the Kahlenberg and the *Wienerwald*. It is remarkably true that the great Schubert just before his death was nearer to Beethoven than to the young Schubert. Absolutely true. This was the novelty with Toscanini that really was completely new to Vienna: a Schubert which was not traditional Viennese, not traditional Schubert. But since Schubert never heard his own C-major Symphony, where can you say that a

Schubert tradition for this symphony exists? It does *not* exist.
And if it had existed in the beginning, since there was no gramo-
phone it would perhaps have been lost. We had our Viennese
style for Schubert; but Toscanini showed us a new style, a new
Schubert. In the C-major Symphony; not in the *Unfinished*:
this he conducted and interpreted in the perfect Viennese tradition, as if he had learned it in Vienna. Of course the powerful
accents, the dramatic *fortissimi*, the more clearly defined contrasts were there; but the tempi, the flow, the expression, the
lyricism were entirely what the Viennese were acquainted with.
Not so the C-major: this was a surprise. And my Viennese con-
temporaries said: "We have never heard it that way. But how
grand it is in effect!" I hardly expected Vienna to accept anything
in this symphony that was not entirely traditional. But though
they were aware that Toscanini's C-major was so different that
it was debatable, they said: "It's not our Viennese Schubert; but
it's done with true Beethoven character. It has a majesty which
we're not used to, and which we don't believe even that Schubert meant; but it's convincing." But how can you put in majesty
when it's not there?

You ask about the coda in the finale—whether he distended
the four unison C's at the climax. I will tell you first about the
coda in the first movement. The final *reprise* of the first theme,
in *allegro* tempo, is always conducted—though it's not written
that way—broadly, majestically, which is *andante con moto*,
you can say, but not *allegro*. Toscanini, without saying a word,
kept the *reprise* in strict tempo without the slightest modification; but he made us hundred men put in such intensity—not
loudness, not three *fortes*, but intensity—that it was *as if* he had
broadened it, though he did not broaden it an iota. (He did the
same thing with the chorale in the finale of Brahms's First: the
first time, at the beginning, it is *piano*; in the *reprise*, in the coda,
it is *fortissimo*, and is always broadened very effectively and
convincingly. Not by Toscanini, who made it impressive and

convincing *without* the modification of tempo. And of course he was right: the *reprise* should have the same face, the same appearance as the original statement; and the changed tempo changes its face.) Now in the finale of Schubert's C-major, at the beginning of the last *Steigerung—Aufbau*—build-up in the coda, Toscanini said: *"Signori, bacchanale di Vienna Prater."* You could call it rhythmically exciting; but *"bacchanale"*! Of all the orchestra, no one had ever heard this word. You say 'bacchanale' in *Tannhäuser*, in *Samson et Dalila*; but he said in Schubert's C-major *"Bacchanale di Vienna Prater."* Well, it was unearthly in achievement, really metaphysical. When it came to the climax—the four unison C's—Toscanini got such a demonic expression on his face that you saw something of an awful power behind it, which made us play with an intensity that another conductor couldn't have achieved, couldn't have got out of us. And the effect was *as if* he broadened, though in reality there was no modification in tempo. (Weingartner also achieved this, by the way, with different means. He was really grandiose in this way, especially with the Schubert C-major. Whereas he usually conducted conventionally, with absolute clarity and geometrical regularity, at the climax of the coda in the finale he began to stab the four C's like with a rapier—which was very effective and also made us play with great intensity.)

So Toscanini's Schubert C-major was a surprise for Vienna; and this was true with Brahms also for us who *lived* with Brahms, *in Brahms* all the time. Toscanini, in the first place, did not start with the First Symphony, or the Fourth, or the Second: at his second concert in Vienna he conducted the *Third*, which is for Viennese the least spectacularly effective. This was a subtle surprise: there comes the greatest star; and he plays first the Beethoven Seventh, which is of the biggest caliber—you could even say more popular than the Ninth; but after that he plays the *Haydn Variations* of Brahms, and then the Third Symphony: this was almost daring for a newcomer. But what an effect it made! What I call *musikalische Plastik*—truly three-dimensional in plastic reality—this was what Toscanini gave us with this symphony—as he did with the Schubert C-major, which also we had never experienced. This Brahms was new, unheard of; yet it fitted into the tradition: it was only taken out of the everyday routine—noble routine, since Brahms is always noble, and yet smoothed down at the corners, at the edges; whereas Toscanini made it sharp and fresh again. And with the Fourth Symphony—the first movement, and the passacaglia, Bach-like, severe, ascetic: people said, "How wonderful to hear once in your life an Italianized Fourth Symphony. It's not our Nordic Brahms; but it's a nice Brahms." And there was no debate; whereas with the Schubert C-major there were debates—spoken, printed.

So the word 'plastic' *is*, absolutely, a most significant word for Toscanini and his interpretive art; and the Schubert C-major was an example very much to the point. Toscanini was a man of few words, and hardly any explanation; but when you were, as a musician, well acquainted with him, he relaxed and unbent and confided; and so I learned that after he established the basic tempo with the very first phrase, what he was most aware of, in lifelong incessant search of, and like with a divining rod hoping to find, was the right *transitional* modification of the tempo in what followed. In the *Haffner* Symphony, after the first proclamation, *forte*, comes a pensive continuation, *piano*; and there has to be this little modification of tempo, which you cannot fix with a metronome, but which is clearly different. Toscanini broke his head and his brain to achieve a nuance of difference which would be just enough and not too little—and convincing. When he was aware that he was not sure—which he expressed quite openly—or when he *thought* he knew, and the playback showed him it was wrong—then it was disastrous. So he played the *Eroica,* and after the first theme and the second theme there was a transition which did not have just this

proportion that he wanted, this slight difference in tempo un-
noticeably going into the next phase of the *plasticus*. And when
the machine reproduced this to him: "Oh, what *stupido cretino
son io!*" First despair and hopelessness; then anger: he took the
record and smashed it: *"Tu bestia—canaille,* you are the witness
of my insufficiency!" But say in ten times he missed—a near miss
—once or twice; the point is that eight times he hit the bull's eye.
Yet he was aware that it's always like with a tightrope-walker:
you can't be sure; there is no net that catches you; and you
may fall to your destruction. It can be wonderful—or it can be
no good at all. He was always aware of this—for any one of us—
and for himself. Yet it didn't upset the work. If another conductor were afraid, he would be inhibited. Not Toscanini; and
this was another thing about him: his powerful spirit.

One peculiarity of his working method which occurs to me
is that when he was working with one group of the orchestra
by itself he often sang with this part the parts of the rest of the
orchestra that was not playing. And I remember also that
forefinger going up near to the tip of his nose in warning and
caution for a perfect balance in a chord or an even *pianissimo*
in a passage.

You ask about the Salzburg *Meistersinger*, which some
musicians said was too fast. In reality it lasted five whole hours!
His *Parsifal* in Bayreuth was the longest ever: no Richard Strauss
or Karl Muck or Furtwängler conducted such a *largissimo Parsifal*. He could be slow if it had to be slow. And his *Meistersinger*
lasted fully five hours; but it *seemed* fast because it was so
lively in expression. For example, at the beginning of Act 3, in
the scene of David and Sachs, he made us play with a much
lighter tone than we were accustomed to produce. He said:
"Come una comedia, non tragedia." And this new lightness of
the tone gave the *impression* of faster tempo, though in reality
it was not faster. The peculiarity of the performance was that he
illuminated the work from the inside, and it became plastic

and alive. This we found remarkable. Because it was taken for granted that his *Falstaff* should surpass all others—even the best of other Italians, like de Sabata, who conducted at La Scala a *Falstaff* which was wonderful. But that Toscanini should conduct such a *Meistersinger!* Of course he had Lotte Lehmann and his Kullman, who was excellent.

The first and third acts, you could say, were of course the highest standard, but well-known standard, no surprises—convincing, and yet what we were well acquainted with—except for the scene of David and Sachs at the beginning of Act 3, which I mentioned. This I dare to say. *But—the second act—*was the literally unheard-of! The poetry of what went on with Sachs and Eva! And Beckmesser! Our Wiedemann sang Beckmesser; and Toscanini—who did not often write such outspoken inscriptions—wrote on his photograph for Wiedemann: "To the best Beckmesser of all my life as conductor." And again those subtle modifications of tempo! In the dialogue of Sachs and Eva the subtlety, the tender polyphony in the orchestra! By then I had heard *Die Meistersinger* for twenty-five years, and had played it, as a member of the State Opera, for fifteen years; but this second act was an entirely new experience for me. In sound and dynamics, in clarity, in expression—this was the ultimate. And afterwards, when we ran up to Toscanini's dressing room, I never saw him as he was then. He said: *"Com' un sogno.* Like a dream. It's a heavenly dream." In such a dream he could speak in an emotional way that was unusual for him: usually if you said something was good, he made a deprecating gesture and said: *"Si, si, va bene, va bene.* It's all right." But this second act —that's when he cried fifteen years later, when somebody played the recording: he looked transported, you could almost say paralyzed: "This happened!" It was the fulfillment of a dream.

And as with the Schubert C-major in concert, he started twice as director of La Scala with *Meistersinger*—in Italy, mind you, with this work which is even today not entirely understood and entirely accepted there. It's too heavy, too *Teutonic*—not German—*Teutonic*. But Toscanini—just like with the Schubert C-major—had the great audacity to play it. Just as during World War I, when the Austrians and the Germans were at war with the Italians, he gave concerts for the benefit, say, of the invalids; and what did he conduct? The Funeral March from *Götterdäm-merung* by Richard Wagner! The concert was of course sold out; but all the people walked out of the hall, and he was alone with the orchestra. This showed the sort of conviction—spiritual conviction—that probably gave his interpretations such power, in addition to their charm. This combination was another thing he had: he could be powerful like a giant—like a Michelangelo—and full of tenderness and charm. This was unique: show me another example.

You ask also about the Salzburg *Magic Flute*. Before Tos-canini finished it he said: "My belief is that this piece is usually in Germany, and in Vienna too"—where he heard the standard performance—"such a bore that it is a pity and unbearable. And I am going to make it *entertaining*." (He said in German *"unterhaltend"*, and in Italian *"con amore e con piacere".*) This meant in the first place: never drag. And not only with Papa-geno: even Tamino is sometimes gay and passionate; and Toscanini put in really moving passion. But of course the tradi-tionalists said: "An Italian, who takes different tempos from Schalk and Bruno Walter. It's all fast, and too fast." They forgot about Strauss, whose tempi in *The Magic Flute* were like Toscanini's. And of course the tempi were not all fast and too fast. But people were used to the great Walter, who put in his heart's blood, and in this way made it so emotionally gripping that it was even sentimental. With Toscanini it was *not* senti-mental; and people were not mature enough for this. For this reason—because it departed entirely from the traditional and conventional—it was not a success—the only thing Toscanini conducted in Vienna and Salzburg that was not an acknowledged success. But of course it was delightful. It could not be otherwise: after all, his heart was in it, and his great understanding and everything else. And such an ensemble: the lovely Novotna, who sang Pamina so sweetly; and the great Scandinavian tenor, Roswänge, with a splendid voice for Tamino, and of course first-class interpretation; and a fine Sarastro, Kipnis. It was beyond any performance nowadays anywhere in the world. Yet for the general public the great Toscanini was in this performance least remarkable—which was a great irony.

But I must tell you what had great success. Once Toscanini, all of a sudden, said: "BurgAHHHser, next time I have in mind to conduct the *Liebesliederwalzer* by Brahms." By then I had been playing in Vienna with the Philharmonic and the Opera for twenty-five years, and chamber music all over; and I had never heard a public performance of the *Liebesliederwalzer* of Brahms. Well, Toscanini came to a rehearsal of the State Opera Chorus—sixteen people, each voice in four. It was in the choral rehearsal room, a little amphitheater; and Toscanini's eye was caught by the yellowed old posters on the wall, of operas in the 1860's: a new production of *Der Freischütz*, prepared, staged and conducted by Richard Wagner; the first production of *Lohengrin*, prepared and conducted by Wagner. Toscanini began to read the names of the singers through the pince-nez which he held before his eyes, and became so absorbed that he forgot what he was there for. But then he listened while the Viennese sang for him Brahms waltzes. *Tja* . . . The choral director had prepared the piece well; the chorus knew it perfectly: it was *theirs*—after all it was *Hausmusik*, everyday music, loved. Then Toscanini went to the piano and said: "I don't ask for any new ideas—only a few things, in tempo and *Agogik*" —he didn't say that word—"flexibility." Of course he wanted more than a few things—some tempi much faster, and much faster articulation to produce clearer diction: ta-ta-ta-ta-ta, like *staccato* between the teeth and the tongue. And then he conducted this piece in the Vienna *Musikvereinsaal*, where never a Hans Richter or Furtwängler or Bruno Walter ever conducted such a simple music, however subtle (after all, it's Brahms). There is always a complete quiet at these concerts: people sit there with a sort of religious concentration and devotion. But after one of the waltzes Toscanini made what we call *eine Atempause*, a very short intermission to take breath; and you heard in the entire hall an exhalation, "Ha-a-a-ah." The people had been sitting pent up, holding their breath in fascination. This was the greatest applause I ever experienced. Mozart says in a letter to his father: "I appreciate most the silent applause, when I enter for my *Magic Flute* performance, and people receive me concentrated and quiet." What we experienced this time with Toscanini was almost a demonstration.

By the way, since it just occurs to me, I tell you this: In Christmas '56, Toscanini's last Christmas, I went with Jonel Perlea—one of our greatest conductors, unrecognized and now very sick, but he still conducts—I went with Jonel Perlea, who had been at La Scala and the Metropolitan, to see Toscanini in Riverdale-on-Hudson. He was practically blind; but he reminisced about Salzburg and *Falstaff* and talked about the shortcomings of Walter and Furtwängler and this and that—how it's never *all* good and therefore it's really *never* good: it's good enough, but never perfect, so it's *not* good. But there was one who was good: Nikisch. And Ernst von Schuch in Dresden: "I heard things—I was transported. He was never a star: he was a star in Dresden, but never international." So Toscanini admitted always: there *were* conductors; but they are not here now; and those who are here now—sorry, it's good enough, but not really good. He reminisced so happily, this time, that when his daughter, after an hour, hinted that maybe *"padre è un po stanco"*—that it was too much for him—he said: "Oh no, stay here. I want to go on talking." And what did he talk about at the end? He said: "Preparation for my ninetieth birthday on

March 25—exactly three months from now. They tell me they prepare something nice; and I am going to enjoy it." He was utterly sure, optimistic. Whereas when he was seventy and we celebrated in Milano, he said: "I am now an old man. And who knows: every new day is a gift of heaven, which I cannot even expect and hope for. I am not sick, but after seventy where are you? Should I even go out and conduct?" But when he was three months less than ninety he said: "I am going to enjoy it." It was one of the gayest of Christmases; and three weeks later it was all over. So I am glad to have been, with my friend Jonel Perlea, among the last to see him. It was so moving, and not only in personal sentiments, which are not important for others, but in the thought that the loss was irreplaceable: where in the world today do you find an Arturo Toscanini?

I can say that we in Vienna, who had a succession of the best, finally had the experience of being lifted to a new height by Toscanini. A few years after the last war I visited my homeland, and listened again to opera in Vienna and Salzburg. One evening I wanted to hear one of the greatest artists of former years, Maria Jeritza, in *Salome*; and as I could not obtain a ticket I took a place with the orchestra in the pit, where I sat enthralled by the flood of sound and the still remarkable dramatic singing of Jeritza. It came to the point where Herod says about Jochanaan: "*Er ist ein heiliger Mann. Er ist ein Mann der Gott geschaut hat.* He is a holy man. He is a man who has seen God." And at this moment an old colleague in the orchestra, with whom I had played for many years, including the years with Toscanini, turned around to me and said: "*Auch wir haben Gott geschaut.* We too have seen God."

Alfred Wallenstein

HAGGIN:

At the opening concert of the New York Philharmonic's 1929-30 season Toscanini presented the orchestra's new first cellist, Alfred Wallenstein, in a performance of Strauss's Don Quixote. He stayed with the orchestra until Toscanini left it; then he left to become a conductor himself—first of an orchestra at WOR, later of the Los Angeles Philharmonic, and more recently of other orchestras here and abroad. It seemed to me that having sat directly in front of Toscanini during seven seasons, he must have a great deal to tell; and it turned out that he did.

WALLENSTEIN:

The first time I heard about Toscanini was in 1921, at a rehearsal of the Leipzig Gewandhaus Orchestra, where Nikisch said: "Gentlemen, I have just come from Milan, where I heard a performance of *Siegfried* conducted by a man named Toscanini that was the greatest performance of opera I have ever heard. Remember this name; because you will hear much of it." And since I was young and impressionable the name stuck with me. In 1927 my wife and I were in Europe, and got to Milan,

175

and picked up a paper, and saw that Toscanini was conducting *Ariane et Barbe-Bleu.* It was the last performance of the season; and we were fortunate in getting the last two seats there were, in the last row downstairs. I remember I went to the performance with my mind made up that I just wanted to hear the opera, because I didn't know it; but I found myself fascinated by one person, Toscanini, and didn't know what took place on the stage because my eyes were riveted on him. I was first cellist in the Chicago Symphony at that time—from 1923 to 1929—and came back raving about Toscanini; and in the summer of 1928 I said to Papi, who was conducting opera at Ravinia Park, and who had talked about Toscanini: "There's one thing I want to do. I want to play with this man." Papi said: "You wouldn't like it. He's very difficult to play with." I said: "I don't care how difficult he is. I've played with everybody else, and I want to play with him; because this is the first time I've heard honesty and truth in music, and I want to have this experience." So Papi said he would arrange an audition; and in January 1929 I came to New York, to the Astor Hotel, to play for Toscanini. I played about five minutes; he asked did I play this, did I play that—and that was it. He couldn't have been more charming; and I was absolutely spellbound: he had this marvelous face, and one of the most beautiful smiles any man has ever had. I mention these things because the personal experiences are the most important in one's life, and Toscanini became not only a conductor for me, but also almost a father in all ways—an amazing man.

You asked about my first experience playing with him, which was the first rehearsal with the New York Philharmonic— of *Don Quixote.* I had arrived in New York with a bad sore throat, which I had during that whole first week; so I had a high temperature and was unable to speak. But after the first rehearsal I came home and talked without stopping until 3 in the morning, telling my wife about Maestro. Everything I had experienced until now was undone by this one experience with him. And contrary to Papi's prediction, I found him the easiest man I'd ever played with—the easiest in all ways—assuming you knew your instrument and could play and had taste. During the entire time I was with him in the Philharmonic—until he resigned; and the same day *I* resigned—there was never one word that he said to the cello section, or to the horn section (Bruno Jaenicke was the leader of the horns). Whenever there was anything difficult I'd get the section together to go over it with them alone. That would be hard to do today; but it was possible then; and we wanted to do our best. So he might say play loud or play soft; but he never had to correct notes or balances. And naturally, when you find that the harder you work the more appreciation you get, it instills confidence and love of the man.

As for what it was like to play with him as a soloist—I think the first season, in addition to *Don Quixote*, I played the Boccherini Concerto and the Brahms Double Concerto—I went beforehand and played the work with him at the piano; and it was never a technical thing he wanted, but mostly a matter of dynamics; and he was very literal: if it said *pianissimo* he wanted it played really *pianissimo*. It was all done here beforehand; and at the rehearsal with the orchestra he didn't say anything to me. Playing with him was unique in one respect: every time I looked up at him, if I was playing an up-beat, it looked to me as if he was on the down-beat—which was a little disconcerting. I remember that once many years later, in Riverdale, Walter Toscanini played an off-the-air recording of the Brahms Double of 1935; and Maestro said: "It's a little fast, don't you think?" And I said: "I'd say it's damned fast!"

It was the same with outside soloists: everything was discussed and settled beforehand; and at the rehearsal with the orchestra nothing needed to be said. I do remember one rehearsal, though, where Ernest Schelling was playing a piece of his for piano and orchestra. Maestro had got the score only two days before—I know that—and was of course rehearsing from memory; and Schelling, who was playing wrong notes, was embarrassed when Maestro stopped and said: "You are not playing what's in the score." And I can give you another example of his perceptiveness in listening. It was in *Don Quixote*—in the windmill variation. There are conductors who happen to know there is a mistake in a part at a certain point, and who stop at that point and tell the player: "You played this note, which should have been that one." But Maestro actually heard: with the *fortissimo* going in that windmill variation he stopped the orchestra and said to the second bassoon: "Weren't you playing B-flat?" "Yes, Maestro." "It's B-natural." I was sitting only three or four feet from this player, and *I* didn't hear it; and I don't think anyone else did. Only Toscanini did; and when a man shows this kind of perceptiveness you are drawn closer to him.

And I do remember one rehearsal, when Rethberg was singing in some German work, and at one point Maestro corrected her pronunciation. She is a German, and her diction is wonderful; and she said to me: "Can you imagine him telling me? And he's right!" This was true with every language, including English, though his own spoken English was far from impeccable. I really think that if he had spoken English as well as he did French or his own language he wouldn't have had occasion to blow up as much as he did. I think it was the impediment in communication that caused many explosions here that wouldn't have happened in Europe. They happened there too, but not to the extent that they happened here—which gave rise to the idea of him as a tyrant and so on. He was anything but that. Once after the war he was conducting a Wagner program in Milan; and at the rehearsal he was so sweet to the orchestra that afterwards I asked him about it. "Everybody was playing out of tune, and you didn't say anything. If it were New York you would be on top of them—as a matter of fact you would walk out." And he said: "Because in New York I know they can do it, but here I know they cannot."

The main point of Toscanini's efforts was very simple: to be honest in music, to give the truth in music as he saw it. He came to the rehearsal knowing the score, knowing exactly what he wanted out of it, because it was in his mind and in his heart. That was it, and what the orchestra had to do; and he got the orchestra to do it by explaining and repeating over and over again. First all the winds in right relationship: the leading voice a little louder, the third horn a little softer, the second bassoon a little more, and so on. Then the strings. Then together —and so you had the whole with perfect balance. But it was all in his mind and heart before he started rehearsing; it was something that had to be achieved; and it was when they didn't get it that the tantrums came. The same with what he wanted in a musical phrase. He was patient going over it twice; but if they didn't get it the third time, then he would lose his temper. And he wasn't satisfied even when it came out right: it could have been better. Yes, *"Non c'è male."*

But he came with knowledge of more than the score he was conducting. I've never known anyone with the range and completeness of knowledge Maestro had. Not only of the operatic literature—many times he'd sit down at the piano at the beginning of the evening and play through operas that aren't heard anymore, singing all the words—but the chamber literature: he knew all the quartets, and sat down and played them all. And the violin literature: once I asked Zimbalist to play some old concerto, to see if one could trick Maestro; and Zimbalist played it, and played some of it wrong; and Maestro said: "That's wrong," and played the whole thing. Then he said: "Let's see what *you* know," and began playing concertos that none of us knew—the *Concerto Militaire* of Kreutzer—that kind of thing. He had the same knowledge of the song literature, and, strangely enough, the poetry of Shakespeare, Shelley, Keats and Byron: not alone that he knew them, but that he could turn to the page of the book for the point he was making.

That reminds me of the time in Bayreuth, during a rehearsal of *Tannhäuser*, when Elisabeth entered for *"Dich, teure Halle"* and the stage was darkened. Maestro stopped and asked: "Why is the stage so dark?" And Siegfried Wagner said: "That's what Father wanted." And Maestro said: "*Father* wanted?! You have the writings of Father?" They had, of course, at Villa Wahnfried; and one person Toscanini didn't want to see was Cosima; so they went straight into the library, and he took down the particular volume he wanted, turned to the exact page, and said: "Here! Read!" And Wagner said that for Elisabeth's entrance there should be the brightest lights possible. There were thousands of incidents like that: it might involve only a rest or a grace-note; but he wouldn't be satisfied until he had seen the source material. Whatever he did he did with this tremendous knowledge of the background of the music. But he also had an instinct, and taste, and an ear. When he reduced the orchestra for a Mozart concerto it wasn't because of what Mozart did or what the musicologists said: it was because his taste, his ear for balance told him one flute couldn't take care of eighteen first violins, sixteen seconds, and so on. Or if there was too much wind sound he would add strings. And I remember that in the first movement of Beethoven's Eighth, at the beginning of the recapitulation, where the first theme returns, there are just the cellos and basses playing against the full orchestra, and it's impossible to hear them in the hall; so he added tympani (but when he recorded the Eighth he took them out!). Those were the changes he made: nothing that would change the character of the music; only reinforcement of something that should come out but didn't come out.

I remember the time when I had given Maestro some scores by young American composers to look at, and I took one of the composers up to see him. Maestro went to the piano and said: "In this passage you have written so; but tell me"—and he showed the composer a manuscript page on which he had re-scored it—"isn't *this* what you really meant?" The composer was completely taken aback: it *was* what he really meant; he told me later it was absolutely uncanny. This was a kind of criticism of composers' work that Maestro did on many occasions, and that was enormously interesting.

The truth he was after started of course with the right tempo. I would go home after rehearsals and check tempos for which there were metronome indications, and find they were right on the head—and not just the first time but every time the passage came back. This didn't mean the performance was metronomic: it had freedom and flexibility and grace and elegance. Also it had the utmost of lyricism—the word he used constantly was "*canta!*"—and it was full of sentiment, but never sentimental. In his feeling for music it was the lyrical line that was important: he thought horizontally, not vertically—that was why Bach wasn't very close to him.

I remember when we got to Berlin on the tour, Maestro as always scheduled a rehearsal to hear the sound in the hall. Just before the rehearsal I was in the Bote & Bock music store, and ran into a well-known conductor who said: "How can I hear a rehearsal?" I knew that Bruno Walter and Furtwängler and Kleiber were coming; so I said: "Simple. Why don't you just come down?" So he did; and later on I happened to run into him again. He said: "Tell me, what does he do to make that piece [it was *Death and Transfiguration*] sound that way?" I said: "You know, I really can't tell you. All I know is that he just has the notes played the way they're written and gets the right balances." He said: "There must be more to it than that." I said: "No, there isn't more to it—just that." And I was telling the truth up to a point: it was true that everything in the part was played just the way it was, so you didn't even have to look at Maestro to find out where you were and what to do (*I* looked

at him simply because it was fascinating to watch what he did).
But it was true that you were bound to be affected by his complete dedication—the fact that he was a man who loved music
above all in life, for whom life *was* a *life of music*. And you were
always on the *qui vive*; you knew you had to be *there* at every
moment, concert or rehearsal. Although the eyes didn't see you,
the ears heard. So anybody who played with Maestro was made
to play better than he *would* play—not physically or technically
better, but emotionally better.

One thing people don't realize is how hard he worked even
here. And when he was head of La Scala he would start at 8 in
the morning with lighting, or rehearsing singers individually;
then he would rehearse with the orchestra from 10 to 1; then
rehearsals again from 2 to 6; then if he had a performance he
conducted that; and after the performance he would go home
and study until 8 in the morning. He did this every day.

Speaking of his Scala years reminds me of the time we were
driving somewhere, and he was tired and had his eyes closed,
and my wife asked Mme. Toscanini: "Who was the greatest
artist among the singers Maestro ever worked with?" And suddenly he came to: "Chaliapin!" Just like that! And this in spite
of what he had told me about Chaliapin years before. He had
Chaliapin do *Mefistofele* at La Scala, and worked and worked
with him; and it was a very good performance. But two months
later he was in Paris and went to hear Chaliapin in *Mefistofele*
at the Opera; and he had forgotten everything and was doing
what he had done at the first rehearsal. You had to stay on top
of these people all the time, he said; then it was all right. But
he still considered Chaliapin by far the greatest.

Yes, I do recall the performances in the Philharmonic years
being more relaxed and spacious and greater: they really were. I
remember especially the last performances—the Mozart G-minor,
which I thought was as near perfect a performance—and yes,
the Schubert C-major at that concert—as I've heard. I think

almost any professional would agree that one can count on one's hand the performances that have completely satisfied one from beginning to end. I can remember only three, really; and those three were with Toscanini. (I'm talking only about the Philharmonic, not about NBC.) One, certainly, was a performance of *Ein Heldenleben*: there were individual flaws, but not collective ones; and it was a great performance because it had tremendous momentum, and none of the sentimentality which the piece itself has already and doesn't need to have dragged out more. Maestro didn't cheapen anything: he had fabulous taste. The others? Well, one was that last concert in April 1936. And one was a concert in Berlin with the *Eroica* and *La Mer*. I remember these as times when everything went right—when every player in the orchestra was just right, and the balance and the sound and everything—the occasions you hope and work for. Oh, I remember another one—Elgar's *Enigma Variations* in London. I've never heard it like that in my life: it was the last concert of the tour; and it was the *most impeccable* playing and performance I've ever heard. It was fabulously beautiful; and the audience just went wild. Now, thirty years later, you find the English saying it wasn't good. I've found a few players in the BBC and other English orchestras who were at that concert and still talk about how wonderful it was; but the majority of the people, who weren't even there, tell you from hearsay that it was too fast, it wasn't English, it wasn't this or that. Hell, it was what Elgar wrote; and the sad thing was that Elgar, who was still living and should have been there, wasn't there. But I remember one rather elderly lady who was there in the first row of Queen's Hall, and got up and came close, applauding and calling out "Bravo, Maestro! Bravo, Maestro!" I wondered who she was; and it turned out that she was Melba. She came backstage; but Maestro had already gone.

If Toscanini had been a composer, the music would still be there; but the unfortunate thing about a great performing musician is that when the man is gone, everything he achieved is gone. There are the recordings: there is the *Falstaff*, one of the great recordings of all time for him. But some of his greatest performances didn't get recorded;[1] and some of the performances that did get recorded give a wrong impression to someone who doesn't know all his work. I don't think he was well served by his recordings—on the basis of sound and other things. The sound of the Philharmonic on 78's was better than anything they got in 8H—yes, the sound of the Philadelphia on 78's too.[2] I wish he had been more attentive to quality of sound; but he wasn't interested. For him recording was the most difficult thing in the world; because it made him tense. Any audience didn't disturb him; but the microphone did; and so the performance he recorded was sometimes a little fast, sometimes a little slow.[3] But whether he was fast or slow, the intensity was always there, and he made a right thing out of the performance. And the people who heard all his work are not misled by these fast or slow performances on the records, and never say, "He did this too fast" or "He did everything too fast," as the people say who know only the recordings. In this way the recordings do him a great disservice; and another disservice is for one of these people who didn't hear the performances and know only the recordings to write a book about him—about what was good and what was bad—on the basis only of the recordings: I find no excuse for such a book.[4]

But as you say, even the recordings are being withdrawn,[5] and most of the Philadelphia Orchestra recordings are still not issued. And I think this is a great disservice not only to Maestro but to music.

Also, I think the engineers can be blamed for the loss of some recordings we might have had. I was present at a recording session at which Maestro began to rehearse at 9, and had a fabulous performance at 10:30; and they said: "Maestro, are you ready to record?"; and he said "No" and went on rehearsing.

By the time they did record, he was tired and the tempo was too slow. They should have taped what he did all along, and pieced it together—which everyone does today—and we would have had that fabulous performance.[6]

When I look back I think that those of us who were privileged to know and work with Maestro and benefit by his all-round knowledge were the luckiest people in the world; and the years in the Philharmonic with him were the happiest years of my life. And as I said at the beginning, he remained as a father and a sort of father confessor. In my early years of conducting on WOR, when I had some technical problem I could call on him and his knowledge of all those problems: "Oh yes, you mean the place so many bars after this theme. Watch out, because you feel this and you must do that." And after the broadcasts he'd call up to tell me this was fine but that wasn't good. Later, when I was conducting in Los Angeles, he came out in 1945 to do a pension fund concert, and stayed with us; and when he got back he wrote us a letter about the visit that was wonderfully warm and sweet. It also contained one extraordinary statement. Mussolini had been dealt with as Maestro felt he deserved; and Hitler had just done away with himself; and as you can see he writes: "No one will find his body," which I think was extraordinarily prophetic. I was in New York when certain well-known people and friends asked him to come back to Salzburg in 1938; and I saw the cable he sent them telling them how mistaken they were and how little realization they had of what was happening, and that he would never go back to any place with a dictator. I also was present when he did the same thing about Stalin—oh yes, they wanted him to go to Russia—there was a big to-do about that. I think he loved freedom more than anybody in the world.

Giovanni Martinelli

HAGGIN:

Giovanni Martinelli could tell me whether Toscanini's dealing with the famous singers at the Metropolitan was different from his dealing with Kipnis, Tourel and Peerce. He was a little reluctant to talk to still another writer; but his good nature won out; and he gave me a little time which was enough for him to tell me what I was interested in knowing.

MARTINELLI:

You ask did Maestro make it difficult for the singer or easy. Difficult—because he wanted singing to be as precise as if you had an instrument. And at rehearsal he used to say: "Do what is written—what the composer wants. If the composer wants *piano*, do *piano*; if he says *pianissimo*, do *pianissimo*." But sometimes it was difficult for the voice to do this. For a singer it is much easier *forte*, loud, than *piano*, fading out, especially with phrasing—beautiful long phrasing.

You mentioned Beethoven's Ninth Symphony. This was very difficult for me because the music was not in my character, and I had to sing in German. What happened? I adjusted the voice and did it. Especially I had to adjust in the passages in

very quick tempo. Of course I studied it before; but I didn't realize what Maestro wanted: such precision—to stick to the principle to do what the composer wants, so you do I won't say a hundred percent but a good ninety percent what he wants.

We did wonderful work—especially when we prepared a new production of *Il Trovatore* in 1915. As you know, everybody says *Il Trovatore* is just a blah-blah-blah-blah; but it's not so; and Maestro wanted to show *Il Trovatore* was a beautiful opera and deserved great consideration. I knew my part, because I sang *Il Trovatore* before; but it was entirely different when the rehearsals started with Maestro. He changed everything—especially the precision of the tempi and the long phrasing. He wanted when was written *Adagio*, do *adagio*; and as well, when was written *Presto*, do *presto*: don't accommodate the tempo to the voice. He obtained beautiful results with the orchestra, and as well with the voices. He told us: "Do what the composer wants. He knew the singers can do it; otherwise he wouldn't have written like that." So we did it: we didn't add anything, and we didn't take away anything. And we knew—I say we, plural, because my colleagues, the soprano, the baritone, everyone—knew that the result would be great, something different than usual, but not extravagant. Toscanini said: "Let's demonstrate that *Trovatore* is a wonderful, wonderful score, a wonderful opera." And we did it: we gave it a beautiful edition, a wonderful edition. So it was a great loss for me when Maestro left the Metropolitan in 1915, my second season, because I was still young. But I had the opportunity to do *Tosca, Madama Butterfly, Aida, Il Trovatore* and *Madame Sans-Gêne* with him.

Before the Metropolitan I worked with him in Rome, in *Girl of the Golden West*, in 1911. That was my first experience with him. *The Girl of the Golden West* was to be done in Rome for the first time after they gave it here at the Metropolitan with Caruso. The tenor in Rome was Amadeo Bassi, who would sing only the first performances, because he had to go to London; so they prepared another tenor—myself. I was very, very green. I was just out of school—only six months from my debut; so you can imagine how green I was. Certainly I was frightened; especially because the score of *The Girl of the Golden West* departed very much from the first melodious operas of Puccini— *Manon Lescaut,* for instance. And of course from Verdi, which I had been singing: I started with *Ernani,* my debut, and then *Ballo in Maschera.* I learned these two operas in ten, twelve days, because the phrases go so easily in your mind. But *The Girl*—except for two short arias—is short phrases with other singers—difficult to go in. And that was the moment when I found myself in great difficulties with Maestro; because he tried himself to give me the cue, but he was not in the right pitch, so I gave the wrong pitch! So Puccini took off his coat and went to the piano to teach me the opera; and then with a couple of orchestral rehearsals I was already well prepared when Bassi went to London. Yes, Maestro was patient; because he knew— first of all that I understood the difficulty, together with the great honor and joy to be associated with such authority. At first it frightens you; then you feel different. It's not exactly fright: your conscience bothers you, are you doing well, are you doing wrong?

In Rome we did also Verdi's *Requiem*—three performances. That was another work! With the *Requiem* I began for the first time to learn and to understand Maestro Toscanini's religion for Verdi—for this Verdi repertoire which I loved myself afterwards. As I said before, I already knew *Ernani* and *Ballo in Maschera*; and now I learned the beautiful phrasing in the *Requiem*—especially the tenor solo, "*Ingemisco*", and then the famous solo in the *Offertorium,* "*Hostias*"—that was really beautiful. We considered that the *Requiem* is a sort of opera, because Verdi put in melodies that could be in *Don Carlo, Ballo in Maschera, Forza del Destino.* There was the same outpouring of beautiful feeling as, for instance, in "*O terra, addio"* in *Aida,* where we poured the melodious voice together with the feeling of the words. But the *Requiem* is a sort of oratorio that has to be treated religiously, not as you sing a phrase in an aria. The phrase has to be correct, without any—what we call, permit me to say—Neapolitan colors. I don't mean like Mozart or Beethoven, but with correct voice, without exaggeration in *portamenti,* without sobbing, without that *pulsus* which Italian singers have when they sing in opera. Correct and precise. This was what Maestro wanted. He wanted to obtain the best, and always what the composer wrote: "Don't do what *you* feel to do."

But Maestro felt phrasing; he felt Verdi's phrasing. When we sang "*O terra, addio*" with Maestro there was a little suspension, a little elasticity—not a stop, but elasticity in the phrasing. The composer could not write this; it had to be in the feeling of the interpretation; and we did it. Or in the third act, when the tenor sang "*Abandonnare la patria*": he couldn't sing straight, "*A—ban—donn—are—la—patria*"; he had to sing with *espansione,* "*Aban—donnare—la patria*". Maestro said: "Is a little slower than we start; then we catch up."

Beethoven's *Missa Solemnis* I sang here later with Maestro. That too has wonderful, beautiful phrasing; and it was easier for me than the Ninth Symphony because it was in Latin. But very difficult for me was to subdue the voice, to tame the voice, in certain passages: no *pulsus.* Oh yes, I was able to do it. For the Maestro—especially for the Maestro, the big Maestro.

It was a great pleasure to sing with Maestro—very great. Because he knew what we can do; he was patient; he tried again, worked again, tried again. They say he was ferocious—cruel with singers. It was not so—no, no. He might shout; he might break a baton; but it was not anger; it was just for the result. And after the work he was a good friend. As I told in the NBC broadcast—the few items—the teasing about my haircut. So he was human like everybody else.

Giovanni Martinelli

[Martinelli is referring to his story of an incident during the break of a rehearsal at the Metropolitan. Holding the hat which he usually put on at this point, Toscanini went to each singer, who put some coins into it. Then, proffering the hat with the money to Martinelli, he said: "Here. Go have your hair cut." In this broadcast Martinelli summed up his experience with Toscanini in the statement that he had learned "the joy to sing, the joy to work, the joy to know . . . the beautiful interpretation of what the composer wanted that Maestro was passing on to us."]

Felix Galimir

HAGGIN:

Though he was for many years an orchestral musician, Felix Galimir in recent years has limited himself to chamber music, part of the time as leader of the Galimir Quartet, part of the time with other groups. And the viewpoint of a chamber-music-player appears on occasion in what he said about Toscanini. Unexpectedly he provided an account of Toscanini's activity with the orchestra that is known as the Israel Philharmonic.

GALIMIR:

I heard Toscanini when he came to Vienna with the Scala in 1929—*Lucia* with Toti dal Monte—a fantastic performance. That of course created great excitement; and they tried to get him in Vienna for a long time; but I think he demanded some fantastic amount of rehearsals, which of course the Vienna Philharmonic thought it didn't need, or didn't want to give him. Until finally they broke down and granted his demands for so many rehearsals; and he came in 1933. There were terrible blow-ups at the rehearsals, because they didn't play well: I mean the Vienna Philharmonic was a wonderful orchestra, but in the rehearsals they took it easy and said: "Tonight we'll play"; and they did play—if there was a good conductor. But Toscanini wanted them to play in the rehearsals; and it took a long time for them to get used to it; and until then there were quite a few blow-ups—I don't remember if he walked out or not. We heard in the conservatory that it was something special; so we tried to sneak into the rehearsals; and I got into one. And *before* the rehearsal—this was a historic event—all the violinists of the Vienna Philharmonic were actually practicing their part—which had never happened since Gustav Mahler left! And at the rehearsal really it was something fantastic: basically the sound was wonderful, and it was *so* precise! We had never heard the orchestra like that, and we probably *will* never. They rehearsed the *Meistersinger* Prelude: I know because I remember the passage of the first violins [Galimir sang it]—high A, which just didn't come and wasn't in tune! And then there were the Brahms *Haydn Variations*; and THAT — WAS — PHENOM-ENAL! It always was probably Toscanini's best piece: there was that variation with the winds—the fifth variation—so fantastic: that we'll never hear again. Years later, in Palestine, when we had a dinner for him, and I told him that I had heard this rehearsal, he said very proudly: "You know, Rosé came to me and said, 'Maestro, Brahms would have been pleased by this.'" He really liked that: he must have felt that Rosé—well, Rosé was quite a personality. That rehearsal of the *Meistersinger* and the Brahms was the only one I heard; and I didn't hear the performances: they were too expensive!

My next experience with Toscanini was in Palestine. The orchestra was formed by Hubermann; and Toscanini was the first conductor; but before he came we rehearsed about two weeks with Steinberg. The orchestra was of course picked very carefully, and consisted of very good players—and some *excellent* players; but there were a few weak spots, because the players had to be Jewish, and in Europe there just were no Jewish brass. The horns were excellent; the trombones were good; but trumpets didn't exist; and double-bass-players—very few. Steinberg was very meticulous; and there was a rehearsal every day. Of course the closer it came to Toscanini's arrival, the more nervous we got; and everybody told stories of how terrible he was, how he threw shoes at musicians, and murdered them, and so on— you know those exaggerations. Then Hubermann came, a few days before Toscanini: he was just as nervous, and wanted to see if it was worth having Toscanini come or he should wire him not to come. He found that there were a few weak spots, but thought it would be possible.

Then Toscanini came. And of course everybody was prepared for big speeches, or for *something*; but he came on the stage and he didn't say anything—not even good morning— nothing! He said, "Brahms"—the Second Symphony of Brahms. We started to play the first movement, and he didn't interrupt once; and at the end of the first movement he said: *"Bene. Andiamo avanti.* Good. Let's go on." And everybody was terribly disappointed: was this the great conductor?—because they expected blow-ups. And in the second movement also, at the end —he corrected a little something, but again, *"Bene."* Then in the third movement, in the beginning, there was one of our weaker moments with the woodwinds; and he didn't like it and got a little angry and said: "Why don't you sing?!" And now everybody looked around and said: "Ah! that's it." After this run-through he started really to rehearse; and at each rehearsal he went a little more into detail; and it was very beautiful—it was a real Toscanini rehearsal. And the concert was a fantastic success: people went completely overboard. They climbed on the roof to get in—it was a small hall—it was incredible.

It happened that at one rehearsal of the Brahms, in the third movement, the first trumpet overlooked the marking "third movement *tacet*", and began to play the fourth movement in the third movement. Toscanini gave him a look; but it was only a rehearsal, and it was a little mistake that could happen. But

we repeated the same program many times: we played it two or
three times in Tel-Aviv, two or three times in Jerusalem, and
then in Haifa. And after so many times it starts to become a
little routine for the player; he doesn't pay attention; and so in
Haifa the trumpeter made the same mistake at the concert.
You remember the fourth movement starts very *piano*, with the
trumpet playing just one note: ta. And the trumpeter played
that one note at the beginning of the *third* movement. Toscanini
got furious: while he conducted he cursed, he threw dagger-
glances at the poor trumpeter, who was dying with fear; he continued to curse all the time while we played the rest of the
symphony; he got faster and faster; he didn't hold the *fermata*;
he ended in a fury, *prestissimo* and *fortissimo*. The audience,
which of course didn't know what was going on, never heard
such fire and such sounds; and there was tremendous applause.
But Toscanini rushed out, kicking over the music stands—*you*
know that exit—and didn't come back on the stage again. The
intermission lasted an hour and a half: he didn't want to continue. Hubermann came; everybody came; nothing helped. Finally he did continue; and then the opposite happened. He was
completely disheartened and didn't want to conduct; and he
conducted almost without any motions. The orchestra went
from *pianissimo* to fantastically loud: he didn't move. And the
public reaction was: what fantastic technique of this conductor
who practically doesn't make any movement, and the orchestra
plays like that! Apparently it made a very good impression on
Toscanini also; and he conducted a second pair of concerts and
was very happy there, actually. The trumpeter? He was through.
A cellist who was also a trumpet-player had to play second
trumpet, and the second trumpet, who was not too good, had
to play first trumpet, for the rest of the concerts. So that was
the first real taste of Toscanini.

We played in Egypt; and Toscanini came back to us the
second year. After the second year I left, and came to America

at the end of 1938. I met Toscanini here; but I don't know whether *he* mentioned me to Chotzinoff, or Steinberg, or who did. I played at NBC for Chotzinoff—and yes, of course, for Spitalny; I substituted once or twice; and in the fall of 1939 I was engaged as a regular member of the orchestra. And except for two years in the army, I stayed until the end.

Let me say this. I've played with many conductors—great conductors—Furtwängler, Walter, Klemperer—I really have played with most of the so-called great conductors of that time. (No, not with Strauss. I heard him of course. His *Don Giovanni* was—in Mozart he was really fantastic. And you know what also? *Tristan.*) With every conductor there were great moments; and maybe one conductor did this particular piece better than the others. But I would say the greatest experience, *playing* with a conductor, was with Toscanini. There was something that electrified you to a point where you had the feeling you played better than you can play. I know that at *any concert* with him —maybe even a concert that did not sound so well outside—the players themselves on the stage, most of them, gave everything; and you came out saying "Ah!" You were proud of the way you played when you played with him; because you could not do anything but give your best: you always were enticed to give your best. And it was not because of fear that you lose your job, or because he was a mean guy—that had nothing to do with it; there were meaner conductors. You had only to look at his face: he was so inspired, that he had to inspire *you*. There was the knowledge he had—the knowledge of the instrument: he knew exactly what can be played and how it can be played—which some really great conductors sometimes either didn't know or didn't care about, but which made it possible for any player to play any note—and every note—in any composition. In Strauss's compositions, for example—you remember the famous rehearsal of *Till Eulenspiegel*—he wanted every note to be played cleanly; and I'm sure Strauss, if he had heard the performance, would have said, "It's too clean." But to play that clean was a pleasure that you can't imagine. An orchestra player felt wonderful. This made it a great experience for any orchestra player to play with him: there was never any possibility—or necessity—to play badly with him.

Then there was something else about this man. He conducted the NBC Symphony how many years?—seventeen years; in those seventeen years he conducted the same composition many times; and every time he tried to do better what he thought was not so good the last time. There was never the slightest possibility of a routine performance—that he would say: "Oh, we've played this many times." I remember an incident in Palestine: when we played for the radio in Jerusalem, they were not experienced in the set-up for the broadcast, and asked him if he would try it for a half-hour; and he was very co-operative, and rehearsed for a half-hour. He played one passage of the Schubert *Unfinished* Symphony—the big climax in the first movement—about twenty times; and not once did he get less excited about the *fortissimo*. He never could think: "Well, let's take it easy now." And this he demanded also from the players—which was very good.

Then another thing. I had a teacher who said: "You should play so that a blind man can see the score." This means that you hear all the notes. And with Toscanini there was never a possibility that you had to fight the trumpets to come through— which very often happens. This, again, made it so pleasant to play: you did not have to force. That didn't mean the climaxes were not perfect: they were always perfect. This was because of another wonderful thing—the proportion. The sense for proportion of this man was really incredible. In Europe, when we played, let's say, the Beethoven Seventh, we used to play the second movement very slowly. Toscanini came and decided it said *Allegretto* and must be *allegretto*; so suddenly you played it very fast; and this was a great shock, after you had played it for

ten years very slowly. But after you were through with the movement the very first time, you had to say to yourself: "Yes, I think
it's right." The sense of proportion was always correct with him;
and this made the Rossini overtures so wonderful. I've never
heard in a Rossini overture the *crescendi* drawn to that point—
when it got loud, louder, always louder, and you thought it
couldn't anymore, but it *still* got louder, until the moment when
it was supposed to be the loudest! And the same in Wagner. In
everything—it was immaterial what—the way the proportions
were made was fantastic: this was one of his best qualities. Yes,
in the shaping. This was an incredible thing. It seems obvious:
you have *piano*, and then *fortissimo*, and you have to go from
one to the other; but *how* you go—and how that face got redder
and redder, and still redder; and you thought now he's going to
burst—but no, it went on! And that made you play.

Aside from the fact that it really was a beautiful thing to
watch him. He had a very expressive beat. I've seen conductors
with more *facility* in the beat; but the *expressiveness* of his beat
was incredible: you really could see everything he wanted in
that beat: the *staccato*, the *legato*, the *espressivo*—everything
was in it. You really had only to look at him, not at the music.
That's why he got so angry when he showed and they didn't do
what he showed. Actually he got angry only when—*either* he
felt one was not prepared, or was negligent; *or* when he felt one
was inattentive, so that he showed something and one didn't
respond. I understand that; and I think he was right: he always
was justified when he blew up—sometimes a little overblown,
but always justified. There was never any doubt what he wanted;
but you had to know your part very well. He always said: "*I am
prepared; why aren't *you* prepared?*" And he was right. In the
rehearsal one should work to make the musical phrases and
details, not to learn the notes.

Another part of his technique was that he always looked at
the players; and with all his nearsightedness I think he saw every-

thing that went on. And what a fantastic look: he could stone you to death with that look! It was a very fiery look! And it was very necessary to get that look sometimes: it inspired you. Of course sometimes it was very disagreeable when he looked at you angry: you got scared. But for inspiration that look was something fantastic. Of course every good conductor always looks at his players; but there was something in Toscanini's look that made it special: it lifted you up and made you do something extra. And contact, yes—incredible contact.

So let's see. A conductor, first of all, must be a big personality: he was. He must have a very good ear: he had a wonderful ear. He must have a tremendous authority: he had. And he must be very musical: he was. A conductor has to be a combination of all the qualities a musician should have; and he had *all* these qualities to a degree that made him great. Another conductor might be greater in one particular quality; but I don't know anybody who combined *all* these great qualities to such a high level as he did.

And the honesty! He was so honest—musically honest, and with himself honest. When he conducted badly, he said it—not at that rehearsal—he couldn't admit that he made a mistake that day—but at the next rehearsal: "I was not good"; and he said it *very often!* When we played the piece the next time he said: "*Anch' io sono stupido.* I didn't do it well. We do it better this time." Which is very nice: it gives you a feeling that you trust a man, when he doesn't only bawl you out, but bawls himself out too.

He always studied the work, and always found something new. And it's true, as you say: only what he did now was right, and what he did different before was a mistake, *stupido.* When the orchestra went to South America, on the boat they heard the short-wave programs that RCA broadcast; and once they heard a performance of the *Semiramide* Overture. Toscanini was cursing: "What stupid players! What bad conductor! Bad!

Bad!" Then the announcement came: "Arturo Toscanini and the New York Philharmonic." A marvelous performance, I know. But he said: *"Stupido! Bruto! Anch' io!"* And as you say, he felt the same way when he listened to someone else. It's natural: when you are so convinced—which every musician must be: before you go on the stage you have to be convinced that what you do is the only possible way of performance—if somebody else performs in any other way you have to disagree. It's very difficult to find something is played differently than you think, and still is good. And very rare.[1]

You ask about the characteristics of his performances. The two great qualities were—one, the shape, that fantastic sense of proportions in the work; the other, the clarity, which made any piece of music, even *Die Götterdämmerung*, sound like a string quartet: you heard every note that it was necessary to hear— which I enjoyed very much. And he had a natural sense of style. A man who actually, when he started to conduct symphonic music, was an opera conductor—how quickly he adjusted. This is a very difficult change which takes real understanding, superior talent—particularly to go from *Italian* opera style to a Beethoven symphony. Yes, actually it was the Schubert C-major that he did first. And he conducted it *very* well, *very* beautifully. The charm! Really, he had everything: he had this charm—personal, for instance: the charm of this man was incredible!

And when it came to Mendelssohn—the delicacy—yes, the elegance—fantastic! Looking back, there are so many great moments. It's a long time ago; but how many great moments there were, particularly in rehearsals with this man, that I cannot get out of my memory. In French music, for instance: there was a rehearsal of *La Valse* by Ravel—and what went on with his hands to get the flavor was incredible: I can't describe it. There was once *Ibéria*—the second movement, *The Perfumes of the Night*: I swear I smelled the perfumes; and I was not the only one. Not to speak of *La Mer*. And—*well*, the Italian operas!

Otello! After that I got tickets to hear *Otello* at the Metropolitan. It was a very good conductor, and it was supposed to be
one of the superb performances at the Metropolitan; but really
you could not listen to it—after the *Otello* that we did. In fact
any Italian opera sounded trivial after his performance. Those
opera performances you don't forget—you can't. The nicest part
was when *he* sang—not the singers with their beautiful voices,
but he with his hoarse voice. There was such expression in his
singing: you felt the whole drama was *in* it. Those were some of
the great performances: I think I will never hear anything like
that *Otello.*

Then German music. His Wagner was absolutely great:
you couldn't imagine better than that. Yes, that *Tristan* which
we recorded—wasn't it wonderful? And Brahms! The Third
Symphony of Brahms! He struggled with it for a long time: I
think he was never really happy with it. But when we played it
the last time, in Carnegie Hall, he was *so* happy. Everybody was
happy. I think he *found* it—he had the feeling "That's it." That
was a wonderful performance: I think it was the greatest Third
Brahms I ever heard or played; it's one of the things I won't
forget. And Beethoven! The *Eroica!* That moment in the Funeral March when he always screamed *"Terribile!"* Yes, the
climax of the *fugato.* That was the most *terribile* thing—I think
everybody among the dead people was scared by it. But there
were so many things that it's impossible to think of all: on every
program we had, there were some things.

As for the change in the later performances which you
speak of, I felt different.[2] I felt that there was a time when it
sounded a little tense, and there was this fear—"Don't make a
retard. Don't slow down"—and it tended to be a little fast.
There's a recording of the E-flat Mozart Symphony where it's
really much too fast and tense; and there were quite a few other
performances like that. There *was* a period of tension; but at
the end I thought it was very relaxed and beautiful. Of course it

was also that Toscanini felt much happier in Carnegie Hall because of the sound. That 8H sound was very clean; but it was not an ingratiating sound;[3] and when we went to Carnegie Hall the playing started really to sound. And I felt that the orchestra itself was a little tense in performances—not in rehearsals—in performances, in the earlier years, but there was a general feeling of relaxed music-making at the end in the performances: "Ah! *now* it's relaxed!"

The things you were told about in the last *Don Quixote* did happen. Toscanini was a little absent-minded; he forgot; he made a few mistakes—in the performance. There was even one bad mishap, which is not on the record: they must have replaced it from the rehearsal. But look: at the age of eighty-five it was very possible that he forgot sometimes a little bit. When he was good he was just as good as ever; but there were bad moments—that was true. Even earlier he made mistakes: I remember the *Bohème* performance—which was in 1945—where he made a bad mistake. It was his fault: I don't know if he forgot, or what happened; nobody knew. Everybody can make a mistake; mistakes happen. His became more frequent only in the last year; and I would not be surprised if it was because he was told it was his last year. I can't possibly make a judgment; but I'm sure this must have been responsible. Anybody would feel *very* bad to be told that; and for a man like Toscanini to get what is it called?—the pink slip! How did we know? Through the grapevine: it was a rumor, and finally it was a fact. It was in the air: we felt it was going to happen.[4] And it was very sad. Because I'm convinced that he would have conducted still another few good years—very good years. And maybe he would have been in better physical shape than he was at the end if he didn't have to stop. When you took away the baton, you took away the thing that kept him young.

Postscript and Notes
by B. H. Haggin

Postscript

On an NBC broadcast a year or two ago one heard Toscanini describing the historic incident in Rio de Janeiro in which —a nineteen-year-old cellist in the orchestra—he took over the conducting of a performance of *Aida* after the conductor had been booed from the podium by the audience. Then one heard the description of the incident which the impresario of the company had given to his son; and finally the description of it by a man who had been in the theater that evening. And the three descriptions differed irreconcilably on a number of details— even on what Toscanini wore.

There is nothing surprising in this; nor is it surprising that a few instances of such differing recollections of a happening occur in the foregoing monologues. In some of these instances the differences can be accounted for; but in any case they are concerned with what is unimportant. Thus, one can accept Burghauser's recollection that he arranged by telephone from Budapest that Kipnis replace the bass from Berlin in the *Missa Solemnis*, but can think he may be mistaken in recalling that Kipnis was waiting at the airport when Toscanini returned to Vienna, and can believe Kipnis's recollection that he was asked, during a rehearsal at the State Opera, to substitute for the

Berlin bass at that day's first rehearsal of the *Missa,* that he went
to the *Musikvereinsaal* where he found Toscanini ready to begin
the rehearsal, and that after this rehearsal he was told of Toscanini's request that he sing in the performance. But the important
thing is not what preceded Kipnis's participation in the rehearsals and the performance; it is what he experienced at the
rehearsals and the performance when he got to them.

The musicians who speak in this book are of course only a
few of those who could speak; but they seemed to me a sufficient
number to achieve the book's purpose. Since some may wonder
at the absence of certain leading players of the NBC Symphony,
I will say that I asked a few of them, but one didn't answer my
letter, one accepted so reluctantly and unpromisingly that I
proceeded no further with him, and one did record what he had
to say about Toscanini, but, when I sent him the monologue I
made of it, decided not to allow it to be published, for reasons
that are worth telling. He wrote that his reverence and love for
Toscanini had already got him into difficulties with one conductor, and he feared that the published monologue would get
him into difficulties with all conductors—not because of the
way he would play for them, but because of what they knew he
had said about Toscanini, and what this might lead them to
suspect he thought of them. As it happened, another musician
wrote at this time to request the elimination of a conductor's
name here and the change of a dangerous word there in his
monologue, explaining that "the conductors who were adum-
brated by Toscanini's brilliance have never forgiven him his
greatness; and this creates a continuing professional problem for
those who worked with the Old Man." He illustrated this by
describing his experience with a conductor for whom he auditioned, who said to him: "You will of course have to forget you
played under Toscanini." The player felt obligated to answer:
"I certainly will respect and co-operate; but I can hardly forget
that I played under Toscanini"; and he didn't get the position.

And further illustration was provided by the Szell-Lang conversation described on pages 225-7.

In addition to Schoenbach of the Philadelphia Orchestra, I saw Mason Jones, the orchestra's first horn when Toscanini conducted it in 1941-42. In 1949 he came to my home with my friend Gordon Kahn, ostensibly to hear my copy of the test pressing of the unreleased recording of the *Midsummer Night's Dream* music, with his marvelous playing of the horn solo in the Nocturne, but really, it turned out, to ask me to try to get Toscanini to autograph a photograph of him rehearsing the orchestra in 1941. I inferred from this that playing with Toscanini had meant something to Jones; and agreed to try. The next time I visited Toscanini I took the photograph with me; and I watched the formidable operation that the autographing of it proved to be: the search for the bottle of white ink, then for the pen, and then the making of each stroke of the inscription with an intensity that was awesome and moving. Though Jones consented to see me now, he said he didn't have much to tell me; and it turned out that playing with Toscanini had meant very little to him. He said he had been very young (only twenty-one, if I remember correctly), with knowledge of how to play the horn, but no knowledge of music; that being in his second year as first horn, he had thought only about making good in that position—which had meant delivering whatever Toscanini asked from his instrument with no thought of anything but that task; and that he had been too busy with this to be impressed by Toscanini, who, he added, had been no hero for *him*: on that stage he had been a Stokowski and Ormandy man. My first reaction was to find it extraordinary that even a young player, and even one so intent on the task of playing his instrument, and even one who was a Stokowski and Ormandy man, should have been completely unaffected by the powerful personality and musicianship that impressed everyone else. And my further reaction was that if Jones had spoken with the same candor in

1949 I would have spared Toscanini the labor of autographing a photograph for someone who wanted it only as an impressive decoration on his wall.

One member of the NBC Symphony who doesn't speak in the book thought that once in a while a Toscanini explosion was just another of his many different ways of getting the orchestra to produce what he wanted—a way of shocking the orchestra into producing it. And he told me something a horn-player had told him once: that when this player had a number of bars' rest which he was counting in reverse—increasingly nervous as he counted "five, four, three"—at one bar before his entrance he would look up and find Toscanini's eye on him; and then he would simply find himself playing, as though Toscanini's hand had reached out and drawn him in.

And I add one item which the players who recalled Toscanini's repeated *"Cantare!* Sing!" failed to mention—the variant on one occasion: *"Cantare! Non solfeggiare!"* ("Sing! Don't do *solfeggio* exercises!")

Notes

¹ (*from page 36*):

It is interesting to read the late Samuel Chotzinoff's account of this incident in his book, *Toscanini: An Intimate Portrait* (Knopf, 1956). Toscanini's demands, he writes on page 108, sometimes interfered with the operations of the commercial programs that earned the cost of the NBC Symphony broadcasts. When it was not working with Toscanini the orchestra was assigned to those commercial programs, of which it could play only a few in any case, since seventy-five or eighty percent of its working time each week was required by Toscanini's rehearsals and broadcast. On one occasion Chotzinoff scheduled the usual two-and-a-half-hour rehearsal for a performance of Verdi's *Requiem* in Carnegie Hall at 4, to make sure that if Toscanini ran over the two and a half hours there would be ample time for thirty of the men to get to NBC at 8 for the commercial program they had to play. But after three and a half hours, Toscanini—who "knew nothing about the '*commerziale*' and would have cared less . . . had he known"—gave no sign of ending the rehearsal; so Chotzinoff had to instruct the personnel manager to signal to the men to sneak out. And though Toscanini made a scene when he discovered what was happening, the next day he recognized the men's need of the extra income from the commercial program, and all was well again.

Every detail in Chotzinoff's account is untrue—including the one that Toscanini knew nothing about the commercial program. It wasn't in his mind while he was rehearsing the *Missa Solemnis*; but he did know about it and did care about it. As Shulman says, it had taken him some time to discover that the men of his orchestra had to play in other programs, and he had disliked it when he discovered it. Chotzinoff not only had foreseen that he would dislike it, but had feared that he might even refuse to come, if he knew, and had therefore been careful to conceal it from him—as he is careful to conceal it from the readers of his book until his mention of it in connection with the rehearsal incident on page 108. On page 79 he writes that he told Toscanini in Milan that NBC "would build him a great orchestra"—which conveyed to Toscanini what it conveyed twenty-five years later to Eugene Lyons, who in his recent biography of David Sarnoff writes that Chotzinoff told Toscanini NBC "would create a great orchestra especially for him."* Chotzinoff's further statements on pages 84-86—that on his return to New York he "started to put together an orchestra"; that a symphony orchestra is not built in a day, and "we had only ten months in which to assemble one"; that by November 1937 "we had assembled a superb body of men"—these statements imply that, starting from zero, he engaged for NBC all the members of an additional new orchestra for Toscanini. And he makes the implied claim explicit on page 86: when Toscanini cabled his withdrawal from the project because he had heard it was costing some NBC men their jobs, Chotzinoff cabled in reply that far

---

*And the letter of resignation that was prepared for Toscanini to sign in 1954 contained a statement about the invitation seventeen years earlier "to become the Musical Director of an orchestra to be created especially for me."

from costing even one man his job, Toscanini's engagement had caused NBC "to take on . . . a full symphony orchestra . . ."

In all this there isn't the slightest hint of the true facts that were given in an article on the NBC Symphony broadcasts in *Fortune* of January 1938: that NBC's contract with the musicians' union for 1938 had required it to increase its staff orchestra from seventy-four to 115 men; that the ninety-two men constituting the NBC Symphony were part of that staff orchestra of 115; that those ninety-two comprised thirty-one men retained from the 1937 staff orchestra, and sixty-one men whom Chotzinoff had engaged as higher-caliber replacements of members of the 1937 staff orchestra (who *had*, then, lost their jobs) and as additions for the 1938 staff orchestra; and that of the thirty hours which the ninety-two were obligated to work during the week, only fifteen were allotted to Toscanini's rehearsals and broadcast, and the remaining fifteen went to other NBC programs, sustaining and commercial.

This fact—that the orchestra built "for him" was actually playing half its working time with other conductors—Chotzinoff, as I said earlier, had concealed from Toscanini because he had known Toscanini would dislike it, and why he would dislike it: the other conductors were unable to hold the players to his technical and musical standards of performance, so that his work in disciplining and teaching the orchestra was constantly being undone; and many of the men came to his rehearsal on Friday after several hours' work with Walter Damrosch for that morning's music appreciation program and with Frank Black for that evening's Cities Service program. The result of Chotzinoff's concealment was that week after week Toscanini was baffled and frustrated and exasperated by the strange fact that the orchestra which delighted him with its youthful energy on other days played "like tired old men" on Friday. Only after some time did he discover why; and it was his growing anger about it that boiled over in response to the crowning outrage at the *Missa* rehearsal. And far from all being well again the next day, it impelled him to absent himself from NBC the next year.

What may have contributed to this action, Hugo Burghauser thinks, was another incident at this time. Though a Catholic who could have remained in Vienna after Hitler's takeover, Burghauser chose—"as a matter of conviction and taste"—to leave, going first to Toronto and then, with the advent of war, to New York. "I thought I had left intrigue behind me in the city of Metternich," he says, "but found it going on around Toscanini at NBC among the bureaucrats who tried to control not only administrative but artistic matters." Toscanini even earlier had invited him to play in the NBC Symphony; and he now recommended him for a position in the orchestra that happened to be vacant. As an experienced player Burghauser assumed he would be considered competent for the position; and he assumed further that with Toscanini's recommendation he would be engaged. But to his astonishment Leopold Spitalny, the union representative who was personnel manager at NBC, growled: "We don't want you here." A violinist who knew Sarnoff mentioned the incident to him; and Sarnoff asked Chotzinoff to look into it—which Chotzinoff did by summoning Burghauser to his office, telling him with cold anger: "I'm seeing you because my boss told me to," and informing him that Toscanini could of course suggest a player but had only the power to say no, while the power to say yes lay entirely with Spitalny and Chotzinoff, and that they had exercised this power to say no to Burghauser. In public Toscanini gave no sign of the outrage and fury that he expressed in private over this humiliating treatment of him, which Burghauser thinks may have contributed to his decision to absent himself from NBC the next year.

² (*from page* 37):

Again it is interesting to read Chotzinoff's account of this incident in his book. As Shulman says, when Toscanini's memory failed him and he stopped conducting, putting his hand to his eyes in an attempt to remember, the orchestra's first cellist, Frank Miller, kept the performance going, Toscanini began to beat time again, the piece was completed, and the audience applauded. But Chotzinoff invents a more dramatic conclusion: when Toscanini stopped conducting "the men stopped playing and the house was engulfed in terrible silence."

[3] *(from page 37)*:

Photo-copies of the Toscanini letter of resignation that Shulman refers to, and the Sarnoff reply, were sent out by NBC and, I believe, reproduced in some newspapers. And the alleged circumstances leading to the exchange were described a couple of years later by Chotzinoff in his book as follows: Only a few days before the first rehearsal of *Un Ballo in Maschera*, in January 1954, Toscanini informed Chotzinoff that he no longer remembered the words of this opera and therefore requested him to cancel the project; then a day or two later he informed Chotzinoff that he remembered the words and would prepare and conduct the performance. This in fact he did. But, says Chotzinoff, it was now clear to the Toscanini family that the time had come for him to stop; Toscanini himself agreed, frowning on any suggestion that he return for another season; at his request a letter of resignation was prepared; and though weeks passed without his signing it, during the week of the final broadcast "he summoned the resolution to put his name to it and send it off."

Though Shulman's doubts about the letter and what it embodied were shared privately by others, the first and only public contradiction of them was the statement on page 213 of Filippo Sacchi's book, *The Magic Baton* (Putnam, 1957): "Only two months after [*Un Ballo in Maschera*] he was informed that the N. B. C. had decided to disband the orchestra, and that they could therefore dispense with his services." The importance of this statement was that Sacchi was a personal friend of Toscanini, who could be presumed to have received the information from him. Moreover, this public statement repeated what had been told privately to a friend of mine by Cantelli, who had seen Toscanini constantly during much of the season of 1953-54, when he was here conducting the NBC Symphony and New York Philharmonic—except that Cantelli had said it was in the late fall of 1953 that Walter Toscanini had told his father of NBC's decision to discontinue the broadcasts and disband the orchestra at the end of that season, and of Chotzinoff's suggestion that his father might, for appearances' sake, wish to resign.

Cantelli's mention of the late fall of 1953 recalled to me that it was at this very time that Walter Toscanini had written me no one would henceforth be admitted to his father's rehearsals, and it was soon after this that I had begun to hear about Toscanini's occasional confusion at rehearsals, which had provided a possible reason for the exclusion of outsiders. And I had myself heard instances of this confusion at two of the rehearsals for the final broadcast, which I had listened to as they came over a telephone line from Carnegie Hall. At that time it had looked as though Toscanini had begun to exhibit occasional failing of his powers; and that this had made NBC unwilling to risk another season.

But in the spring of 1966 another person in close touch with the situation—a friend of both Toscanini and Sarnoff—told me what Sarnoff had told him at the time: that Sarnoff and Chotzinoff had gone up to Riverdale to offer Toscanini a contract for the following season, but had been intercepted by Walter Toscanini, who had requested them not to offer his father the contract and had told them he wouldn't let his father sign it. At first I was at a loss whether to believe Sarnoff or Cantelli; but a friend pointed out that I could believe both:

Sarnoff could have been dissuaded by Walter Toscanini from offering his father the contract; and Toscanini then could have been told what Cantelli said he was told—that NBC would discontinue the broadcasts at the end of that season.

This certainly could be what happened. But if Sarnoff was ready to offer Toscanini a contract for the following season, Toscanini cannot have exhibited any failing of his powers; and one must assume that Walter Toscanini's reason for requesting Sarnoff not to offer his father the contract was the family's belief that conducting another NBC Symphony season would make too great demands on Toscanini's diminishing physical strength. What this failed to take into account was Toscanini's mind. Felix Galimir is not the only one who maintains that it was not the lapses of memory and the confusions that necessitated discontinuing the broadcasts, but the shock of the discontinuing of the broadcasts that caused the lapses of memory, the confusions and the mistakes of the last year— among them the mistakes that one musician remembered in the broadcast performance of *Don Quixote*.

FOR WILLIAM CARBONI'S STATEMENT

[1] (*from page 54*):
Carboni is referring to Toscanini's absenting himself from NBC during the season of 1941-42 because of the rehearsal of the *Missa Solemnis* at which thirty-five men of the orchestra had to sneak out to play a commercial program. It must be pointed out that he returned to NBC after that year's absence. And it must also be pointed out that he acted as he did in 1941 because he had discovered what Chotzinoff had concealed from him; but that he didn't discover it every time.

In July 1947 the time of the NBC Symphony broadcasts was changed, for the season of 1947-48, from Sunday at 5 to

Saturday at 6:30. (NBC had been unable to get a commercial
sponsor for the NBC Symphony, and Ford wanted to buy
Sunday at 5 for another program.) I pointed out in my *Music
on the Radio* column in the Sunday *Herald Tribune*—which
Toscanini read—that the new time was one when people were
busy with their children and their dinners and therefore unable
to listen; and a few weeks later I published objections to the new
time from readers all the way to the west coast. The change
was made in October for the last few broadcasts of the NBC
Summer Symphony; and a couple of weeks before the start of
Toscanini's series in November I visited him.

After we had been talking for some time he said suddenly:
"Is very interesting: they say only 7,000,000 listen to NBC
Symphony on Sunday, but 11,000,000 listen on Saturday."

Since nobody could be listening to his broadcasts that
hadn't even begun, I asked: "How do they know that?"

"NBC make investigation," he said.

Again, NBC couldn't have "investigated" how many
people were listening to the broadcasts that hadn't begun; so
I asked: "Who told you that?"

"Chotzinoff."

In its July announcement of the change of time NBC had
stated that "a number of additional stations are expected to
carry the broadcasts" (which, I had written, they would do
because not enough people listened at 6:30 on Saturday to make
the time commercially valuable); and NBC probably had derived from the number of stations a total potential audience of
11,000,000. If Chotzinoff had been pinned down, he undoubtedly would have said this advance estimate was the "investigation" he had referred to; but he had apparently given Toscanini
the impression that NBC had conducted a real survey of a kind
which had definitely established that 11,000,000 people actually
were listening. And so Toscanini had accepted the change of
time which cost him part of his audience, and which he would

have objected to, and might have refused to accept, if he had known the actual nature of the "investigation" Chotzinoff referred to.

FOR ALEXANDER KIPNIS'S STATEMENT

[1] (*from page 63*):

In Bayreuth in 1928, Nikolai Sokoloff, who had played under Muck in the Boston Symphony, visited him one morning and took me along. Muck was greatly changed from the dark-haired, vigorous, proudly erect man I had seen walk out on the stage in 1917: he was gray, shrunken, wrinkled, with a ghost of a smile flickering over his face as he talked pleasantly. I discovered that he conducted the Hamburg Philharmonic in the winter; and I went to Hamburg in November to hear his performance of Brahms's Third. He allowed me to attend the rehearsal, where he spoke as quietly as he conducted. And after the rehearsal he talked with me in his room pleasantly—not at all the terrifying person one had heard about in his Boston Symphony days.

When I mentioned Toscanini he said: "Toscanini is a fine musician, very serious and earnest; I honor him. I knew him in Italy, and we made several voyages together. He never went to concerts; but he came to every concert in Boston." Evidently this friendly attitude could not survive his displacement as reigning monarch in Bayreuth by Toscanini in 1930.

Twenty years later Toscanini revealed that he had gone to the concerts in Boston only to hear the superb orchestra. Muck, said Toscanini, "was terrible! . . . Everything so slow! Muck was Beckmesser of conductors!"

[2] (*from page 66*):

In the performance of Toscanini's 1937 Salzburg *Magic*

Flute that is preserved on records it is the Queen of the Night's second aria that Toscanini performs in an unusually fast tempo, in which nevertheless the singer sings it perfectly. The *Allegro moderato* section of her first aria he performs in the usual moderately fast tempo; and it is not his tempo, therefore, that causes her to go to pieces in the florid passages.

[3] (*from page 67*):

Kipnis was answering the statement in our conversation in which I pointed out that *The Magic Flute* itself was not an opera which people talked about as they did about *Don Giovanni* or *Die Meistersinger* or *Tristan*; but I ventured the guess that if *The Magic Flute* had been one of the operas Toscanini performed here with the NBC Symphony, the performance would be one that people would be talking about as they did about the *Otello*, the *Fidelio* and the *Traviata*. Actually, I added, I *had* talked about Toscanini's enchanting *Magic Flute* ever since 1937; and so had the English critic Spike Hughes in his *Toscanini Legacy*. This had been on the basis of our memories of it; but recently I had been able to hear a recording of the performance, and had again found it enchanting. And my recollection, finally, was that at the dress rehearsal and the performances I heard in 1937 the audience every time had been tremendously enthusiastic.

FOR JAN PEERCE'S STATEMENT

[1] (*from page 119*):

Again Chotzinoff tells it differently—and again with the caricaturing malice of his entire book. On page 138 he has Toscanini—about to fly to his dying wife in Italy, overcome with grief, answering no, his life is finished, to Chotzinoff's reminder of the *Ballo in Maschera* planned for next season—

still weeping as he says to Chotzinoff: "*Addio, caro,* I pray you to engage for *Un Ballo* Bjoerling . . ." And on page 142 he includes "a last-minute substitiution of Jan Peerce for the indisposed Bjoerling" among the difficulties he ironed out before the first rehearsal of *Un Ballo* the following season. According to Chotzinoff, then, Bjoerling was Toscanini's first choice, and his replacement by Peerce was a routine matter handled by Chotzinoff.

FOR SOL SCHOENBACH'S STATEMENT

[1] (*from page 121*):

Alfred Wallenstein agreed with Schoenbach, saying that Toscanini would try to find English words, and then would resort to Italian words, which most of the men didn't understand; but that the men of the New York Philharmonic and NBC Symphony—as against the men of the Philadelphia—knew enough about the kinds of things he talked about to be able to understand what he was trying to say.

[2] (*from page 124*):

Toscanini once said: "Beethoven is very exact—but even Beethoven sometimes write different"; and he cited the *pizzicato* note that Beethoven wrote now as an eighth-note, now as a quarter, now as a half.

[3] (*from page 124*):

Each pair of concerts in which Toscanini conducted the Philadelphia Orchestra in 1941-42 was followed by recording sessions, in which they recorded Schubert's C-major, Mendelssohn's *Midsummer Night's Dream* music, Berlioz's *Queen Mab.* Tchaikovsky's *Pathétique,* Strauss's *Death and Transfiguration,* Debussy's *La Mer* and *Ibéria,* and Respighi's *Feste Romane.*

None of these was issued by RCA Victor until 1963, when at last the recording of Schubert's C-major was released. Several months before the release it was broadcast by WFMT in Chicago and WRVR in New York, with an introduction by the music critic of the Chicago *Sun-Times* professing to give authoritative inside information on the history of the Philadelphia recordings, the reason why they hadn't been issued, and the reason why the Schubert C-major was now being released. He had, he said, heard the test pressings Toscanini received; and they "were really pretty horrible: the noise level was as high as the levels of the music in the pianissimo passages"; but the new tape processed from the original masters conveyed "all the familiar warm, round sound of the Philadelphia Orchestra." In other words, the beautiful sound that couldn't be heard because of the noise from the original test records—this sound was made audible by the new tape. Actually the *Sun-Times* critic was merely embroidering the Victor account in the brochure accompanying the Schubert recording when it was released: that the recording hadn't been issued in 1942 because wartime processing had resulted in "mechanical imperfections [i.e. noises] which neither the Maestro nor the company could accept"; and what made its release possible now was the engineer John Corbett's "[restoration of] the recording to its original state" through "750 hours of work and through the miracles of new electronic transfer techniques"—the result being, according to Roland Gelatt of *High Fidelity*, the revealing of "glories in the groove that were never suspected in 1942."

After the WRVR broadcast of the recording I told the musical director of WRVR that the *Sun-Times* critic's introduction had been incorrect in what it said and had left a great deal unsaid; and he asked me to prepare a correction. I did; but a few days after I recorded it he informed me that he had shown it to Walter Toscanini, who had requested him not to broadcast it, and that he had acceded to this request. I published some of the facts in my review of the recording; and I give all of them—or rather, all known to me—here.

In September 1942 I listened with Toscanini to test pressings of the 12-inch 78-rpm sides of Strauss's *Death and Transfiguration*, Debussy's *La Mer* and Berlioz's *Queen Mab*. All of these begin very softly; and even in those soft passages there was no unusual, obtrusive noise from the records that prevented us from hearing the musical sound, or that even disturbed us. (My recollection of this is confirmed by the account of the occasion in a letter I wrote to a Victor engineer named Sinnott on September 26, 1942: there is mention of the magnificent sound from the records, but no mention of noise.) What caused Toscanini to reject the sides he did was not their noise but the imperfect balance in the sound—either as performed or as recorded—that caused him not to hear this or that instrument he expected to hear. Thus, at the end of the first movement of *La Mer*, his face registered his delight as he exclaimed: "Is like reading the score!"; and he approved those two sides. But a moment later, listening to the second movement, he cried out in anger and stopped the record when he didn't hear one of the woodwinds; and this side he rejected.

At this time it was expected that Toscanini would remake the rejected sides with the Philadelphia Orchestra; and there was the same expectation about the sides which Victor itself rejected because of mechanical defects. But at this very time the president of the musicians' union, James Petrillo, ordered its members not to do any recording until the record companies agreed to his demands; and this prevented the remaking of the sides. It was not until two years later that recording was resumed; and by that time the Philadelphia Orchestra had transferred from Victor to Columbia. The orchestra would have been available for the correction and completion of its Victor recordings with Toscanini; but Walter Toscanini told me at that time that Victor wanted the Philadelphia Orchestra record-

ings abandoned and new ones made by Toscanini with the NBC
Symphony, and that "we are trying to get Father to forget the
Philadelphia recordings." He didn't say why Victor wanted this;
and one could only conjecture that it didn't want Toscanini's
name to promote a Columbia orchestra, and rather than have
this happen preferred to sacrifice recordings which documented
the collaboration of this great conductor and great orchestra
in some of the greatest performances Toscanini ever put on
records; and that for Victor's purposes one Toscanini performance was as good as another, a performance of *La Mer* with the
NBC Symphony as good as one with the Philadelphia Orchestra.
The argument that the Philadelphia was now a Columbia
orchestra wouldn't have counted for much with Toscanini; and
Victor could hardly argue that the performances were poor;
but it could, and did successfully, argue that the Philadelphia
Orchestra recordings were mechanically defective beyond hope
of remedy.

Quite possibly, Victor, in persuading Toscanini, also persuaded itself that the recordings were atrocious—in particular
that the musical sound couldn't be heard because of the noise—
and that therefore they couldn't be issued. But it wasn't true:
the surface noise was stronger than the usual surface noise from
78-rpm records; but it didn't prevent one from hearing the
musical sound: one's ear separated it from the musical sound,
which was clearly audible and marvelously beautiful. In the
statement I recorded for WRVR I demonstrated this with
passages from vinylite and shellac test pressings of several sides
of the Schubert C-major—including one especially noisy side,
on which nevertheless the quiet opening of the second movement could be heard. What Corbett's skillful and patient work
had achieved was not to make audible a sound that had not
been audible before, but to reduce the accompanying noise as
much as it could be reduced without loss in the sound.

What I have said about the Schubert recording is true

of the others: the noise doesn't prevent one from hearing the beautiful sound and marvelous playing of the Philadelphia Orchestra in Toscanini's great performances. And the musical public should compel Victor to issue the Debussy *La Mer* and *Ibéria*, the Berlioz *Queen Mab*, the Mendelssohn *Midsummer Night's Dream* music, and the Tchaikovsky *Pathétique*, all of which are greater than those Toscanini recorded with the NBC Symphony.

[4] (*from page 127*):

I had been told of other incidents at Cantelli's rehearsals with the Philadelphia Orchestra, but not of this one. I asked David Walter if Cantelli had misbehaved in this way with the NBC Symphony; and his answer was "Never."

[5] (*from page 129*):

After the Saturday morning "love feast", at which Toscanini had rehearsed Beethoven's *Pastoral*, Gordon Kahn of the viola section remarked: "I'm a little surprised at the things he's letting pass," referring to flaws in execution which his orchestra player's ear had noticed. I mention this because of the explosion the next morning: I had the impression that Toscanini was raging not just about what had gone wrong in the Septet, but also about all the things he had let pass in the symphony.

[6] (*from page 130*):

Actually, Richard Aldrich of *The Times*, in his review of the Metropolitan Beethoven Ninth, credited Toscanini with the qualities of a great symphonic conductor and described with evident approval the unbroken melodic line, the plastic shaping of phrase that did not lose sight of the proportions of the whole, the rhythmic vitality of a performance which rose to heights of eloquence. And in the 1927 Philharmonic performance not only was the orchestra finer but the soloists were Elisabeth Rethberg, Louise Homer, Richard Crooks and Fraser Gange.

FOR JOSEF GINGOLD'S STATEMENT

1 (*from page 133*):

As against Gingold's statement that at this first rehearsal Toscanini took the NBC Symphony straight through the Brahms First, leaving the work on detail for subsequent rehearsals—his usual practice in this situation, as appears in Felix Galimir's account of his first rehearsal with the orchestra in Palestine—Chotzinoff, on pages 92-3 of his book, writes that after playing through the first movement of the Brahms, Toscanini said, "*Da capo!*" and began to rehearse it "in earnest"; and Chotzinoff then gives a picturesque description of the hour and a half of work on detail that happened—like the performance of the *Tannhäuser* Bacchanale coming to a halt in a hall "engulfed in terrible silence" at the last broadcast in 1954—in Chotzinoff's imagination.

2 (*from page 133*):

In conversation after the interview Gingold said: "Bruno Walter came to conduct us and began with an all-Mozart program. He did one of the big divertimenti, the D-minor Piano Concerto, in which he played—and the G-minor Symphony. Toscanini had come for the rehearsal. We saw the Old Man there, and remembered his wishes; and we played for *him*: with *molto arco*. Walter stopped us and said: 'Gentlemen, gentlemen, please, please, I beg you. Not so much bow, not so much bow. [Gingold imitated Walter singing the opening phrase delicately.] Little bow, very short. Once again, please.' Again we played with *molto arco*; and Walter stopped us and said: 'Gentlemen, gentlemen, please, please, I am unhappy. Do me the favor: short notes, please; little bow.' The third time; and again we played for Toscanini—which, I must say, was not right. Finally, the fourth time, some of us had the courage—the conductor asked for it, and we had to do it—we played as Bruno Walter asked us to. At that, Toscanini yelled something, banged his fist against the wall, and rushed out of the rehearsal. Walter knew exactly what was going on behind him. He was very calm, and said: 'Let's start once again'; and we played it exactly as he asked. The rumor was that they never spoke to each other after that. But I don't think the Old Man acted very nicely."

[3] (*from page* 133):

I had hoped Copland would tell me about Toscanini's rehearsal of *El Salón México*; but he said that for some reason he wasn't there. As for the performance, which he did hear, he would say it was o.k. That is, it seemed a straightforward performance of a piece in which Toscanini didn't feel at home. The continual change of meter made him nervous and unhappy; and he deprecated the performance when Copland spoke to him in the greenroom. Copland thought it was because he was unhappy about the performance that he didn't play the piece again; but I told him that most of the American pieces Toscanini played in the forties he did only once.

[4] (*from page* 135):

The surprise and doubt Gingold saw on my face when he spoke of Szell's tremendous admiration for Toscanini was caused by my recollection of the highly qualified admiration Szell had expressed on two occasions. One was a radio interview, on the anniversary of Toscanini's death, in which Szell began with the astonishing statement that the first Toscanini performance he heard, in 1927, was, unfortunately, one of "the Verdi operas he conducted least interestingly—to wit, *Aida*." More generally, Toscanini's performances "were always most impressive, and in most cases very instructive, partly in the positive, partly in the negative way . . . There was very often a tendency to rigidity and to a relentless drive even when the music wanted to breathe a little more freely" (this from Szell!). But he credited Toscanini with having "put a definite end to the arbitrariness of a whole generation of conductors before him." Thus his performances were "an education in discipline"; yet because of the rigidity the Toscanini influence could be "murderous for the one who went along blindly, and without any discrimination and any sense of criticism"; and Szell "could think of very remarkable performing musicians who were permanently or temporarily damaged or inhibited by too strong a Toscanini influence." Asked what distinguished Toscanini from other great conductors, Szell replied: "His relentless sense of continuity . . . Everything was pulsation and life from the first to the last note." This was interesting to recall a few months later at one point in a conversation between Szell and Paul Henry Lang in *High Fidelity*. Lang complimented Szell for his not excessive attention to detail, as against "the recording by a very distinguished conductor of advanced years who brought out every little detail with the utmost clarity—to the point where eventually it seemed mere meaningless precision"; and Szell replied in agreement: "Because probably the big general line was lost" (which, if true, would have made this performance unique among Toscanini performances). But the high point was Szell's reply when Lang asked who he thought were the great conductors of the past. After speaking glowingly of Nikisch and Strauss, Szell added that a man like Toscanini could not be left unmentioned—but not, it turned out, because of his performances. "Whatever you may think about his interpretation of a specific work," said Szell, with the implication that the specific interpretations offered much for men of superior taste like Szell and Lang to shake their heads over in pained disapproval, "that he changed the whole concept of conducting and that he rectified many, many arbitrary procedures of a generation of conductors before him is now already authentic history."

⁵ (*from page* 139):

Moldavan, who went to Bayreuth for Toscanini's performances of *Tristan* and *Tannhäuser*, told me that the German musicians there had resented the intrusion of an Italian in this shrine of German art where hitherto only Germans had performed—until Toscanini's first rehearsal of the orchestra, when he reduced them to stunned silence by detecting in their playing mistake after mistake in the orchestral parts that had for years gone undetected by the German conductors.

FOR HUGO BURGHAUSER'S STATEMENT

¹ (*from page* 155):

Burghauser later told me some of the details of these "objections and difficulties". After Toscanini conducted his orchestral concerts in Salzburg in 1934, the administration there—which was part of the administration of the State Opera in Vienna—asked him to conduct opera in Salzburg the following summer; and the agreement was reached that he would conduct *Fidelio* and *Falstaff*. But in Vienna the previous year, the enormous excitement over Toscanini's appearances—and even such a detail as the special 'Caruso' scale of prices for them—had been regarded rather sourly by certain eminences of the Viennese musical world, who had felt their own public image to be adversely affected, and had begun to plan a behind-the-scenes counter-campaign. Early in the fall of 1934 the Musical Director of the State Opera, Clemens Krauss, announced a new production of *Falstaff*, to be conducted by him. It was entirely legitimate for him to do so; and for Toscanini the announcement had no significance or importance; but those connected with the State Opera and the Salzburg Festival, who knew that

227

it was customary for productions in Vienna to be transferred in their entirety to Salzburg, saw at once that Krauss's intention to conduct the new *Falstaff* in Vienna was in effect an intention to conduct it also in Salzburg the following summer, and created a conflict with the agreement that the opera was to be conducted by Toscanini. He was asked if perhaps he would be willing to conduct another opera with *Fidelio* in place of *Falstaff*, and answered: "No *Falstaff*, no Toscanini." After which the authorities, in Viennese fashion, did nothing further, hoping that, with almost a year until the festival, something would turn up that would remove the difficulty. (The chief authority, the general Administrative Director of the State Opera, could not act against Krauss, because it had been Krauss who, astutely, had had him appointed to his position the year before.)

Meanwhile Toscanini was in Vienna for his concerts with the Vienna Philharmonic and the performance of Verdi's *Requiem* for the murdered Chancellor Dollfuss. And a series of incidents almost wrecked the *Requiem* project and delayed the performance several weeks. In the *Musikvereinsaal*, where the Vienna Philharmonic gave its concerts, Burghauser, as its chairman, arranged everything connected with Toscanini's rehearsals, watched over him, anticipated or smoothed out difficulties;* but in the State Opera, where the *Requiem* was to be performed, he was merely a member of the orchestra, and as

---

* On one occasion when something had gone wrong, Burghauser rushed upstairs to the librarian of the Society of Friends of Music and said: "Quick, give me the manuscript of Mozart's G-minor!" With the manuscript he rushed back to Toscanini's dressing room, and said: "Most unfortunate, I agree. But I thought you would like to see this, which I have to return in a few minutes." At the sight of Mozart's writing on the manuscript, Toscanini, forgetting his anger, became transfigured; as he began to read, and discovered what, strangely, he hadn't known—that Mozart had scored the work originally without clarinets, and had later rewritten the woodwind parts to include them—he exclaimed: "*Che meraviglia!*"; and when he came to the end he kissed the manuscript reverently before handing it back to Burghauser.

such had to obey Krauss's orders that in the opera house he was to remain with the orchestra and have no contact with Toscanini. On the day of the first orchestral rehearsal, therefore, Burghauser sat with the waiting orchestra, while Toscanini walked alone from the Hotel Bristol across the street to the stage entrance of the State Opera, where the man at the door asked him what he wanted and—being told *"Ho una proba"*—answered: "No stranger may enter here!" So Toscanini returned to the hotel, while the orchestra waited in the Opera. After a time a search party was sent out, and found Toscanini in a fury in his hotel suite, where he now refused to return to the Opera for the rehearsal. So it was agreed that he would from now on rehearse in the *Musikvereinsaal*, where he felt at home and would, it was thought, be in no danger of further hostile acts instigated by powerful persons.

But his first piano rehearsal with the solo soprano at the *Musikvereinsaal* was wrecked by another such act. The co-repetiteur from the State Opera who should have been there to play the piano did not arrive (because, it turned out later, he had not been notified of the rehearsal). So Toscanini himself had to sit down at the piano, put his pince-nez on his nose, and begin to play for the soprano. He had said: "Give me a good Aida"; and she was the company's Aida, with an excellent voice, said Burghauser, but without commensurate intelligence. Soon after they began, Toscanini stopped and asked her to sing a phrase in one breath, instead of breaking it to take breath; and she answered that she was accustomed to doing it her way, and showed him her score in which Bruno Walter had marked it to be sung that way. Toscanini, still quiet, told her she would have to sing it as he asked. There were a few more such exchanges, increasing the danger of a storm; and then an abrupt movement of Toscanini's head caused his pince-nez to fall off his nose to the floor. Before Burghauser could get there, Toscanini was on the floor groping nearsightedly for the pince-nez, which he found; and sitting down again he put it back on his nose, only to discover that he could see nothing because the lenses had fallen out. In exasperation and fury he jumped up and stamped his feet; and at the terrible sound of the lenses being crushed, the soprano burst into tears and fled from the room. It took more than a month to find another suitable soprano who was willing to follow Toscanini's directions; and it was not until November 1 that the performance of the *Requiem* took place (in gratitude for which, the Austrian government gave Toscanini a first edition of the early version of *Fidelio*, with Beethoven's inscription to his landlord: *"Seinem werten Freunde, Baron von Pasqualati, vom Verfasser, Ludwig van Beethoven"*).

Back now to *Falstaff*. When the time came that something had to be done about the conflict created by Krauss's intention to conduct in Salzburg the *Falstaff* that it had been agreed Toscanini would conduct, and the administration of the State Opera still did nothing, there was only one recourse left: to inform the new Chancellor, Schuschnigg, of the situation and ask him to take action. He was, in the first place, a genuine music-lover who could recognize the artistic importance of Toscanini's participation in the Salzburg Festival; but in addition he recognized its financial importance, and the disastrous financial consequences if Toscanini withdrew. And so he decided that the agreement between the Salzburg administration and Toscanini would be fulfilled and Toscanini would conduct *Falstaff* at the festival (which caused Krauss to withdraw from the festival, and the next year to resign his position in Vienna and go to Berlin).

But the "difficulties" didn't end at that point. At the first orchestral rehearsal of *Falstaff* in Salzburg, Burghauser found a young, inexperienced substitute in the chair of the first oboe, who was "ill"; and his inadequate playing caused Toscanini to walk out after a few minutes. Luckily the missing first oboe was located and was in his chair at the next rehearsal. But disaster threatened as late as the first stage rehearsal. In Vienna the preceding fall, the last choral rehearsal for the *Requiem* had taken place at the State Opera; and on the way to the rehearsal room Toscanini had had to pass through the auditorium. The stage rehearsal of the first scene of the third act of *Falstaff* was in progress; and inevitably Toscanini stopped to listen and to look through his pince-nez at the stage. What he expected to see was Falstaff sitting outside the inn, shivering after his immersion in the river, warming himself in the last rays of the sun, and sipping hot wine; but what he saw instead was Falstaff in his room, in bed under a mass of bedclothes. Outraged, Toscanini turned to Burghauser and exclaimed: "Criminals! They should be put in prison for daring to change what Boito and Verdi did so well. If they want something different let them write their own *Falstaff* and leave the *Falstaff* of Boito and Verdi in peace. If this scenery appears in Salzburg I walk out of the theater!" Burghauser reassured him, and subsequently impressed on the administration the necessity of having the correct outdoor set for Toscanini the following summer. But in Salzburg, when the curtain rose for the first scene of the third act, there again, to everyone's consternation, was the bedroom set; and Toscanini, infuriated, rushed out of the theater. Miraculously, a correct set was produced overnight; and after that *Falstaff* proceeded without further "difficulties" to its marvelous realization in Toscanini's performance.*

² (*from page 160*):

When I told Burghauser about having heard Strauss con-

---

* In his book, Chotzinoff has Toscanini objecting to the set of the interior of Ford's house. "Do you call *that* . . . an Elizabethan house!". . . When, on the following day, the curtain went up on the new interior of Ford's house, the Maestro said triumphantly: *"Ecco!"*

duct not only *The Magic Flute* but *Così Fan Tutte*, in which he improvised delightfully witty accompaniments on the piano for the recitatives, he said: "In 1949, the year of his death, I had some hours' conversation with him in Montreux; and I said to him: 'I have one request.' He asked what it was; and I begged him to write out those enchanting accompaniments for the recitatives in *Così Fan Tutte*. But he pointed to the *Vier letzte Gesänge* and the Duettino for clarinet and bassoon, which he had to finish. So the accompaniments for *Così* were lost."

[3] *(from page 164)*:

Burghauser described what happened at Novotna's first piano rehearsal with Toscanini for *The Magic Flute* in Salzburg. The pianist failed to appear; and before Toscanini could go to the piano himself, Bruno Walter, who was present, offered his services. The opening chords of *"Ach, ich fühl's"* enabled him to set his exceedingly slow tempo, in which Novotna had to continue when she began to sing. Toscanini paced back and forth impatiently, and after a few moments interrupted, exclaiming: *"Ma, caro Walter,* is *Andante,* and you play *adagio!"* Walter, embarrassed by the presence of Novotna and Burghauser, said: "My dear Maestro, you know I am always in agreement with you; but in this case I differ with you and think my tempo is correct." To which Toscanini answered heatedly: "And I, my dear Walter, am never in agreement with you!"

Years later Toscanini talked about the tempo of Pamina's aria. Clasping his hands as he acted her agitation, he exclaimed: "Pamina say, 'I lose my Tamino! Where my Tamino?!' Must be *andante,* but is always *adagio!"* And on another occasion he said: "When I conduct *Flauto Magico* in Salzburg I am afraid about my tempi; but Rosé [the old concertmaster of the Vienna Philharmonic] say once, 'At last!' I tell Bruno Walter, 'You will not like my tempi in *Flauto Magico.'* He say, 'Is very interesting'; but afterward he make again slow tempi."

Notes for Alfred Wallenstein

[1] *(from page 184)*:

Wallenstein is referring to certain great concert or broadcast performances which, as he says, were not recorded by RCA Victor on those occasions. They include the Mozart G-minor and Schubert C-major at Toscanini's last Sunday afternoon Philharmonic concert in 1936, which Wallenstein spoke of earlier; and to these can be added the 1936 Beethoven Ninth with the Philharmonic, the 1938 Strauss *Don Quixote* with the NBC Symphony (and Feuermann), which was superior to the 1953 broadcast issued by Victor, the 1940 Verdi *Requiem* and Beethoven *Missa Solemnis* with the NBC Symphony, both far greater than the later ones issued by Victor, the 1942 Berlioz *Romeo and Juliet* with the Philharmonic, the incandescent Haydn *Clock* Symphony and hair-raising Funeral Music from Wagner's *Die Götterdämmerung* at the 1945 Philharmonic pension fund concert. But as it happens, all of these except the Berlioz *Romeo* were recorded, though not by Victor. Because the 1936 Philharmonic performances were broadcast by CBS, they could be, and were, recorded privately off the air; the NBC performances were recorded by NBC itself; the 1945 Philharmonic performances were recorded by the recording company in Carnegie Hall for Walter Toscanini. They could be issued by Victor; and all—even the early ones with poor sound—should be.

But there is another sense in which it is true that Toscanini's recordings don't give us his best performances. Almost all the performances on Victor records today date from 1944 and thereafter, with a few Verdi excerpts and 'pop' numbers recorded with the NBC Symphony from 1939 to 1943 and the Schubert Ninth recorded with the Philadelphia Orchestra in 1941, but with none of the performances recorded with the New York Philharmonic in 1929 and 1936 and with the BBC Symphony from 1937 to 1939 (some of which are to be had on imported Odeon records). The significance of this is that the performances before 1944 were in Toscanini's earlier performing style—relaxed, expansive, articulating and organizing and shaping the substance of a piece with much elasticity of tempo, and inflecting the phrase with much sharply outlined detail; whereas the performances roughly from 1944 on were in the later simplified style that was swifter and tauter, setting a tempo that was maintained with only slight modification, and giving the phrase only subtle inflection. And while the performances in this later style are great performances, the ones in the earlier style are even greater. One discovers this when one listens to the 1941 Schubert Ninth after the 1953 performance, to the 1936 Rossini *Semiramide* Overture after the 1951 performance, to the 1940 Verdi *Requiem* and Beethoven *Missa Solemnis* after the 1951 *Requiem* and 1953 *Missa Solemnis*. Moreover the years from 1944 on include a period roughly from 1945 through 1947 when many of Toscanini's performances were tense and driving—one example being the 1948 Mozart Symphony K.543 on LM-2001, another the 1945 Sousa *Stars and Stripes Forever* on 11-9188 and VCM-7001 as against the relaxed performance broadcast in 1943. And as Wallenstein points out, the recording microphone disturbed Toscanini, made him tense, impelled him to set a faster tempo than that of the performance at the concert.

² (*from page 184*):

Even worse than Studio 8H was Studio 3A, in which (on the insistence, I was told, of an NBC executive that some use of the studio appear on the NBC books) Victor had Toscanini record Mozart's *Haffner* and Haydn's *Clock* in 1946-47, producing two of the most atrocious-sounding Toscanini recordings ever issued.

And actually a few excellent-sounding recordings were made in 8H—on the occasions when the microphone was placed at the optimum location for the studio that had been determined by an engineer named Johnston, and the chairs were pushed all the way back to increase the studio's resonance. These things were done at one session in 1945 for Gershwin's *An American in Paris,* and made its recorded sound spacious, warm, clear and clean. But at the same session Sousa's *Stars and Stripes Forever* was recorded with a microphone on each side in front of the orchestra and one in the rear of the hall—which is to say, with none at the Johnston location; and the result was coarse *tuttis* without depth and spaciousness and textures not cleanly defined in quiet. The superb Debussy *Ibéria* of 1950 was achieved by placing the microphone at the Johnston location and pushing the chairs all the way back; the lessened sharpness of presence and impact of the *La Mer* recorded the day before was the result of placing the microphone a few feet back of the Johnston location and pushing the chairs only part of the way back.

Nor were all the poor recordings made in 3A and 8H. In Carnegie Hall Victor produced in 1940 the excellent-sounding Brahms Piano Concerto No. 2, but in 1941 a Tchaikovsky Piano Concerto No. 1 that was thin, shallow, harsh and noisily clouded with reverberation, and in 1947 a Tchaikovsky *Pathétique* without luster and spaciousness because the microphone was placed too far back and the side boxes and parquet were covered with draperies, a Mendelssohn *Midsummer Night's Dream* even dimmer and weaker because the microphone—for this lightly scored music!—was placed even further back. As late as 1952 Victor produced a Beethoven Ninth without the spaciousness and luster of the *Pastoral* it had made a few months earlier; as late as 1953 a *Missa Solemnis* in which the chorus predominated over the orchestra and soloists because their microphone (the principal microphone behind Toscanini) was placed too far away.

What all this means is that whereas it would have been unthinkable that anyone should change what Toscanini produced at a concert, when he produced the performance for a recording Victor's supervisor of the recording could change its sound by his placing of the microphones and his other decisions affecting the acoustic characteristics of the hall; and the mistakes of a number of supervisors did alter and damage the sound of many of the performances imprinted on the records. Nor did it end there. When it happened that a superb facsimile of the performance—of Beethoven's Eighth, of Musorgsky's *Pictures at an Exhibition*, of Bizet's *Carmen* Suite—*was* imprinted on the tape, and Toscanini had approved it, then a Victor music editor—assigned to make from this original the tape master used in the processing of the metal parts for the final disc records—could, and did, make the changes that resulted in the ear-piercing, raucous *Pictures at an Exhibition* on LM-1838, the harsh Eighth on LM-1757, the shallow, blowzily 'brilliant' *Carmen* Suite on LRM-7013. The worst of these editors went so far as to inflict on the clear, bright, solid Debussy *La Mer* already issued on LM-1221 successive doses of 'enhancement' by echo-chamber resonance that produced the glossy, blurred and blowzy *La Mer* on LM-1833. And the transfer of 78-rpm recordings to LP provided this editor and others with the opportunity for various forms of electronic 'enhancement' that spoiled good recordings and made poor ones worse—an atrocious example being the 1964 version of the 1946 Tchaikovsky *Romeo and Juliet* on LM-7032, *Toscanini Concert Favorites*, in which the solid, bright, clear sound of the original 78-rpm recording was deprived of its solidity by a cut in bass, of its brightness by the treble-filter used to eliminate surface noise, and of its clarity by the addition of echo-chamber resonance.

As I write, many of the recordings are being newly edited for the reissue commemorating the hundredth anniversary of Toscanini's birth, arousing the hope that the new records will at last let music-lovers hear what he produced and wanted them to hear.

[3] *(from page 184)*:

But there were exceptional occasions when Toscanini produced a better performance at a recording session than at the concert or broadcast. One instance was the Haydn Symphony No. 88 he recorded in 1938, with a slow movement even more overwhelmingly powerful than the one he broadcast. And another was the Beethoven Ninth he recorded in 1952, whose first movement was controlled, steady and powerful, as the first movement he broadcast had not been.

[4] *(from page 184)*:

Wallenstein doesn't name the author of this book, but he can be referring only to the abominable Marsh book; and he nodded recognition and agreement when I pointed out in addition that Marsh had brought to his evaluation of the recorded performances no adequate or accurate critical perception and judgment (the recorded performance of the Prelude and Finale of *Tristan und Isolde*, he writes, "is over-refined, the antiseptic souvenir of passion rather than its full-blooded actuality . . . [This] is easily understood when we see that these two pieces rank fourth and fifth in frequency [of performance] in Toscanini's repertory: they have had all the life played out of them"; and one phrase in the Finale is "played in a cool, polished and unfeeling manner, more appropriate to Verdi . . ."). Also that he had, to my knowledge, never heard Toscanini conduct the NBC Symphony in a hall before the last season of 1953-54 and never been present at a working rehearsal, but had felt able to make statements about what he hadn't experienced that one NBC Symphony musician pronounced untrue or nonsensical and others contradict in their monologues ("He would rush a work rather than run the risk of letting it go slack even for a moment . . . In general, as he grew older he tended . . . to grow nervous when confronted with long stretches of music in a slow pulse pattern"; "In his later seasons there must have been times when the only thing that saved Toscanini from disaster in some performances was the phenomenal virtuosity of his orchestra, which could play anything at virtually any tempo"; because of his language difficulty, Toscanini, "with his American orchestras ... did not talk a great deal [at rehearsals]: they simply played for many minutes at a time, going over works again and again until the Maestro was satisfied"). Also that he had certainly never heard Toscanini conduct the New York Philharmonic, or heard Mengelberg do so before him, but had felt able to make statements about them which I was in a position to pronounce untrue ("A peer of these great ensembles [Stokowski's Philadelphia Orchestra and Koussevitzky's Boston Symphony] was the New York Philharmonic ... under Willem Mengelberg, to which Toscanini came as a guest conductor in 1926 ... Although it always responded to Toscanini with sensitiveness and fine playing [it] apparently did not begin to take on all of the characteristics it was to exhibit under him in later seasons until 1927-28, when he led it for a longer period"—the facts being that under Mengelberg the Philharmonic was not a peer of the Philadelphia and Boston Symphony, but that from its first performance with Toscanini in 1926 it exhibited the dazzling sonorities and execution that made it the peer of the other two). Also that he had never exchanged a word with Toscanini, but had felt able to make statements about him as a person without any basis of first-hand knowledge ("Toscanini brooks no peers"; "Young conductors were able, under certain conditions, to make friends with the Maestro and enjoy a pleasant relationship with him until they became potential rivals, after which the friendship abruptly ceased"—the examples being Rodzinski and Steinberg, whom nobody else has ever thought of as potential rivals of Toscanini).

[5] *(from page 184)*:
The newly edited versions of Toscanini's recordings that

Victor is issuing in 1967 may include some of those withdrawn in recent years.

⁶ (*from page 185*):

It was not the engineer who asked Toscanini if he was ready to record, but the man supervising the recording session—the producer, as I believe he is called nowadays.

FOR FELIX GALIMIR'S STATEMENT

¹ (*from page 199*):

Preparing, in October 1944, to broadcast Beethoven's *Eroica* in November, Toscanini listened to his performance of November 1939, and—he told me—blushed at what he heard. The 1939 performance was in his earlier expansive style marked by great elasticity of tempo; and by 1944 there had been the change to the later simpler style involving only slight modification of the set tempo. But for Toscanini this was not just a change from one way of playing to another: it was a change to a right way, to the only right way, and from a way, therefore, that had been shamefully wrong. And I had suggested to Galimir that this habit of mind, rather than the jealousy Toscanini was accused of, was responsible for his unfavorable comments on other conductors: his intense conviction at a particular moment that *this* was the right way to play something made any other way—his own in the past, another conductor's now—appear to him wrong. Actually, it was not true that he spoke only ill of other conductors, out of jealousy. He spoke well to me of Nikisch, of Schuch, of Ansermet; he told me I must come to Cantelli's rehearsals, where I watched him nodding and smiling in approval of what he was hearing. And when he spoke ill of a conductor to me, it was because of something he had heard the conductor do that was wrong: Muck's excessively slow tempo in

Beethoven's First; Beecham's in Haydn's No. 99; someone else's whipping up of the tempo of the finale of Berlioz's *Symphonie Fantastique* for excitement; Koussevitzky's coming to the *fermata,* the rest and the trill near the end of the Adagio of Mozart's Divertimento K.287, and failing, through sheer ignorance, to interpolate the cadenza which they indicated.

² (*from page 200*):

Our minds failed to meet at this point. By early I meant the last New York Philharmonic and first NBC Symphony years, say through 1943, in which Toscanini's performances were unhurried, expansive, spacious, and shaped and articulated by modifications of tempo (e.g., the 1940 Verdi *Requiem* and Beethoven *Missa Solemnis,* the 1941 Schubert Ninth with the Philadelphia Orchestra). And by late I meant the years from 1944 on, in which the performances were swift, taut, smoothed out, with only the slightest, subtlest modifications of tempo (e.g., the 1951 *Requiem,* the 1953 *Missa Solemnis* and Schubert Ninth). The performance of the Mozart E-flat which Galimir speaks of was done in 1948; and what he thinks of as early is the period roughly from 1945 to 1947, in which there were performances as fast and tense as the one of the Mozart E-flat—as against the relaxed performances of the fifties.

³ (*from page 201*):

In the months preceding the first NBC Symphony broadcast, when the orchestra was being drilled by Rodzinski, Chotzinoff—operating as NBC's musical ear, and hearing the dry, flat, hard sound of the orchestra in acoustically dead Studio 8H—was in a position to insist that the studio was unsuited to orchestral performance. But on this subject he is not known to have said a word in private or in public; and so for several years Toscanini's performances went out over the air with this unnatural sound, which in addition was made airlessly tight by the audience that filled the studio. In 1941-42 Stokowski had a shell installed, which changed the unfilled studio from acoustically dead to harshly reverberant; but with an audience present the sound still was flat and tight—against the orchestra's normal spacious, warm, luminous sound at the occasional benefit concert that Toscanini conducted in Carnegie Hall. And his performances continued to go out over the air with this "not ingratiating sound" until the broadcasts were moved, in 1951, to Carnegie Hall.

[4] (*from page 201*):

Galimir is referring to the threat to the NBC Symphony program during those last years from the belief of NBC's head, Sylvester Weaver, that this program should, like every other, pay for itself. The suitable comment on this was made by NBC itself repeatedly in the fall of 1946, when it kept informing listeners to the NBC Symphony broadcasts that their cost was being borne by the network itself out of revenue from commercially sponsored programs, and that they were thus part of "a balanced service of the world's finest programs" which, "sponsored directly or not," were "all dependent on the sound American plan of financing radio by advertising revenue." Which is to say that in 1946 NBC rightly considered its expenditure on the NBC Symphony broadcasts a fulfillment of its part of the bargain of the American system of broadcasting —the bargain that in return for the use of the public domain to make money, the broadcaster undertakes to spend part of the money for programs of public service. That was NBC's position also in the early years of the NBC Symphony broadcasts, when, if I remember correctly, it declared them to be unsuitable for commercial sponsorship. And it should have been NBC's position in 1954, when it discontinued the orchestra and its broadcasts because it couldn't get a sponsor for them without Toscanini: under the American system NBC had an obligation to the public not only to continue them with Toscanini as long as he wished, but to continue them without him—with Cantelli, with other gifted younger conductors, with some of the older men.

Actually, moreover, the cost of the NBC Symphony broadcasts was not money spent on a public service program, but money spent to acquire for NBC and RCA the prestige of Toscanini's name, which NBC profited by in its sale of time and programs to advertisers (as CBS profited by the prestige of the New York Philharmonic), and which RCA profited by in its sale of radios, phonographs and records, including those Toscanini made with the NBC Symphony. It was, in other words, an investment which right from the start brought a financial return even with the broadcasts unsponsored. The *Fortune* article of January 1938 spelled this out: with the amounts paid to Toscanini and the other conductors, and the amounts above contract minimum paid to higher-caliber players, the entire excess cost of the NBC Symphony program for performers came to $250,000. With fifteen of the orchestra's thirty hours of work each week available for other programs, unsponsored and commercially sponsored, *Fortune* estimated that the sale of the orchestra in various groups to advertisers would by itself recover the extra $250,000 by the spring of 1938. The network time, Saturday from 10 to 11:30, had a nominal value of $47,000 on the NBC rate card; but *Fortune* pointed out that few advertisers wanted to buy time on America's night out, and that in fact no advertiser had had to give up time for the program. And *Fortune* also pointed out the possible financial benefit of Toscanini's prestige to NBC and RCA that I have mentioned. All this at the beginning, when the Toscanini broadcasts were not commercially sponsored; and in later years there was the additional financial return from commercial sponsorship. I haven't cited this in disapproval: one must be glad when a broadcasting company operating under the American commercial system chooses to invest in the program of a symphony orchestra and is rewarded by financial return on its investment. What I contend is that even when there was no such financial return, and the program didn't earn its cost, NBC, under the American system, had in 1954 the obligation to offer the program that it acknowledged in 1946.

Concerning those NBC statements in 1946 about the "world's finest programs . . . dependent on the sound American plan of financing radio by advertising revenue," one could say then that the British plan of financing radio by license fees from owners of sets had proved equally sound and had given the British public even finer musical programs—the BBC's systematic presentation of the entire musical literature, as against the American networks' programs limited almost entirely to the big-name orchestras and soloists and the Metropolitan Opera. Specifically the BBC, solely out of regard for music, had set up its BBC Symphony ten years before NBC, with regard for the commercial value of Toscanini's name, set up the NBC Symphony. And today one can point out that the BBC Symphony still exists and enriches the musical life of the British public, whereas the NBC Symphony does not.

In his recent biography of Sarnoff, Eugene Lyons writes about his efforts on behalf of high-quality music on the air, which attained their climax for him in Toscanini's broadcasts with the NBC Symphony. Lyons reports how Sarnoff had to defend the program to his associates by pointing to the return in prestige and profits to NBC and RCA from their association with Toscanini. But he contends that while those arguments had validity, "they were also rationalizations. . . . No matter how logically he justified superior programs, he was in fact responding to his own hungers for beauty, music, culture . . ."—hungers which appear to have ceased in 1954.

Acknowledgments

I am indebted to

The musicians who speak in the book, for their generous and patient co-operation.

William H. Youngren, for his critical reading of what I did with the material they gave me.

Roger Dakin, for the editorial advice I asked on several matters.

Margaret Nicholson, for, among other things, her suggestion of the introductions to the musicians' statements.

Robert Hupka, for the unpublished photographs he made available, and his help in fitting them into the book.

B. H. H.